V JOBS

As jobs disappear, what remains is despair   *169*

A land of broken glass—and broken promises   *179*

Futures of three men get junked in a vacant lot   *187*

Youths spin their wheels in the streets of despair   *195*

The lots are empty as dying economy tightens grip   *203*

VI PRIDE AND COMMUNITY

Roots of the underclass: Racism and failed policies   *211*

Too proud to trade welfare for minimum wage   *221*

A system unable or unwilling to respond   *231*

Churches offer hope, but only for the hopeful   *239*

A memorial to dreams gone sour, social neglect   *247*

Community's housing in full state of collapse   *257*

VII THE CHOICES

Despair, dependency tow underclass into the vortex   *267*

VIII AN EDITORIAL

Courage and brains can grind a millstone into dust   *293*

The authors   *303*

Acknowledgments   *307*

About the photographer   *307*

The American
MILLSTONE

An examination of the nation's
permanent underclass

The American
MILLSTONE

An examination of the nation's permanent underclass

By the staff of the

Chicago Tribune

CONTEMPORARY
BOOKS, INC.
CHICAGO • NEW YORK

Chicago Tribune photos by Ovie Carter
except where indicated.

To the people
of North Lawndale

Contents

Preface   *ix*

I THE TRAPPED SOCIETY
The American millstone   *3*
A family tradition with no hope for tomorrow   *15*
North Lawndale blues: Day with the down and out   *27*

II CRIME
Crime in the ghetto: Everybody pays the price   *39*
Violence rules the day in troubled North Lawndale   *53*
Parole system putting crime back on the streets   *63*
Addicts slip out the back door of reality   *71*

III FINANCIAL INCENTIVES
Even money can't seem to cure poverty   *81*
Checks bring basics and a dead-end emptiness   *91*
Welfare warfare: The victim is the family   *101*
A social worker's losing battle to help hopeless   *113*
Another child is born without a fighting chance   *123*
In the delivery room, poverty cycle starts again   *131*

IV EDUCATION
Schools outclassed in a battle with failure   *139*
Poverty and crime hold education hostage   *149*
Escape is a struggle, but some will pay the price   *159*

Preface

In order to lift a millstone, you first must see it

This book is a collection of Chicago Tribune coverage during 1985 of a story unique to the American experience. It is about people who constitute a segment of an underclass that is mostly black and poor and hopelessly trapped in the urban centers of Chicago and other large cities of the nation.

Neither the existence of this group nor its circumstance is news. What is new and significant is that over the last decade this group appears to have gained political and social acceptance as a permanent fixture of the world's most advanced society without much understanding of, or concern about, the consequences.

In these and related stories published in 1983 and 1984, Tribune reporters and editors have tried to examine the lives of these Americans and to document their impact on the past, present and future of the rest of us. The Tribune editorial board also arrived at some conclusions on what might be done to change things. Those, too, are included in this book.

It was from the beginning an ambitious, seemingly impossible undertaking certain to hurt people's feelings, attract criticism of the newspaper and possibly raise more questions than it would answer. And in a city of hot political blood and raw racial nerves, it had to be approached cautiously, sometimes in an unorthodox fashion. It is provocative to lift up a rock when so many are being thrown.

But who better than a newspaper with the resources of The Tribune serving a city such as Chicago, where daily life offers a laboratory study of virtually any problem or issue that confronts a modern world? And it did not take long for the more than two dozen reporters, editors and photographers involved in this project to conclude that they were examining the most serious and far-reaching domestic issue facing the American people today.

Ultimately, the term "millstone" was chosen to glue together the puzzle of what we found. No other word better describes the weight of the burden this issue places on America's ability to govern itself in the future, or conveys more urgently the need for riddance of this burden from the American conscience.

By choosing North Lawndale, an almost all-black community with rich history on the city's West Side, as the site for much of their reporting, Tribune reporters were able to find within a few square miles stark examples to illustrate virtually all sides of this complex and sensitive issue and to personify problems that others cannot truly appreciate when presented in the abstract. This has resulted in some hurt feelings, some misunderstandings in some quarters about the newspaper's motives and some baseless allegations that the community has been exploited in the interest of selling newspapers.

Tribune reporters found life and death of all descriptions in North Lawndale, including some amazing and enlightening success stories. And we found instances of courage and commitment by individuals that are truly inspirational and beyond anything we had imagined. But for these few rare exceptions, the real story of North Lawndale was not pretty, successful or uplifting. So it was not presented that way. To do so would have been to condone and abet the kind of deliberate distortion and blind ignorance that decimated communities like North Lawndale in the first place and made their restoration virtually impossible.

Stories as complex, painful and extensive as this one do not sell newspapers. Our motivation to do the American Millstone series was singular—to give Chicago and the rest of America a new perspective on something gone dead wrong in our society.

James D. Squires
Editor
The Chicago Tribune

I

THE TRAPPED
SOCIETY

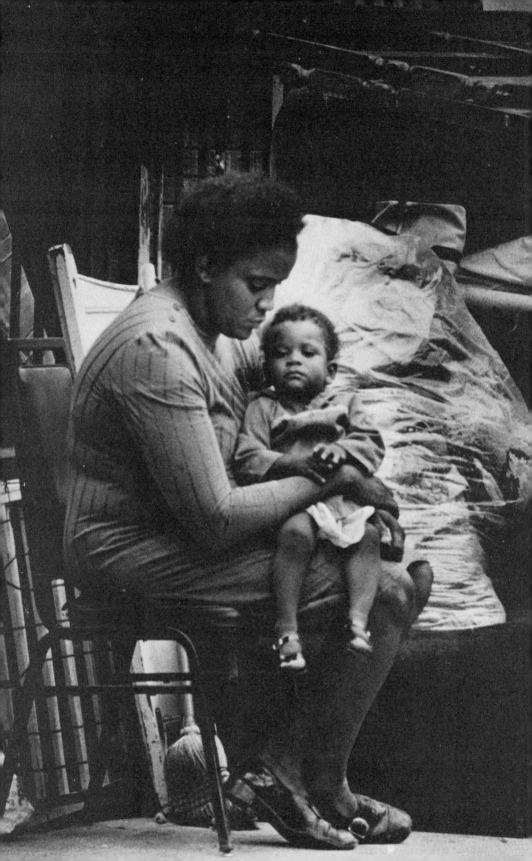

The American millstone

In a nation of riches, a permanent underclass

A new class of people has taken root in America's cities, a lost society dwelling in enclaves of despair and chaos that infect and threaten the communities at large.

The group defies most convenient labels and definitions, but it has its parallels in other societies and in other times. It is most often described in the United States as black, but there are similar groups in other countries without significant black populations, reflecting the fact that at the core the problem is economic.

Its members don't share traditional values of work, money, education, home and perhaps even of life. This is a class of misfits best known to more fortunate Americans as either victim or perpetrator in crime statistics.

Over the last quarter-century in America, this subculture has become self-perpetuating. It devours every effort aimed at solving its problems, resists solutions both simple and complicated, absorbs more than its share of welfare and other benefits and causes social and political turmoil far out of proportion to its numbers.

The existence of an underclass in itself is not new in this

Left: After she was evicted from her apartment, a woman sits amid her belongings with her 14-month-old daughter.

country. What appears to be different today from past decades and centuries is what gives every indication of being the permanent entrapment of significant numbers of Americans, especially urban blacks, in a world apart at the bottom of society. And for the first time, much of the rest of America seems to be accepting a permanent underclass as a sad, if frightening, fact of life.

As researchers and social scientists work to identify and document this trend, it is becoming increasingly apparent that the urban underclass is inextricably entwined with a broad range of more familiar and often debated societal ills that the political system has so far found incurable.

Among the conclusions drawn from reporting by Tribune staff members in Chicago and across the country on such social concerns as crime, street gangs, prisons, hunger, housing, welfare, inner-city schools and this new, apparently permanent, underclass are the following:

● Most of the violence, both random and predatory, emanating from the underclass is directed at members of the same group or other poor people trapped by circumstance within easy range. But chills are sent through entire cities by the mindlessness and casual amorality of the rapes, beatings, robberies and murders.

● Public schools, often cited as the best hope to break the cycle of poverty, usually are among the first victims. As violence stalks the corridors, education succumbs to fear. If they are able, the best, or most realistic, leave for safer schools. The rest drop out of the system or mark time in an agonizing standoff with their tormentors.

● Public housing, conceived as a steppingstone out of poverty, has frequently deteriorated into islands of terror populated in large part by brutal gang members, single mothers, pimps, prostitutes, drug dealers and children, whose chances of escaping the urban jungle are overwhelmingly diminished by the negative role models who dominate their environment.

● Racism and poverty are basic ingredients in the cauldron that gives birth to most of the inner-city underclass. But most poor people and most black people avoid and abhor the web of antisocial pathologies that seems to ensnare thousands in the nation's major cities.

● Traditional poverty alone does not account for the enduring presence of this new group at the bottom of American urban life. In addition to the welfare payments that form a base for its survival, an underground economy produces usually untraced and untaxed cash from enterprises ranging from jobs that bring under-the-table pay to prostitution, drug dealing, thievery and fencing. For some, at least, the money earned would be sufficient to buy their way out of the abyss. But because their income frequently depends on the favorable climate of that environment, few seem to leave.

● The illegal nature of many of the careers acceptable within the enclaves of the underclass lands a disproportionate number in prison. There, they often thrive in a milieu not unlike the one they left and return to their neighborhoods as folk heroes, free of the stigma that might follow them elsewhere.

● Because the lifestyles of those deeply embedded in the underclass are so out of tune with society in general, the group appears to have an impact far beyond its relatively small percentages in the community. Much white and black flight from the cities, with the resulting loss to the tax base and to the stability of institutions, can be traced to the perceived threat from this group and its intractable problems. Politicians of all colors and at all levels of government find it almost impossible to win support for improvements in welfare, housing, schools, transportation, day care or almost anything else that might be perceived by a hostile public as benefiting the most visible of the black urban underclass.

● To understand the far-reaching implications of the problem, or to formulate any kind of action to deal with it, society must understand how the new underclass developed and gave birth to its most virulent offspring.

Unquestionably, racism and poverty were the midwives. But the rapid progress in civil rights and social programs in the 1960s laid a groundwork of great expectations that embittered those somehow left behind. The assassination of Dr. Martin Luther King Jr.; the futile, neighborhood-destroying riots; the militant campaigns to define black manhood, which encouraged many to shun menial jobs for more dignified work that constantly eluded them; the cancerous growth of the drug culture; the disappearance of smokestack industries from the cities; the accelerated decline of the black family; the increased availability of welfare; the quantum leap in illegitimate pregnancies, which produced contracting generations of mothers in their early teens, grandmothers in their late 20s and great-grandmothers in their early 40s—all these gave rise to the permanent underclass.

The people who study this group believe there is a pattern to the behavior, one bordering on the pathological. It is a compressed, inner-city world dominated by values foreign to the rest of society, which witnesses only the most violent behavior when it reaches the headlines or television news.

The Reagan administration, with its cutbacks in social programs, has quickened the arguments about how to approach the problem. Any national response, even one to ignore it, ultimately will involve billions of dollars in outlays or losses.

Conservative social policy, which has been on the rise since the decade began, is attempting to use the group to discredit many of the welfare programs of the last two decades, make severe cuts in federal involvement and generally influence the government to take a strictly limited role in the future. They see this as a law-and-order matter, and the response has been to build more prisons and hire more police.

The debate is racially sensitive, because the emphasis is on the poorest of the poor, most of them blacks who live in the core of America's cities. The question is not one of race but of racism, of economics and politics and perhaps of capitalism itself. Similar problems have emerged in other developed capitalist societies: Britain, Ireland and other parts of Europe.

The jobs have gone away and most of the people who find themselves at the bottom rung of capitalism's ladder have no escape. The days when cities needed vast pools of manpower for smokestack industries are gone. The people who were drawn by that magnet, and their children and grandchildren, remain. And they are plagued by problems that have become too acute to ignore in a society that claims equality and opportunity as its goals.

Significantly, many black scholars and sociologists are raising hard questions about historical racism and the urban economy, and their effects on black family life.

Sociologist William Julius Wilson of the University of Chicago has called the existence of a black underclass "one of the most important social transformations in the last quarter of the 20th Century."

Others, such as U.S. Sen. Daniel Patrick Moynihan [D., N.Y.], have looked at what they consider the genesis of the problem, the dissolution of family life in America.

"We're seeing chunks of our society collapsing," Moynihan said recently while describing the pressure on the family as "a huge social change that we barely anticipated."

This concern is not a rehash of the poverty debate of the mid-1960s, though the U.S. response in the War on Poverty is one of the controversies. Welfare and welfare dependency, the most current arguments assert, also are central to the issue.

Evidence from a 10-year study suggests that within any decade, one-fourth of all Americans receive some public welfare. They experience "spells" of poverty caused by divorce, death or temporary unemployment. Their problems pass.

But for the underclass, welfare is not extraordinary aid.

It is as common as air and, some believe, a symbol of collective failure.

The members of this group are, and have been, consistently poor amid the nation's progress. Its members are on welfare from generation to generation, and attempts to change that have ended in frustration.

Beyond that, there is an isolation in attitudes and values that set the members of this group apart from the rest of society.

Researchers find it difficult to describe them. Much debate also centers on the size of the group.

An influential voice in President Reagan's first term, Martin Anderson, once proposed that up to one-tenth of the U.S. population was becoming "a caste of people almost totally dependent on the state, with little hope of breaking free."

But researchers at the University of Michigan believe that about 5 million people fit a model of dependence on the bottom rung of society.

Statistically, they add, that is not an alarming figure.

Interpretations vary wildly of how accurate or significant those numbers are, but most agree there is a certain cancerous vitality to it, spreading from a core group in the ghettos of the nation's big cities.

Those in this group are not infirm, mentally incapable or physically handicapped. Nor are they necessarily criminal, though there is something pathological about their behavior. No one knows why some are violent and others are not.

Some call them the "unfortunates," untouched or ignored by a flawed social welfare system. Others insist they are the product of that welfare system.

Political and ideological bias clouds almost all discussions and academic papers about this group.

As Wilson notes, there is even intense disagreement on what to call the group. He, like many others, favors the word "underclass."

That debate itself is a reflection of the struggle in American society among those who say that something happened within the last 20 years that not only proved the failure of the Great Society and well-intentioned social programs, but also changed the fundamental characteristic of urban America, especially the inner city.

Unquestionably, racism infects and affects large portions of American urban life whether in housing, employment or law enforcement. Some believe there is a cynical, but sophisticated, form of racism that talks only in economic terms, using words such as underclass as code words for race.

But most recent studies, by the Congressional Research Service, the Brookings Institution and the Bureau of the Census, all point to deepening disparity between whites and blacks. The number of children in poverty, female heads of households, illegitimate births, the slowing of the infant mortality drop and the likelihood of death by violence are all weighted disproportionately on blacks.

Significant social changes also have taken place in the last 20 years, said M. Carl Holman, head of the National Urban Coalition, including a "hardening of public attitudes toward those who have not made it." He also worried that the attention given to an "underclass" may smack of hypocrisy as an attempt to isolate a small, perhaps irredeemable, segment of society and then "write it off."

Many factors contribute to America's urban plight, Holman said, including the national decline of auto and steel production and other smokestack industries that employed many blacks.

Jobs also have become increasingly white collar, and moved to the suburbs, the Sun Belt and overseas.

Martha S. Hill, at Michigan's Institute for Social Research, believes "the term 'underclass' applies to blacks not by definition but by default." She includes four major groups in it, unemployed urban youths, drug addicts, welfare mothers and criminals.

"Blacks are not the majority," she said, "but they have a higher [statistical] representation." And the problem is compounded by the historical confinement of poor blacks to inner-city neighborhoods because of unemployment and housing discrimination.

Holman lists the underclass as "the chronically unemployed, the generally unskilled, uneducated, unqualified. Their numbers are disproportionately black and Hispanic and they tend to be much younger or older."

The debate fuels political preconceptions among liberals and conservatives and is used by them to advance points on political power for both Democrats or Republicans.

Other approaches point to root causes in the economy, in more sophisticated forms of racism, in the drug culture and in crime statistics. But many look at the family life of America.

In a speech last May, Wilson, the head of U. of C.'s sociology department, said that "many of those who represent traditional liberal views on social issues have been reluctant to discuss openly or, in some instances, even acknowledge the sharp increase in social pathologies in ghetto communities."

New studies assert that, unlike previous reports about slavery breaking down family ties, it was not until the last 30 to 40 years that black families experienced such turmoil. In a paper last year, "The Black Underclass," Wilson reported that "of the 27,178 families with children living in Chicago Housing Authority [dwellings] in 1980, only 2,982, or 11 percent, were husband-and-wife families." The current figure is only 8 percent.

He also cited the increase in births of illegitimate black children, from a national rate of 15 percent in 1959 to more than 50 percent now. In Chicago, the illegitimacy rate in black births has climbed from 67 percent in 1978 to 75 percent currently.

Next month Wilson is launching a two-year research project

in Chicago's inner-city neighborhoods to study the underclass among blacks, Mexican-Americans, Puerto Ricans and whites. The ambitious project will begin with 1,250 families in the city's poorer neighborhoods.

In a recent article on the black family, Eleanor Holmes Norton, former chairman of the Equal Employment Opportunity Commission in the Jimmy Carter administration, said that less than 25 years ago, three-quarters of black households were headed by traditional husband-and-wife families.

Now, about 43 percent of black families are headed by women only and 70 percent of children in those families are being brought up in poverty. She also warned that unless a way is devised of penetrating the ghetto, a new group "without work and without hope, existing at the margins of society, could bring down the great cities, sap resources and strength from the entire society and, lacking the usual means to survive, prey upon those who possess them."

Similar warnings have been sounded before, from Moynihan's seminal and, at that time, infamous report on the black family in 1965 and three years later in the Kerner Commission report that followed the riots in Detroit.

The term "underclass" has become fashionable, and its combination of two simpler words has become enormously loaded with emotional freight. In the national debate that ultimately determines billions of dollars in programs, policymakers choose sides, defending it or attacking.

For many, such as Anna Kondratus of the Heritage Foundation, even the existence of welfare programs creates a division, with groups seeing the programs as symptoms of failure or of progress.

Sar Levitan, the director of the Center for Social Policy Studies at George Washington University, said that "in this current talk of an underclass, there has always been one, but the complexion changes." Now, fewer "are elderly and more are women and children," he said.

The word almost has a tonal sensitivity—the way "underclass" is spoken may suggest concern or hypocrisy. It is often trotted out as a euphemism to talk about crime and welfare and drug taking and other problems associated with the inner city. With rare exceptions, it is used to describe chronically poor blacks in large cities.

Throughout the years sociologists have become very nimble in describing the very poor. The word "lumpenproletariat," a favorite term of Marxists, has a meaning similar to "underclass," but it sounds so foreign.

The "lower class" or "lower classes" is too broad and too vaguely imperial in one sense and Marxist in another. The "culture of poverty" is a '60s term and generally associated with the War on Poverty and the Great Society, two movements that seem dated now.

Underclass is a new word that is more descriptive of a condition than of people, although Wilson calls it the grouping of families and individuals "who are outside the mainstream of the American occupational system."

Among them he includes some long-term welfare recipients, some untrained or unskilled workers and some criminals.

Another researcher, Sheldon Danziger of the Wisconsin Poverty Institute cares less for the term. He believes it is similar to appreciating good art. He knows it when he sees it. "Take me out and I'll point to a member of the underclass," he said recently, but the academic words now in vogue are just too vague.

"There is a notion of antisocial behavior and there is a notion of poverty," he said. "Where those two cross is the underclass."

The word has sprung from the urban earth like an Arthurian sword, and both Reaganomic conservatives and liberals have seized it to wound their opponents. The conservatives, such as Anderson, Charles Murray and others, prefer to swing it around, saying that little can be done, to justify welfare cutbacks and minimal assistance programs to aid a small and basically incorrigible core of needy.

Liberals use it to condemn the conservatives for lack of feeling, or refuse to use it, perhaps out of guilt that so little has been done after all the promises of two decades ago.

Just as the estimate of the number of homeless people in the United States ranges from 200,000 to 4 million, depending on the source, it is impossible to quantify, except in the broadest terms, who are the members of the underclass.

"There's an enormous amount of imprecision," said Dr. James Wright, assistant director of the social and demographic research institute at the University of Massachusetts. The way it is used, he said, includes the poor, the dispossessed, released felons, the chronically mentally ill, runaways, the homeless—"the whole bottom strata."

The "underclass" term became currency for researchers looking at the failure of many federal and state welfare programs.

At the White House, the official interpretation is that the Reagan administration has committed itself to balancing excesses of the welfare system with systematic and deep cutbacks.

Officially, the federal human resources budget for 1985 totaled $475.8 billion, said Ed Dale of the Office of Management and Budget.

Of that money, $102.3 billion is targeted to the poor, $70.4 billion in means-tested programs and $31.9 billion in human development funds, block grants and other aid. Add to that, he said, about $15 billion more in state funds for programs such as Medicaid, Aid to Families with Dependent Children and food stamps. The great bulk of the money is for Social Security [about $200 billion], Medicare [$70 billion] and unemployment insurance [about $20 billion].

That represents about 49.6 percent of the federal budget, Dale said. Its growth of more than $160 billion since the last year of the Carter administration reflects the rapidly aging population of America, as most of the increase goes to Social Security and Medicare.

But that national commitment to the nation's poor and elderly is in tandem with these figures from the Bureau of the Census: The poverty rate for 1984 was 14.4 percent, or 33.7 million people. Of those, 22.9 million were white [11.5 percent of the white population] and 9.4 million were black [33.8 percent of the black population]. The poverty rate for people of Spanish origin, who may be counted as white or black, was 28.4 percent, or 4.8 million people.

Those figures, released in August, were hailed by the administration as the most significant one-year drop in poverty in nearly a decade. Indeed, 1.8 million people went off the poverty rolls from the year before. But that hardly offsets the nearly 11 million people who went into poverty from 1978 to 1983.

Murray's criticism of welfare in his book "Losing Ground"

has made him the darling of the conservative movement to change and slash federal involvement. His theme, echoed throughout official Washington circles, is that programs from the War on Poverty encouraged the break-up of families, downgraded the traditional American work and education ethics and encouraged illegitimate births among women on welfare.

Welfare creates its own dependency from generation to generation, according to Murray, and many believe that is the beginning of the underclass.

Others disagree. Greg J. Duncan, at Michigan's Institute of Social Research, said Murray's assertions are challenged by the school's "Panel Study of Income Dynamics," which has tracked about 5,000 families, including 20,000 people, for more than a decade.

He said the study reveals the percentage of people who are persistently poor is very small, about 2.2 percent, and that generally it is not a condition handed down through generations. Still, there is little in-depth research on that group, which does live in poverty from generation to generation. It has remained off the screen for most sociologists, who deal in much broader groups.

Levitan, a believer in the Great Society, defends the programs. "Some . . . worked tremendously," he said. "Infant mortality was cut in half between 1970 and '80."

But other programs were extravagant failures, and many Democratic politicians now think they failed twice by not reforming them before the Reagan decade.

The social consciousness of the mid-1960s was not sustained, they believe, and now, opportunities for new legislation and funding are lost.

What remains, however, is growing awareness and concern about a small group of people who live desperate lives in America's cities, an underclass that has contradicted traditional American belief that all problems can be solved.

A family tradition
with no hope for tomorrow

Somewhere along the line, Dorothy Sands was left behind

The burned carcass of a dog lies in the vacant apartment below.

The school year is four weeks old, but Carla, 15, still hasn't gone to class.

William, 14, feels angry most of the time and thinks about running away.

Sean, 11, has started to draw street gang graffiti on his arms.

LaWanda, 18 and pregnant with her second child, sleeps with her latest boyfriend on a dirty mattress on the living room floor.

Something has happened to the family that lives at 1554 S. Kolin Ave. Something ugly has taken root. Eleven people live together in three rooms, each so caught up in the realities of surviving for today that the promise of tomorrow is that things will stay the same.

Welfare dependency has been passed down like an inheritance through three generations. The cycle began in 1957 when Dorothy Sands' mother, Ora D. Streeter, migrated to Chicago from the South. The woman left her abusive husband and her job and applied for government assistance so she could set up a household to rear six small children on her own.

Left: Dorothy Sands [bottom right] with some members of her family in North Lawndale: At top, from left to right, William, Sean, Carra and Carla; at bottom, Roseanda and Dorothy.

Today, 28 years later, this family has never been off welfare, never once breaking away from a vicious cycle that is already nipping at a fourth generation, Dorothy's grandchildren, a girl, 7-year-old Roseanda, and a boy, Carra, who is 2.

Once again, a tragic assimilation is taking place.

Dorothy, 37, and her family live worn-out lives in a worn-out, three-story building on the city's West Side. They live in an area called North Lawndale, a ghetto of invisible walls where more than half of its 61,500 people live on some form of public assistance and where nearly 97 percent of the population is black.

Over the years, Dorothy remembers listening as President Lyndon Johnson talked about the Great Society and Rev. Martin Luther King Jr. preached about his Dream. But with her eyes, she saw that she was losing ground, slipping deeper and deeper into a seemingly hopeless abyss of rock-bottom poverty—and taking her children and grandchildren right along with her.

What has happened here is far from unique. Dorothy's situation is representative of that of a growing number of urban blacks who have fallen into what appears to be a permanent underclass of Americans who have few prospects for improving their lot. She has been ignored over the last two decades by civic leaders eager to talk about successes of black society but unwilling to address what may be a most dramatic failure. She has been untouched by the myriad social agencies in place to help the urban poor. And she has been abandoned by more fortunate neighbors who have followed their jobs out of the ghetto or moved up into the middle class.

There was a time, long ago, when Dorothy worked at a menial job without telling her welfare caseworker, trying to earn a few extra dollars to make ends meet. But those days are over, a bleak indifference having settled in.

Somewhere along the line, Dorothy Sands gave up. She lost her initiative, her self-reliance and the instinctive feeling that she might be able to change her life if she tried. Somewhere along the line, she allowed herself and her family to slide into the minimal living standards that $868 in monthly government support payments and food stamps can provide.

Somewhere along the line, she was left behind.

On the living room wall, a cockroach crawls over the peeling
paint and onto a picture of Jesus that hangs cockeyed in a
plastic frame. Beneath it, on a dirty mattress on the floor,
LaWanda, 18, is asleep under the covers with her new
boyfriend. She is pregnant with her second child and has not
been to the doctor for a prenatal check-up. She does not drink
much milk or eat regular meals. She smokes.

Most of the time, she sleeps. Her sister Carla, 15, tiptoes to
her bedside and steals a cigarette from her pack, then takes it
to the kitchen for a smoke. Four weeks into the school
semester, Carla has not spent a day in class.

In this family, no one goes to work. There are apple cores on
the sofa, cookie wrappers by gym shoes on the windowsill and
cigarette butts on the floor. In the kitchen, a cat named
"Meow" is pawing through the garbage that has spilled over
the top of a container and onto the floor.

No one can remember the last time they showered or took a
bath. The problem, as they explain it, is that the plaster
tumbles into the tub when the water is turned on. They asked
the building manager to fix things, and for a while they took
turns cleaning up the tub. The manager, South Side Realtor
Otis Flynn, acknowledges that, despite the requests, he did not
make the repair. The family solved its dilemma by deciding to
do without that step of daily hygiene. They just "wash up."

Most nights, the children stand over the sink and scrub their
clothes by hand because they have only a few items. Dorothy
rations the soap. Hung over an electrical cord strung across the
kitchen window, the clothes drip onto the floor, but they are
rarely dry by morning. Dorothy's boys, William, 14, and Sean,
11, try to wake up early so they have time to get ready for
school. One plugs in the iron and they take turns pressing their
blue jeans dry. The other plugs in the hot plate in the kitchen,
and they rub the dampness out of their shirts and socks over
the orange glow. Roseanda, 7, whose nickname is "Poochie"
because Dorothy thought she was an ugly baby, is not as
patient as her uncles. Often, she just pulls the wet socks onto
her feet. "Sometimes she's kind of stupid," Dorothy explains.

All but one of the seven other apartments are vacant, but the
building is not empty.

Before bed, Dorothy parcels out some of the nails she said she snatched from a carpenter's workbox, and sends William or Sean downstairs to the vestibule to nail shut the building's front door. Invariably, it is pried open or pushed in.

Some nights they hear footsteps in the vacant apartment above them as the men from across the street walk to a closet and retrieve the big, white plastic tub labeled "pork chitterlings" that holds paraphernalia for free-basing cocaine: a vial, spoons, matches, soda and a bottle of 100 percent grain alcohol. They hear laughter and an occasional scream through the rotting floorboards as the men get high.

In the vacant apartment below them lies a stray dog that has been dead since three neighborhood boys brought it to the building one night and torched and beat it. Wide-eyed, the children discovered it one afternoon after school. The next day, when the real estate agent came to collect rent, Dorothy told him about the dog. Even when several days passed, Dorothy was content to complain that the "landlord left it there." No one in the household took the initiative to remove it. Flynn said he "just forgot."

Dorothy takes $275 out of her public aid check each month to rent this ramshackle apartment, which has no gas hook-up for cooking or heat. The eleven who live there include five of Dorothy's six children: LaWanda; Angie, 16; Carla; William; and Sean. There is LaWanda's son, Carra, and Roseanda, the child of Dorothy's oldest daughter, Barbara, 22, who lives elsewhere in the city. Also residing in the apartment are LaWanda's boyfriend and two teenage girls, both of whom say they prefer Dorothy's apartment to their own homes.

Two weeks out of the month, Dorothy says, they have enough money to eat eggs for breakfast and cheap meat for the evening meal—if anyone feels like cooking. Most of the time, meals are quick ones, like hot dogs, rice or beans. They have no kitchen table.

The tragedy of this household can be seen most vividly in the way the family relates to Carra. Times when they are patient and loving seem fleeting.

His Aunt Carla thinks something is troubling him, but she said she does not understand what it could be.

"Sometimes he just walks out the back door and sits on the back porch," she said. "He just sits there for a long time, staring off into space."

Carra, at the age of 2, already calls women "bitches."

Dorothy laughed one afternoon when asked how he picked up the word. "He got it from me," she explained. "Because that's what I call these girls when they are bad."

LaWanda and Carla play a game to get the boy to say the word.

"Who she?" they say, pointing to LaWanda. "Ma" is the reply.

"Who she?" they say, pointing to Carla. "Ca."

"Who we?"

"Bitches."

Everyone, including Dorothy, laughs.

The boy has only a few other words in his vocabulary, and when he does speak, his diction is so poor he can barely be understood. He is toilet trained "some of the time," his mother says. When he makes a mistake, no one bothers to change him, leaving him in wet shorts until they dry.

His nickname is Fella "because he is bad," Dorothy says. Much of what this child hears is negative, in voices loud and menacing. One recent afternoon, it seemed as though every frustration in the household was erupting on young Carra. Dorothy was yelling at him because he stepped into her room. LaWanda paddled him because he wouldn't sit still. William chased him through the apartment, hitting him on the back with a cord because he touched a bicycle tire he was told to leave alone. When the boy refused to put on his shirt at the command of 18-year-old house guest Stacey, the girl grabbed him by the shoulder and pulled him close. Then she hit him with a belt.

Amid all this confusion, Dorothy is usually in her room, perched on the edge of her bed and dividing her gaze between the activity she watches through her bedroom window and the cartoons, soap operas and game shows on her color television, one of three sets in the apartment. It is from this position that Dorothy runs her house. A stout woman with square shoulders and heavy arms, she has a kind smile, which seems out of place considering her voice, a bellow that gurgles up from her belly and then pushes out through her teeth. *LaWanda! Put some pants on that boy!* She does not take her eyes off the TV screen.

Dorothy occupies one of the three rooms, and it is strictly off limits except by invitation. She used to lock her door when she left to run errands, but her daughters picked the lock one day and raided all her personal items. Now she keeps her special things—her perfume, green olives and records—locked in her closet with a padlock whenever she leaves. Hers is the only room in the house with any order, always swept and dusted. She has the only real bed. The girls sleep on canvas cots lined up side by side in the front room, and the boys, along with LaWanda, take turns rotating between cots and an extra twin mattress on the living room floor.

On top of her bureau, one of the few pieces of furniture in the house, is a 12-inch knife she took to bed with her one night after seeing a strange man lingering at the back porch. The next morning, she was watching cartoons at 10:30 when one of her daughters drifted into her room. She watched TV for a while, then casually announced that she had heard someone jiggling the back doorknob during the night. They seemed unconcerned.

Though Dorothy did not finish high school, she brags about the education she gets by looking out her bedroom window. She watches the dope peddlers work the corner at 16th Street and Kolin, tall men in leather jackets and gold chains who boldly hawk packages of marijuana and cigarettes dipped in embalming fluid that Dorothy said she was told sold for $10 apiece. At night, when she hears the whistle, she knows someone is creeping into her building to make a buy. Dorothy still talks about the drug raid in the evening last June when plainclothes officers from the Marquette District came up the back stairs with picks and sledgehammers, yelling and cursing as they broke through two layers of burglar gates—"like they was mining for *gold!*" Dorothy exclaims. The festivities ended when eight people were led, handcuffed together, down the back stairs.

But such illicit activity does not seem to bother her much, because she has been surrounded by it for so long. She still gets angry telling a story of her son Sean and a friend once finding 25 "happy sticks," marijuana dipped in PCP, while playing outside. Sean told his mother they were worth $10 apiece on the street. Sean took the friend to a man who dealt drugs, Dorothy said, but when Sean wasn't there, the man convinced the other boy that they were plain marijuana cigarettes. The boy sold all of them for just $9.

"That would have been two hundred and fifty *dollars!*" Dorothy exclaims, shaking her head. "If that boy was mine, I would have whupped his ass for being so dumb."

Dorothy was reared in a tiny, one-room shanty across from a graveyard in Louise, Miss., a rural area about 50 miles north of Jackson. Her family was among the poorest of the Southern sharecroppers who picked cotton for the white man who lived in a big house and owned the farm. In her home there was just enough room for a bed for the children at one side, a bed for the adults at the other and an old wooden table wedged in between.

It was not a happy home. The children did not like their stepfather. When Dorothy was small he left her unattended, and as she loaded wood into the stove her skirt caught fire. She suffered second- and third-degree burns on her legs, injuries that required her to spend a year recuperating from burns and having skin grafts. The fire and the way the stepfather beat her mother are Dorothy's vivid recollections of childhood. Full of liquor, he would come home in the middle of the night and beat Ora D. until she was black and blue. Her wide-eyed children stood by and cried.

In 1957, Ora D. decided she and her children deserved something better.

One morning, as soon as the stepfather left for the fields, she assembled the children, combed and dressed them and gathered up their few belongings in a small bundle. An old gray pick-up truck came for them, stirring dust as it rumbled up their road. One by one, she grabbed her children and hoisted them into the truck, explaining that they were going to join relatives up North. "We were all excited," Dorothy recalls. "Everyone was always talking about Chicago."

The driver took them as far as the bus station, and for the next two days they rode through the changing countryside, looking out the bus windows at farms, horses and gardens as they made their way north. "For us," Dorothy remembers, "it was something like going to a new world.

"Our mother told us that in Chicago we would get away from our stepfather and start a new life," Dorothy recalls. "In a way, we did, and in a way, we didn't."

They settled first on the South Side of the city with Ora D.'s mother in a small apartment on East 63d Street. She was a working woman, a counter cook at a downtown restaurant who had migrated North some time before. Not long after they arrived, Dorothy and her mother, while riding on a Jackson Street bus, discovered that the stepfather had followed them to the city and was sitting in a seat behind them. Eventually, he and Ora D. set up a household, and he supported the family by working at a watch factory. But as soon as the day-to-day realities settled in, so did the drinking and the beatings.

A year later, the couple separated, leaving Ora D. in charge of the children. With arthritis in her legs, Dorothy's mother did not feel as though she could hold a job. She signed up for public aid.

By the time Dorothy was in high school, her mother had moved the family to the West Side, where rents were lower. Dorothy, the most mature of the children, was assigned the household tasks of cooking, cleaning and caring for her brother and sisters. She had little time for herself. She made it to 9th grade at Farragut High School, thinking briefly about becoming a nurse.

But when she was 15, the same thing happened to her that had happened to her mother at the same early age: She became pregnant, her sexual interlude the product of a schoolgirl's crush. "I was tired of taking care of children," Dorothy remembers. "I didn't want a child." When her mother found out, she did not hit her daughter, as Dorothy had feared she might. She cried.

Dorothy dropped out of school to have her first baby, Barbara. Like her mother, she signed up for public aid. Her first check, she remembers clearly, was for $23.

In 1965, Dorothy met a radiator repairman named Carra Little, and they shared a relationship for 11 years. When the courtship began, he made her two promises: He could not father any children and he did not drink. Both proved false.

Dorothy began taking birth-control pills, not wanting more children. But she did not understand how they worked, swallowing one before each act of intercourse. After the birth of her second daughter, Dorothy asked doctors to tie her tubes. They refused, saying they could not perform such an operation because she was not married and not yet 21.

Little fathered the rest of her children. "Something inside just said, 'Well . . .,' '' Dorothy remembers. "I was just stupid, immature about a lot of things. When you are young, you don't really think about the future. You say, 'If I have another baby, then I have another child.' ''

After Sean was born, she had herself sterilized.

With Little in the home, some of the burden was taken off Dorothy. He liked to roughhouse with the children and watched them from time to time. But the environment was tumultuous. Like her mother, who now is dead, Dorothy put up with a lot from her man—drinking, beatings and philandering. One night after he came home drunk and began pummeling her face, she considered leaving. Instead, she grabbed a telephone and slammed it against his head and decided to stay.

They never married. "When he wanted to get married, I didn't want to, and when I wanted to, he was dead," Dorothy says matter-of-factly. Little suffered a fatal heart attack in 1976.

Whatever stability the family had when Little was alive seemed to disintegrate when he died. The children became hard to handle. Nothing seemed to get done unless Dorothy yelled and "whupped" and yelled again. She married a man "just because he asked me," only to separate five months later. There was so much chaos in the household that Dorothy's oldest daughter, Barbara, was seven months along before Dorothy noticed that she, just like her mother and her grandmother before, was pregnant at 15.

Everything began to take a toll. "A lot of times, the kids would be in the house fighting and I would be sitting in my room. I was devastated by Carra's death, mostly because he was not around for the children. My mind would be telling me to jump out the window. *Jump out the window!* I started going to church and praying.

"And then one morning," Dorothy says, "I got up and I looked out that window and I said, 'Dorothy, you ain't no damned fool.' ''

From the hallway, Dorothy can sense that someone is in her room. She turns around, her big shoulders twisting, and in one fluid motion her body follows through. Scuffing her house slippers on the dusty wood floor, she walks across the hall to find that William has changed the channel on her TV.

"Get out of here!" she yells.

"Dorothy, I just watching the game," the 14-year-old explains.

"Get out of here! I don't trust you!" William crouches on the floor, shielding his head with his arms until he peeks up and sees that she is not going to let him have it. He jumps up, smiling, and darts into the front room.

When he heads off for school in the morning, William says, he sometimes feels as though he should just keep walking and never come back home. He knows something is wrong. To get pocket change, he admits to having bullied neighborhood kids for "protection money," and he hops turnstiles at the "L" stations for a free ride when he is broke. Most of the time, he says, he feels angry.

"It's just terrible here," he confides in a whisper. "It's like we just don't know how to take care of ourselves or how to keep what we have."

William, an average student in school, says he feels it is his obligation to try to replace his father, whose crumpled photograph is taped to a wall. "I get depressed when my sisters start fighting. I try to settle it. Sometimes it's like we all take it out on Fella because he is so bad."

He is asked what he wants to do with his life. "I know I don't want to go past high school. I know that. School is boring. Maybe I can be a mechanic." Heroes? "None," he says flatly, staring into the television screen. "I can't say I look up to anyone."

Sean is the one who gives Dorothy the most concern. "He is vulnerable," she explains, "and he likes money too much." The 11-year-old flunked 2d and 5th grades and has started to draw street gang graffiti on his clothes and arms. He fights. "If the price was right," Dorothy says, "I wouldn't be surprised if he could be persuaded to sell drugs."

With Carla now 15—the age when so many women in this family have become pregnant for the first time—Dorothy keeps an eye on her, careful to put her "on punishment" when she catches her sneaking out of the house to go to the park. Carla said that her sister LaWanda has promised to take her to a clinic so she can get some birth-control pills.

One evening last November, during a quarrel, William brushed up against Dorothy as though trying to fight. The two ended up in the kitchen, William cowering as Dorothy threw him against the refrigerator. He cut his head. Shortly after, Dorothy checked herself into a hospital psychiatric ward for treatment.

"I felt like I was going over the deep end," she explained. "I had hurt my child. I was feeling angry and useless and hopeless, to tell you the truth." Two weeks later, she went home.

Unlike her grandmother, who worked hard all her life, and her mother, who had the courage to uproot her family and bring them north in search of a better life, Dorothy lacks the strength and motivation to make major changes. She sometimes talks about escaping all that is falling apart around her by moving to a better place. But when she moves, it will probably be just across the alley or across the street.

"I just don't have the energy," she explains. "Public aid won't pay for you moving, and it costs too much to pay someone to do it for you."

If she could change one thing in her life, Dorothy says, she would not have had children. "They lock you into something that, when you are young, you don't have the wisdom to think about."

Dorothy Sands says she is looking forward to getting off the public aid rolls, a system that has helped her lead a life that scrapes the bottom for the last 21 years.

"I want to get on disability," she says, speaking about the Social Security payment plan for disabled workers, gesturing to her disfigured legs. She covers her mouth, chuckling, as she thinks about what she is about to say:

"Because," she confides, "you can get more money then."

North Lawndale blues: Day with the down and out

Alcohol, drugs, crime and the underground economy

By the time Calvin Barrett leaves the apartment, it is past 10 a.m. Adjusting the tilt of his black cloth cap, he bids goodbye to the person he calls his "woman" and struts through the front door, out onto the sidewalk and into what has become his daily routine.

Along Douglas Boulevard and then south on Lawndale Avenue, he walks nine blocks to the liquor store at 16th Street, where he buys breakfast for $1.40.

It is a pint of white port wine.

Barrett is 36 and an ex-convict, released from Stateville Penitentiary in 1981 after doing two years for burglary. After a couple of months on the street, he committed another burglary and was sent back to prison. The taxpayers already have invested more than $50,000 in Barrett, the bill for his two stints in prison and the "hundreds" of days he estimates he served in Cook County Jail as a teenager.

Today the taxpayers are paying for his liquor.

Barrett lives in North Lawndale, a community on the West Side where there are no jobs to speak of and where street crime is commonplace. Even though its population has dropped

Left: Jimmy Murphy, 20, with his radio, toothpick and hat, waits for the future on Lawndale Avenue.

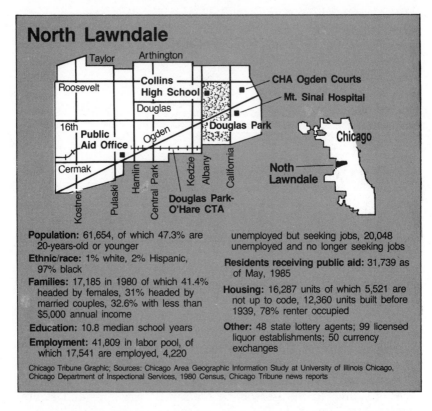

North Lawndale

Population: 61,654, of which 47.3% are 20-years-old or younger

Ethnic/race: 1% white, 2% Hispanic, 97% black

Families: 17,185 in 1980 of which 41.4% headed by females, 31% headed by married couples, 32.6% with less than $5,000 annual income

Education: 10.8 median school years

Employment: 41,809 in labor pool, of which 17,541 are employed, 4,220

unemployed but seeking jobs, 20,048 unemployed and no longer seeking jobs

Residents receiving public aid: 31,739 as of May, 1985

Housing: 16,287 units of which 5,521 are not up to code, 12,360 units built before 1939, 78% renter occupied

Other: 48 state lottery agents; 99 licensed liquor establishments; 50 currency exchanges

Chicago Tribune Graphic; Sources: Chicago Area Geographic Information Study at University of Illinois Chicago, Chicago Department of Inspectional Services, 1980 Census, Chicago Tribune news reports

by more than 30,000 in the last decade, the number of people living there on welfare has risen by more than 45 percent.

Like 5,034 others in this community, Calvin Barrett derives part of his income from general assistance, the welfare program for single men and women with no dependent children. He receives a monthly check for $151.55, plus $79 in food stamps, which he can sometimes sell for a little more than their cash value.

But that is not the only way he supplements his welfare check. He admits to "a little cheating" and a few "hustles," commonplace in this community. Unemployment is so endemic that half the residents older than 16 have completely dropped out of the legitimate labor pool.

Sometimes Barrett sells "slum jewelry," as he calls it, rings and necklaces of cheap metal and worthless stones that he buys from a wholesaler for less than a dollar apiece. But he says he has been a little cool about this scam ever since the "diamonds" fell out of a ring and shattered on a barroom floor shortly after a customer had handed over $75. Barrett fended off the man by throwing pool balls at him as he escaped out the tavern door.

Sometimes he goes to a meat wholesaler at Halsted and Lake Streets, where he buys cuts of meat for $10 that he later sells to his North Lawndale neighbors for as much as $25. Today, if the liquor doesn't take hold of him first, he will ride the bus over the Eisenhower Expressway to the Garfield Community Service Center, 10 S. Kedzie Ave., where he can get a free box of government food—canned fruit, crackers, beans, and instant milk—and then barter the contents off for food stamps, or sell them for cash.

Barrett is a fixture in a vacant lot at 16th and Lawndale, where men with similar backgrounds gather every day to drink away their time, none bothering anymore to look for honest work. They used to sit on an old couch under a shade tree in the lot until a garbage truck came by one day a few weeks ago and hauled the ratty piece of furniture away.

Here in North Lawndale, where many of the residents belong to the black underclass, it is not difficult to find people like Barrett, whose lives have been swallowed up by the urban wasteland around them and who have been down and out for so very long that their basic instinct is to adapt, not escape.

Not all those who have been left behind rely on social programs or on the underground economy for their livelihood. Some are honest, hard-working people who have invested in homes or businesses here and who make their own way above the poverty line.

But the undertow in this community, where nearly 97 percent of the population is black, cannot be ignored. Vacant lots, crumbling buildings and boarded-up businesses are on almost every street. In North Lawndale's 3½ square miles, there are 48 lottery agents, 50 currency exchanges, 99 liquor stores and dozens of store-front churches with names like "Instant Deliverance."

Lose a job, lose a husband, lose your motivation and there is something waiting to reel you in.

In many respects, North Lawndale typifies what has happened to the black slums of urban America over the last two decades as jobs have left, the economy has soured, housing has crumbled and the ranks of those dependent on government handouts have soared. The lives of many here are mired in a daily routine of alcohol, crime, drugs and the underground economy.

But it is a place where tax dollars are hard at work.

Every day in this community, $247,000 is spent in government assistance programs, four times the statewide per capita average. Every day, more than $134,000 goes for government payments for medical services, five times the statewide per capita average.

Each day taxpayers spend about $14,000 for fire protection and ambulance service in this community. Although police protection costs $40,000 a day, the murder rate here is 5 times the national average, sexual assault is 6 times the average and other serious assaults are 10 times the average.

But the cost may be far greater in human terms.

On a typical day in North Lawndale, anything can happen. Here is one of those days.

● ● ●

Waitress Doris Bell is dressed in jeans and a white sweater as she pours coffee to the regulars who have gathered at 7 a.m. at Paul's Snack and Deli, a smoke-filled greasy spoon at the corner of Pulaski Road and 16th Street. Teenagers are filling the video games with quarters as they wait for the bus to take them to school. Lottery tickets are selling briskly. Men in soiled work uniforms sit shoulder to shoulder at the counter, swapping stories about a fight the night before that started in a car wash and then moved into a pool hall.

"It was a bunch of them fighting, knocking each other out and cutting each other up," one man explains.

"Gonna get themselves killed over nothin'," another adds.

Some will go to work today, including a truck driver and a laborer. A 35-year-old man without a steady job for several years is making his daily checks with the contractors who have breakfast in the restaurant, asking whether there are any odd jobs to be filled.

Over the last 10 years, steady work has steadily left North Lawndale. In that time, 7,519, or 80 percent, of the manufacturing jobs have left the community. Wholesale and retail jobs have dropped by 44 percent. Work in the service sector, the fastest growing sector in the nation's economy, has declined by 1,087 positions.

People do what they can to get by.

Cobblestones cut out of the alleyways are sold to contractors and rehabbers for $5. Bricks stripped from crumbling buildings go for 40 cents apiece. A valid bus transfer begged from a passenger leaving a bus can be turned into a 50-cent gain. Tokens given out by the welfare office to encourage recipients to go to job interviews also can be turned into cash at the bus stops. A dollar buys a token and a dime.

Aluminum cans fetch a penny.

"It took me a good 30 minutes to get these," says a man who identifies himself as Stanley and who estimates he has maybe $5 worth of cans in his two garbage bags. His scavenger work, he explains, is to supplement the sum his wife receives from public aid for their two children. "Got to make a living some way," he says.

At DMS Metals, 1101 S. Fairfield Ave., where people like Stanley sell their cans, owner David Schwartz claims he has found everything from dead puppies at the bottom of bags to sand filtered into each can as people try to cheat on the weight and get a few pennies more.

On any given day, 20 to 200 people come through to sell their cans, Schwartz says. He tells of one regular who bent down in the darkness of an early morning to pick up what he thought was a can and came up with the cold, stiff hand of a corpse, a man who had been shot through the heart in a gang killing the night before.

Beverly makes her money a different way.

She is standing at Roosevelt Road and Kilbourn Avenue, smiling as she strikes a strategic pose in her low-cut dress. She waves discreetly. Today, like most days, it is easy to find Beverly and other prostitutes standing on the street corners and walking up to the few remaining factories at shift changes, advertising brazenly.

"Let me tell you," Beverly complains, "I have had better days."

On a good day, Beverly says, she can make $180 in just two hours, but today business is bad, and she has made only $25. A flash of anger in her eyes, she blames other streetwalkers who are getting a little mean with the men who pay for their time.

"With all the girls sticking them up, they're afraid," Beverly explains. "They don't know how it is when they see an honest girl like me. I straightout flatback. By that I mean I screw for my money."

One of her competitors, Diane, is a slim woman with a sensuous profile in a silk blouse and a pair of designer jeans. Her face, however, is a testament to the rigors of her lifestyle: She has bags under her eyes and gaunt cheeks, and she is missing a couple of teeth.

Diane, 33, says she "got into all this" when she was 17 and started dancing in a nightclub in Memphis. She says she does no business for less than $20, does not work for a pimp, and her profits go solely for food, rent and a cocaine habit that she says costs $100 a day.

"I don't work for anybody but the drug man," Diane says.

Look around. There ain't nothing here," says Michael Worsham, 33, as he boards a bus for work on the corner of Roosevelt and Kedzie for what will probably be the last time. The truck driver, fearful of violence in the area, is leaving North Lawndale for Hyde Park after 20 years. "I got two growing daughters," he says. "I want to make sure they grow."

Others whose service jobs bring them into this urban combat zone must stay behind and cope.

CTA bus driver Ken Cleveland drives his bus through the heart of the community on the Roosevelt line. A year ago he made the mistake of arguing with a passenger about a fare and ended up with a broken hand. He sizes up his passengers before deciding whether to quibble over an expired transfer, allowing many to walk right on past him when they pull their coat back to expose a gun.

Cleveland guesses that he's felt the barrel of a pistol maybe 10 times in the last 2 years, guns drawn mostly in arguments over expired transfers. Once a passenger told him in a menacing voice that he was going to "get" him. A while later, guiding his bus to a stop, he saw the passenger standing on the sidewalk, pointing a pistol and yelling, "I'm going to kill you!"

When the man pulled the trigger, Cleveland says, the gun did not fire.

"Now that's scary," the bus driver exclaims.

"Attention cars in 10. Attention cars on citywide. Stripping auto in progress. 1531 S. Albany. It's a brown auto."

Patrolman Lamont Lee of the 10th District, which includes most of North Lawndale, steps on the accelerator of beat car 1011, runs a red light at Ogden Avenue, goes west a block to

Albany, then guns the engine as he heads the wrong way on a one-way street. He stops abruptly when he spots the car near 15th Place.

Lee, a husky man of 6 feet with a slight paunch, carries two guns, a regulation pistol and a 13-shot automatic on his hip. He maneuvers himself out of the squad and over to the 4-door Buick LaSabre with a suburban Hinsdale sticker. The hood, the trunk and all four doors are open and all the tires are gone. The ignition is mangled, the radio gone and file folders lie strewn about the back seat.

The thieves are nowhere to be found. "In this neighborhood, they can take them apart faster than they can put them together in Detroit," Lee remarks.

An 18-year-veteran of the force, Lee was born and raised on the South Side and lives today in the integrated neighborhood of Hyde Park. "I never even knew the West Side existed until I took this job," he says.

Back in the squad he cruises the neighborhood, pointing out a few landmarks, like a tavern with no name on Kedzie just north of 16th that the police have nicknamed "The Bucket of Blood" because of the frequency of calls about stabbings and shootings there.

Drugs are big business in North Lawndale. Storefronts double as "shooting galleries" where addicts inject themselves with heroin; abandoned buildings are warehouses for drug operations. It's no secret in the neighborhood that when the back gate is ajar at one apartment building on South Drake, the "store" is open for business.

Later in the day, in front of a three-story CHA building at 1407 S. Spaulding, violent crimes detectives John Dahlberg and Tom Blomstrand make their way through the crowd and into foul-smelling apartment 104. The windows are boarded, the front room empty, and in the bathroom Ernest Pratt, 29, is lying dead on the floor.

A packet of liquid PCP and a syringe are beside him.

At Fadi's Food Mart at Homan and Ogden, owner Mike Nassar recently installed a state lottery-ticket machine. In its first week of operation, more than $3,000 in lotto tickets were sold. According to Nassar, 75 percent of his grocery sales are paid for with food stamps.

Nassar, 23, is one of a growing number of Arab immigrants

who have taken over liquor and grocery stores in North Lawndale. His only trouble so far has been with a customer who tried to make off with a lemon and a tin of sardines.

Other storeowners are far more cautious. They work from behind bulletproof shields or cages of wire and mesh. Today, as always, some have pistols tucked into their belts. "All the store owners around here have one," said another Arab shopkeeper.

Arabs prospering where blacks have failed is just one of the economic changes that have taken place in North Lawndale over the last three decades. After significant numbers of blacks began migrating into the area in the late 1940s, which touched off a flight by the predominantly middle-class Jewish population, the neighborhood began a downward spiral that has never been reversed.

In January, 1966, Dr. Martin Luther King Jr. rented an apartment in a three-flat on the corner of 16th and Hamlin to call attention to the social problems of North Lawndale that had long been ignored.

Today, that spot is a monument to broken dreams. The building has long since been demolished; the lot is vacant, littered with broken liquor bottles and overgrown with weeds. Across the street, amid a graveyard of abandoned cars, young men sit laughing and drinking. They are unaware that Rev. King ever lived here.

Whatever hopes there were that conditions for poor blacks would improve were dashed in 1968, when riots sparked by Rev. King's assassination ripped through the community. The rioting, which drove out white-owned businesses, left a legacy of burned-out buildings, vacant lots and a climate of despair.

It is difficult in 1985 to find an area in North Lawndale that is not spotted with vacant lots. Over the last 15 years, 1,766 buildings have been torn down. One-third of the area's housing stock is listed as substandard, yet apartments rent for an average of $250 a month.

North Lawndale was once dubbed "the greatest Democratic ward in the country" by President Franklin Delano Roosevelt, who was commenting on its ability to "deliver" for the city's Democratic machine. The 24th Ward, which encompasses most of North Lawndale, has always been good about delivering the vote. It was the first West Side ward to elect a black alderman, a black committeeman and a black state representative. For Mayor Harold Washington, the ward delivered a resounding

99.5 percent of its vote in the 1983 election. Last year, Walter Mondale won 98 percent.

Yet for a community that has had such an impact at the polls, it shows few signs of benefitting in return. The scene near Ald. William Henry's office on Roosevelt is telling: In the vacant lot next door, hustlers sell cheap jewelry and piles of old clothes. Across the street are a tavern, a pool hall and another vacant lot where men drink while sitting on rusty cars.

Sometime around 8:30 p.m., Dewitt Patterson walks calmly into the kitchen of his sister's cramped third-floor apartment on Central Park Avenue. He selects a butcher knife, then goes into the bathroom and locks the door.

While his sister and nephew watch the two-hour season premiere of Miami Vice on the televison in the living room, Patterson plunges the 5-inch blade into his throat.

At 8:35, a call for help goes to paramedics Brian Cheevers and Richard Galas in Fire Department Ambulance 34. Six minutes later, they are on the scene, lifting Patterson from his puddle of blood and onto a stretcher, giving him oxygen and carrying him down three flights of dark, unsteady stairs.

At Mt. Sinai Hospital, nine blocks away, the ambulance radio in the emergency room crackles the advance alert: "Traumatic arrest. Stab wound to the neck." As Patterson is rushed through the emergency-room doors, a medical staff of 20 are waiting.

For 40 minutes, five doctors, two anesthesiologists, two respiratory therapists, five nurses and assorted aides labor to revive him. They take turns compressing his heart by hand. Intravenous lines are connected, drugs injected, tubes pushed in. But the butcher knife has severed his windpipe and major blood vessels in his neck.

"From the look of him, you could see that he was dead," said Diane Kimball, head nurse that evening. "We did our best."

Later, back at her apartment, Patterson's sister is interviewed by detectives Dahlberg and Blomstrand. Since last March, when Patterson left his wife and three children in Memphis, she and other relatives had watched helplessly as he wrestled with bouts of depression that hampered his search for a steady job, the sister says. He had been a boxcutter in the South, but factory after factory in Chicago had turned him away.

For the detectives, there is some question whether Patterson killed himself or was murdered. Earlier in the day, two other officers had handled a case of battery at the same address. Police suspect that the two violent incidents might be related.

After reviewing the evidence, Dahlberg and Blomstrand conclude that Patterson's death was a suicide after all. They offer their condolences to the family and radio headquarters for an evidence technician to photograph the scene.

"The family is going to need to use the bathroom," Blomstrand says. "Could you make it a priority?"

"We'll try, but we're backed up out there," a voice over the radio responds. "We always are."

Before midnight, the emergency room at Mt. Sinai will handle about 150 patients, including three young girls, ages 9, 10, and 11, who were sexually abused by their stepfather; a 21-year-old shot through the arm by a man wearing a ski mask; and a 23-year-old woman who overdosed on heroin and had to be restrained with leather straps when she began kicking and screaming.

Doctors and nurses also will tend to Darrell Bolden, 17, shot in the foot by gang members who mistook the youth for a rival, and a CTA bus driver who was hit in the head by a rock as he drove along Homan. They will restrain a violent 16-year-old high on PCP after he lashes out at nurses with his fists, and stitch a cut on the back of his head. They will still have time for a regular, Leroy Smith, a chronic alcoholic who will say he has suffered a seizure but who will leave, content, after being fed an evening meal.

Before midnight, ambulance 34 will answer 14 calls.

Eight police vehicles will speed twice to a tavern called "The Pad" at 3211 W. Ogden Ave. The first report will claim that there is a man there with an Uzi submachinegun, the second that a man has a shotgun. Both reports will prove false.

Just before midnight, Dahlberg and Blomstrand take note of the lights of the Chicago skyline to the east as they climb into their black Ford LTD at Central Park and drive west on Roosevelt Road. About a mile later, they spot a slow-moving Chevy Nova with a flat tire. They follow it for moment, then Blomstrand rolls his window down as they pull up alongside.

"Hey," he yells, "do you know you got a flat?"

"Sure," replies the driver, a white teenager with a toothy smile. "But if you think I'm stopping here to fix it, you're crazy. Four more blocks and I'll be in Cicero. Then I'll stop."

II
CRIME

Crime in the ghetto: Everybody pays the price

Blacks suffer most, but urban terror touches us all

In 1972, it was the De Mau Maus, a gang of black terrorists who, in a five-month crime spree, killed 10 whites in robberies, home invasions and random shootings in Chicago's supposedly safe suburbs and along its well-traveled expressways.

In 1981, it was a white 18-year-old Cicero woman who was stripped, beaten, robbed and sexually assaulted by at least seven black youths during a rhythm-and-blues concert at the International Amphitheatre, four days after Christmas.

In 1983, it was the Mahaffey brothers, Reginald and Jerry, two black men who climbed in the open bathroom window of a Rogers Park apartment, raped a 30-year-old white woman, beat her and her husband to death with a baseball bat and severely beat the couple's 12-year-old son.

Crimes such as these, in which ghetto violence reaches out of the inner city and into the middle class, are not common. But when they occur, the frightening news stories get bold headlines and wide readership and spark renewed fears and prejudices that adversely—and unfairly—affect the vast majority of blacks, both poor and affluent, who are law-abiding.

Left: Cops raid an apartment in the inner city. Blacks are more likely to be crime victims than whites, and black men are six times more likely than white men to go to prison at least once.

Tribune photo by Michael Fryer

For years, whites and middle-class blacks in Chicago and around the nation have fled from a black underclass mired in poverty and routinely plundered and victimized by a subclass of criminals.

When those criminals prey on the innocent ghetto poor, little notice is taken by society. But the reaction is much different when underclass violence bursts out of the ghetto.

Then whites and middle-class blacks are forced to recognize that, no matter how far they may run, no matter how much they may try to ignore the crime that makes life in the underclass a dangerous daily existence, there is no escape.

In fact, the number of black-on-white crimes is small—minuscule, really, when compared with crime statistics for the inner-city neighborhoods, called "snake pits" by police and social activists.

Yet, for all of society, the effect of underclass crimes—whether black-on-white or black-on-black—is profound.

Underclass crimes cost the wage earners of America billions of dollars a year in police, court and prison expenditures.

They turn many of Chicago's public schools into places where the fear of crime and injury is routine for students and teachers and cause many parents—white and black—to move their children to private schools or move their families to the suburbs.

They feed white prejudices and fuel the slow-dying embers of discrimination and are used by many whites to justify their refusal to differentiate between blacks who follow the law and those engaged in crime.

They corrupt the political process, making it difficult for many white voters to look at a black candidate without considering the color of his skin, making it politically expedient for a white-dominated Chicago City Council to maintain a constant running battle against a black mayoral administration.

And they underline the ugly reality of modern urban life that many whites live in constant, if little acknowledged, fear and guilt because of the existence of the underclass and the threat of underclass crime.

Many whites are scared of the lone black youth on an empty subway platform, scared of the group of black teens walking down the sidewalk, even scared of the middle-aged black man sitting on the park bench.

Much of the city frightens whites. Many white suburbanites, in fact, are afraid to walk on any Chicago street, day or night. Most city residents, more savvy, know there are safe communities. But they also know there are ghetto neighborhoods that are best avoided at night and other inner-city war zones where it is dangerous for anyone—white or black—to appear at any time.

Even in their quiet, comfortable, "safe" neighborhoods and suburbs, whites fear the threat of underclass violence. Over and over, they have read how, with no logical pattern, ghetto crime has reached into the most peaceful of communities to destroy the cherished tranquility with violence and death. Over and over, they have known the bitter taste of their fear.

The victims of the De Mau Maus, for example, were four people slain during a home invasion in Barrington Hills, a family of three murdered on their Monee farm and three men killed in separate shootings along Chicago-area expressways—a college student, a truck driver and a soldier from Kentucky asleep in his pick-up. All 10 were many miles from the ghettos of Chicago when they were put to death.

Middle-class blacks, many of whom live close to the underclass, face similar fears, but without as many prejudices. In fact, middle-class blacks are often the victims of those white biases.

Random acts of violence by whites, such as the murders committed by Richard Speck and John Gacy, send chills down the spine but are usually dismissed as the actions of insane or, at least, highly disturbed individuals.

Yet when random violence is committed by blacks against whites, it is often perceived by whites as a reflection on all blacks—even when the criminals are clearly aberrant.

"You're brought up to be afraid of them," explains a housewife in the Far Northwest Side neighborhood of Edison Park who is married to a police officer. "You're always afraid they're going to hurt you. The mass of poor blacks, that's what you fear."

So many whites—and middle-class blacks—have run from the underclass and have tried to pretend that it doesn't exist.

Roger Fox, research director for the Chicago Urban League, notes that many whites have "tired of civil rights" and the social agitation of blacks for an end to the racial prejudice, poverty and educational deprivation that have afflicted them for centuries. "A lot of people have become indifferent," Fox says.

Yet the underclass and its problems continue to grow, and Fox warns, "If we make things bad enough, the problems are going to come back and hit us."

"You can ignore crime if it's in the ghetto," says Winston Moore, former director of the Cook County Department of Corrections and now chief of security for the Chicago Housing Authority. "As long as blacks commit crimes against blacks, the penalty is very lenient.

"Whites don't want to pay for anything. But they'll pay now or pay later, and the price they pay later will be more than they can afford."

The heavily segregated nature of Chicago and its suburbs has enabled most whites to avoid underclass crime, but it also has helped create urban neighborhoods in which crime is a day-in, day-out, fear-breeding fact of life and, for many, a way of life.

"You have a breakdown of all of the controls," says Rev. George Clements, pastor of Holy Angels Catholic Church, 607 E. Oakwood Blvd. "We don't have the men in the home. There's nobody holding the youngsters accountable. They're running amok.

"We have so many of the children being born out of wedlock to mothers whose own mothers bore them out of wedlock.

"The children run our communities—the terrorist gangs, the teenage thugs."

Such crime makes life a hazardous gamble for everyone in the underclass—whether law-abiding or criminal, whether gang member, store owner, welfare mother or minister.

It sets a tone for neighborhoods in which disorder, destruction and dependency are normal, while industry, stability and hope represent deviant behavior.

It exacts a high cost in property loss, business flight and charges for goods and services and a higher cost in injury and death.

Consider this: The eventual cause of death for 1 of every 21 black men born in America will be murder. For white men, the odds are six times better: 1 of every 131. Black women have a greater chance of being murdered [1 in 104] than white men. And the odds undoubtedly are much more deadly for blacks who live in the underclass.

Similarly startling are the results of a Tribune analysis of crime statistics and census data for overwhelmingly white and overwhelmingly black areas of Chicago.

In the analysis, five police districts [the 2d, 3d, 5th, 7th and 15th], which have a total population of 550,000 that is 96 percent black, were compared with two police districts [the 8th and 16th], with a total population of 404,000 that is more than 91 percent white. Four of the black districts are on the South Side, and one is on the West Side. The two white districts cover huge corners of the city on the Northwest and Southwest Sides.

The comparison found that people in the black police districts were 11 times more likely to be victims of violent crime in 1983 than those in the white districts and 14 times more likely to be murdered or raped. In 1983, 251 people were slain in the black districts, but only 13 in the white districts.

Everyone in the ghetto is afraid. "Every day, it's constantly on their minds, the fear of being hurt," Father Clements says.

For example, Sister Jean Juliano, one of several Daughters of Charity who work at Marillac House, 2822 W. Jackson Blvd., on the West Side, notes: "There is a general fear on the part of seniors to come out on the streets, especially on the 1st and 3d of the month when their checks come in.

"They know there are young punks waiting to knock them down and take their wallet or purse. They're afraid to death to open their doors, especially at night. They have become prisoners in their own homes.

"The young punks around here have no respect for anyone. They'd cut their own grandmother's throat."

Such crime hits members of the underclass especially hard because of their poverty.

The Tribune analysis found that residents of the five black districts were nearly six times more likely to be living below the poverty level than those in the two white districts.

In the black districts, 29.7 percent of the population was living below the poverty line in 1979, a figure that is probably much higher today because black unemployment in Chicago has doubled since then. In comparison, only 5.4 percent of the people in the white districts were living in poverty.

The black districts were also much more densely populated, and that means it is much more difficult for members of the underclass to avoid coming face-to-face with crime.

In 1983, there were 24 times as many violent crimes per square mile in the black districts as in the white districts, even though the black districts had more than twice as many police as the white districts.

A multitude of local and national studies show that the more deeply a person is stuck in the underclass, the more likely he is to be a crime victim or a criminal.

Blacks, for example, are more likely to be crime victims than whites; so are the unemployed, the poor and people who are single.

In addition, black men are six times more likely than white men to go to prison at least once during their lives. In fact, 1 of every 50 black men in the United States older than 18 spent at least some time in prison during 1982 alone.

The Illinois Criminal Justice Information Authority conducted a study of 12,872 homicides in Chicago over a 17-year period and found that 70 percent of the victims and 68 percent of the killers were black.

The poor have always been with us, but not the levels of violent crime that exist today in the ghettos of Chicago and the rest of America.

Experts note that, even at the height of the Capone gangster era, the city's murder rate was a fourth of what it is today. In those years, during the depths of the Depression, it was possible to walk safely almost anywhere in the city and, on hot nights, to sleep in the parks and on the lakefront without fear of violence. No longer.

A major reason cited for today's heightened danger is the disintegration of the black family.

"In the ghetto, the rock-bottom poverty ghetto, there are very few intact families, very few people with stable, steady lives," says John McDermott, a longtime civil rights activist who is now urban affairs director for Illinois Bell.

"It is a society in which crime is almost socially acceptable. There are no longer significant social strictures against it. That has led to the most horrendous crime."

To some extent, at least, the problems can be traced to well-meaning welfare programs that, according to McDermott, have been "like an acid that's eaten away at the family structure."

Further exacerbating the problem has been the economic recession of the early 1980s, from which Chicago blacks have yet to recover. In 1979, black unemployment in Chicago was 11 percent, just double that of whites. Last year, it was nearly 23 percent, compared with a white rate of 9 percent.

In addition, underclass youths find themselves in schools that are not only dangerous but woefully inadequate.

The Chicago public school system spends $8.2 million a year on security, but in 1984 there were 528 assaults by students on fellow students—an increase of 39 percent over the previous year.

A 1985 study of Chicago schools by the Chicago Panel on Public School Finances accused the school system of employing "an operative policy of educational triage," using a term usually associated with separating battlefield casualties for treatment.

In releasing the study, G. Alfred Hess Jr., the group's executive director, noted: "Academically adept students were encouraged to enroll in the system's elite or selective schools, while inner-city youths were abandoned to, and neglected in, a few schools which received the most poorly prepared students."

The inner city has become "an environment where, if you steal a bike and come home, your mother doesn't ask any questions because she knows she could never afford one for you," says Dennis Rosenbaum, a social psychologist at Northwestern University.

"You're reinforced and condoned for criminal behavior. They see signs of incivility, signs of disorder around them—garbage and litter, bars on the windows, rats. Nobody seems to respect each other.

"We're talking about people who live in a different world."

Members of the underclass know this. They look at television and see the world of middle-class values and possessions, but they know their opportunities to enter that world are few because of poor education, lack of jobs, racial prejudice and the absence of cultural supports.

This breeds a self-hate that, experts say, is one explanation for underclass crime remaining concentrated in the ghetto as much as it has.

Another reason is that, in Chicago and its suburbs, blacks and whites have very little contact. Studies have found Chicago to be the most segregated major city in the United States. In the course of a day, there is only a 1 in 25 chance that a black in Chicago will see a white in his neighborhood or that a white will see a black in his community, according to a 1983 study cited by the Illinois Criminal Justice Information Authority.

Although the great majority of crimes by blacks are committed against other blacks, a 1977 national study found that most robberies by blacks were against whites. Nonetheless, in Chicago, apparently because of the segregation of the races, blacks were responsible for only 24 percent of the murders of whites who were killed in robberies between 1965 and 1981.

On the other hand, lack of contact with middle-class whites—and with middle-class blacks who have escaped the inner city—has left underclass youths with few role models except drug pushers, gang members, pimps, small-time criminals and unwed mothers.

"The frustration and grimness of life in the ghetto forces young blacks to aspire to these roles," says Pierre de Vise, a Roosevelt University urbanologist. "Young people would prefer to be middle-class people, but that seems so far from reality."

To get away from the depressing reality around them, many in the underclass flee to alcohol and drugs, in particular heroin.

Drug use "is one of the leading causes of all our criminal offenses," says Sanford Neal, commander of the nearly all-black Austin district on the Far West Side.

Winston Moore, the CHA security chief, blames the increase in inner-city drug use and the increasingly violent nature of underclass crime on the white and black middle classes, which have been indifferent toward ghetto crime and lenient toward ghetto criminals.

"There's no justice when poor people commit crimes against poor people. Nobody cares," Moore says. "A person can commit a very serious crime and go to the penitentiary and be out in a couple of years.

"We cannot control our streets until we control our penitentiaries and our jails. If they are running amok in the penitentiaries, they'll run amok on the streets."

Most important, Moore says, "The black community has to learn responsibility." Black leaders, he says, must speak out against crime, black fathers must be required to take care of their children, and law-abiding blacks must actively fight against the presence of criminals in their neighborhoods.

In coming years, experts predict, the underclass will act as an ever-heavier dead weight dragging down the Chicago economy.

Already, the costs are very high. This year, taxpayers in Chicago will spend nearly $500 million for police protection, while it will cost Cook County residents nearly $300 million for the county court system and other law enforcement programs. Taxpayers throughout Illinois will spend $400 million more for the state's prison system.

What this means is that each Chicagoan who has a job has to pay at least $600 a year to protect himself, his family and others from crime, much of which stems from the underclass.

Earlier this year, the Chicago Panel on Public School Finances studied the financial implications for society of high school dropouts, many of whom have grown up in or end up in the underclass.

Of 29,815 members of the class of 1982 in the Chicago public high schools, 12,616 dropped out before graduation—42 percent.

The annual costs to society of these 12,616 dropouts alone were $7.3 million in lost taxes, $50.5 million in welfare payments and $1.6 million in crime costs. In addition, the dropouts could expect to earn $51 million less a year than if they had finished school.

Over the course of their lifetimes, these dropouts would be expected to cost society nearly $2.7 billion in welfare payments, crime costs and lost taxes, while earning $1.8 billion less than graduates.

But the cost of the underclass is not computed only in money. It is also measured in increased fear and restrictions on social freedoms that could result from a society angry over underclass crime.

"If the underclass continues to grow, we will become a more militaristic state and rely on more oppressive measures of control," says Roger Fox of the Urban League. "There will be greater hostility, greater animosity, greater fear on the part of both sides.

"What the middle class in the suburbs and in the city are going to be forced to face is that they can't run anymore."

One short, wayward life; one horrid crime

Just after 6 p.m. on July 24, 1984, Kevin Tyler left his mother's 7th-floor apartment at 4555 S. Federal St. in the Robert Taylor Homes public housing project, went outside and started walking north.

He was on his way to another Chicago Housing Authority apartment at 4410 S. State St., where he lived with his girlfriend, their two infants and her two other children.

Tyler had lived in the Robert Taylor Homes since infancy. Nearly everyone in his mother's building knew him. They had watched him grow into an aimless young adult without a job. Day after day, he could be seen loitering with other young men at the building's entrance or sitting on the benches nearby.

Tyler, thin and relatively short, was a product of life in the urban underclass. He had been a gang member since grade school, had dropped out of high school when he was a freshman and had recently signed up for general assistance but had not received any payments.

Tyler's mother had six children, five boys and a girl. His sister, Barbara, had died several years earlier of cirrhosis of the liver at age 27. In February, 1985, his brother Louis would be found bound and strangled in his apartment near 48th Street and Michigan Avenue.

During his troubled life in the ghetto, Tyler had done little to come to the notice of society at large—with one exception.

On the night of Dec. 29, 1981, at a rhythm-and-blues concert at the International Amphitheatre, an 18-year-old Cicero woman was stripped, beaten, robbed and sexually assaulted by at least seven black youths.

Her two male companions were beaten and robbed, and her girlfriend narrowly escaped the attackers.

"They were just like animals," the girlfriend said. "I was screaming and kicking, biting and pulling hair, trying to keep them off of me."

One of the attackers was Tyler.

On Nov. 19, 1982, the leader of the attack was sentenced to 120 years in prison; another man involved in the incident got a 60-year sentence.

Tyler had been one of five men who pleaded guilty earlier. Originally charged with attempted rape, deviate sexual assault, robbery, aggravated battery and conspiracy, he entered his guilty plea to a simple charge of aggravated battery and was sentenced to serve 90 days in Cook County Jail and two years' probation.

On this warm July evening in 1984, as Tyler walked to his girlfriend's apartment, he had been off probation for more than a month. He had, however, recently changed gang affiliation, and that caused what happened next.

As Tyler neared another project building, at 4444 S. State St., two 16-year-old boys rushed at him with baseball bats.

He tried to run, but the bat-wielding attackers caught him and beat him repeatedly while a crowd gathered to watch.

Eight hours later, at a nearby hospital, Tyler died. He was 100 days short of his 21st birthday. His death drew no notice from the outside world.

It shouldn't have happened in land of opportunity

An editorial from the Sept. 22, 1985, edition of The Tribune:

That tacky TV show, "The Jeffersons," had at least one feature worth remembering. Movin' on up, began its theme song. That's been the story, and the glory, of this nation. Penniless families came here from around the world and moved up. They converted swamps into great cities, turned rocky fields into rich farmlands and parlayed janitor jobs into comfortable homes and kids in medical school.

The drive to move up produced the Model T, the Apple computer and the Big Mac. It propelled the son of slaves to international fame as a scientist and a sharecropper's daughter to the presidency of a major advertising agency.

This country didn't achieve true equality of opportunity, but it did try harder and moved further toward that goal than any other nation on Earth. And with the civil rights legislation and new social programs of 1960s, it looked as if the last barriers to upward mobility—to moving on up—would fall for all people.

Yet somehow, at the very time America was making its heaviest legal and financial commitment to economic and racial equality, its social fabric was ripping apart. Its great cities, traditionally the springboard for moving up, were developing a class of people mired permanently at the bottom. That sad irony was the central theme in reports on "The American Millstone," a Tribune series that examines the underclass and its impact on the nation.

It shouldn't have happened here, in the land of opportunity. Even the word "underclass" sounds harshly un-American. And, shut off from mainstream concepts of job and family and responsibility, this new underclass formed a set of values distinctly foreign to American tradition. Independence is your first baby and its accompanying welfare check. Crime pays; in fact, it may be the only thing that pays. Schools are centers of violence and failure that put you down instead of helping you up.

This is not just an alternate culture that society as a whole must learn to tolerate and subsidize indefinitely. It's too dangerous to be shrugged off. Its problems and pathologies are sapping the strength of cities like Chicago, poisoning the political climate at all levels of government, fostering racism and dooming millions of children to lives of hopelessness and despair.

The doomed children: That's the saddest part of the whole phenomenon. No one, no matter where he or she stands in the political spectrum, should ignore the tragedy of young children who will never realize their potential because they never had a chance. No society can afford this waste. No thinking, feeling person can accept it.

Yet there is a growing acceptance of the underclass as an unfortunate but unavoidable offshoot of modern urban life. Some traditional liberals as well as conservatives are saying, "We've tried everything and nothing worked. Seal them off as best we can and concentrate on helping the deserving poor."

Two things are wrong with that reasoning. First, there can't be any status quo. The teenage pregnancies, the drug culture, the joblessness and the violent crime that are pervasive among the underclass will sop up ever greater amounts of tax resources, if only to build more courts and prisons. The financial drain on cities and states will shortchange schools, parks and other services needed to attract industry. The crime, or the fear of crime spilling out of the ghetto, will drive more middle-class families and job-producing businesses to calmer parts of the country.

And, second, it's simply not true that this nation has done all it can to help the underclass. It has not supplied the one key that will unlock the chains: It has not reached out to the doomed children and given them a chance to develop their minds and their spirits.

The way to do that, as a wealth of pilot projects has proved, is through early childhood education. A network of early learning centers serving urban ghettoes and involving parents as well as children would do more to lift the American millstone than any other domestic initiative. It would give the children of the underclass the motivation and stimulation that other children routinely get in their formative years. It would give them the resources to move up and the drive to use those resources.

Job training, supportive services for young mothers, efforts to prevent early pregnancy, tough law enforcement, better grade schools and high schools—all are needed to treat the wounded victims of the underclass. But the number of wounded will continue to escalate if nothing is done to save the children.

The question is not whether this nation can afford to educate the little boys and girls born into chronic dependency, but how long it can afford not to.

Violence rules the day in troubled North Lawndale

Prevalence of crime breeds indifference among poor

It was almost 3 a.m. when Tommy Lee Allen and Donnie Riddle rounded the corner at 16th Street and Kedzie Avenue and spotted Charles Jackson. They knew him as "the cripple" who sold drugs. Sitting in his wheelchair, he was an easy target.

"We are gonna get some money," Allen whispered to Riddle. "I feel like killing the old boy."

Jackson, 36, who lost both legs in connection with a gunfight several years before, protested as the two ex-convicts steered him down the street and into a vacant lot behind a storefront church called the Holy Sanctuary.

They threw him out of the wheelchair and rifled through his pockets, finding just a half-filled pack of cigarettes. They kicked him in the face, stomped on his chest and threw bricks at his head.

Then they took turns bashing him with his wheelchair until he was dead, court records show.

Another senseless crime had been committed on the streets of North Lawndale, an urban battleground where a violent crime occurs an average of every 3 hours and a murder occurs every 12 days, often at the slightest provocation.

Left: Looking for revenge, a man with a shotgun returns to a pool hall where he had been beaten up. The murder rate in North Lawndale is six times the national rate.

The murder of Jackson, on Aug. 24, 1983, is typical of the black-on-black atrocities that occur with alarming frequency among the underclass. For many of these people, spontaneous violence has become a reflex way of dealing with everyday frustrations.

During the 12-month period ended Aug. 31, statistics show, 1 in every 8.5 residents of North Lawndale was the victim of a serious crime and 1 in 21 was the victim of a violent crime. The citywide rate, by contrast, was only 1 in 50 for violent crimes. The national rate was 1 in 182.

The murder rate in North Lawndale is twice the citywide figure and six times the national rate. The incidence of rape and serious assault also are double that of the city as a whole. The many residents of the neighborhood who are hard-working, honest people run those risks along with those in the under-class.

Children growing up in areas such as North Lawndale absorb a casual indifference to even the ugliest crimes. They learn at an early age to live by a twisted set of rules. Because most boys have little contact with their fathers, their first male role models frequently are gang leaders, drug dealers and pimps.

Two street gangs with extensive criminal operations recruit members off the streets and play lots of North Lawndale. Many boys join before their teens and are put to work delivering narcotics and guns.

"This neighborhood is like another world," said James Linn, a former Cook County prosecutor who worked on the Jackson case and other vicious killings in North Lawndale. "These cases leave you with the feeling that life is cheap there."

Underclass violence, largely limited to the ghetto, occasionally reaches into other neighborhoods, and only then does it receive widespread publicity.

Five days after Jackson was slain, Dean and Jo Ellen Pueschel were bludgeoned to death with baseball bats during a burglary in their Rogers Park apartment. Their 11-year-old son was stabbed, beaten and left for dead, but survived.

Two brothers with long criminal records, Reginald and Jerry Mahaffey, were convicted of the murders and sentenced to death. Reginald Mahaffey lived in North Lawndale.

As rare as interracial murders might be, they have an impact far out of proportion to their number. They play a pivotal role in shaping white America's perceptions of blacks, and they work against efforts to improve life for the poor.

When underclass lawlessness reaches beyond the ghetto, the

most frequent result is property crime. Police say a growing number of property crimes in more affluent city neighborhoods and in the suburbs are being committed by ghetto residents.

"We have to understand that we can't hide from these people," warned Judge Claude Whitaker, who hears all juvenile cases from North Lawndale. "They drive cars. They go into other areas. We can't hide."

There were 84 homicides in North Lawndale from Jan. 1983, to last Sept. 13. Most occurred between 8 p.m. and 4 a.m., and most of the offenders and victims were black males ages 18 to 24.

Twenty of the victims were stabbed, 51 were shot and 10 were beaten. Three children died in an arson fire allegedly set by their father during a fit of anger. All but 16 of the homicides were solved.

Perhaps the most disturbing thing about these killings is how random and instinctive they seem.

● Late one night, after a disco party at his video game room on Cermak Road, Roger Griffin fell asleep sitting upright on a sofa. When three men who had attended the party returned to steal stereo equipment, Griffin did not awaken. But the intruders, ages 19 to 24, became concerned that Griffin might link them to the theft.

Wielding screwdrivers from Griffin's toolbox, they took turns stabbing him in the head and chest, then divided the $21 they found in his pockets. Griffin died four days later. One of his killers received a 60-year sentence. The others were given lesser terms.

● Maria Martinez, 74, a grandmother from Humboldt Park, was en route to Sportsman's Park Race Track in Cicero and waiting to transfer trains at the Central Park Chicago Transit Authority station at about 8:30 p.m. Two young men came up from behind and ripped a gold chain from Martinez's neck, then threw her down a flight of stairs. Martinez died after being in a coma for several weeks. A 20-year-old is awaiting trial.

● At the "Quick" car wash on Roosevelt Road, manager Waymon Hall told Jerry Fisher to stop making calls on the pay telephone. Fisher, 37, left but was back in minutes, brandishing a .38 revolver. "You want to tell me to leave now?" he asked.

Hall's father grabbed Fisher from behind and there was a struggle for the gun. It discharged, killing Fisher. The state's attorney viewed it as a case of self-defense and no charges were filed.

● Truely Hunter, 72, was beaten in a robbery attempt and

died 50 days later. His convicted killer, Michael Caeser, 18, had had the sort of problem-filled unanchored childhood that is common among many underclass youngsters today.

The son of alcoholic parents who lived off public aid and physically abused him, Caeser was removed from their custody when he was 12, then was shuffled through eight foster homes. Caeser, a gang member who admitted using drugs daily, did a brief stint with the federal Job Corps training program in Wisconsin, but he never had held a full-time job. He is awaiting sentencing.

Very few homicides in North Lawndale, or in underclass communities nationwide, get reported by the major news outlets. Though the public knows little about the specifics of ghetto crime, it pays a heavy price for not curtailing it, as the aftermath of Jackson's slaying shows.

This one murder will cost taxpayers more than $1 million.

It took 23 police officers and personnel from the medical examiner's office to complete the investigation. One of the killers was represented by a public defender at taxpayers' expense.

The killers spent 14 months in Cook County Jail awaiting trial. At an average cost per inmate of $523 per month, this phase of their incarceration cost more than $14,000.

Tommy Lee Allen, 25 at the time of the killing, pleaded guilty to murder and was sentenced to 45 years in prison. Donnie Riddle, 19, was convicted in a jury trial and sentenced to 65 years.

Even if both are model prisoners and paroled after serving half their sentences—as early as the law allows—they will still serve a total of 55 years, which will entail an expenditure of at least $880,000, based on today's cost.

The cost of crime and violence in underclass communities can be measured in other ways:

● Every day, more than $40,000 is spent policing North Lawndale. On a typical day, about 140 police officers are routinely assigned to duty there.

● Last year, the emergency room at Mt. Sinai Hospital, the only one in North Lawndale, handled an estimated 25,000 cases. Almost half were traumatic injuries, and many involved violence. Hospital officials estimate that 60 percent of emergency room services there are paid for by public aid, at a cost of more than $1.6 million a year. Hospitalization and treatment add considerably to the expense.

● North Lawndale has only 2 percent of the city's population but about 10 percent of the calls by Chicago Fire Department ambulances go there.

● Many victims of ghetto slayings are on welfare, and public aid pays for their funerals and burials as well—up to $900 each.

Although the rate of violent crime in North Lawndale is more than double that for the city as a whole, the rate for property crimes is not much higher. In the 12-month period ended Aug. 31, the incidence of burglary was only 16 percent above the citywide rate. The incidence of thefts involving more than $300 in cash or goods was below the citywide figure.

These figures underscore the depressed economic state of North Lawndale, where there is relatively little to steal. But they do not reflect the growing number of property crimes that ghetto residents commit in other areas.

It is not possible to measure precisely the amount of crime committed by underclass people in Chicago's more affluent neighborhoods and in the suburbs. But city and suburban police maintain that ghetto residents, often motivated by the need to pay for drug habits, are responsible for an increasing amount of auto thefts, burglaries, robberies, purse snatchings and shopliftings in other areas.

Of 1,983 automobiles stolen in west suburban Cook County in a 13-month period in 1984 and 1985, 27 percent were recoverd in the city—almost all of them in North Lawndale or nearby ghetto areas, said Lt. George Nicosia, commander of the Cook County Sheriff's Police investigative unit.

Many of these cars were stolen and stripped by rings of urban gang members, who also specialize in thefts at suburban shopping malls, according to police.

Trips to more affluent areas for property crimes sometimes lead to violent crimes against whites or more affluent blacks. The Mahaffey brothers traveled to the North Side with plans to burglarize a store. When their van broke down, they decided instead to burglarize a home. That twist of fate cost the Pueschel couple their lives.

People who must deal on a regular basis with violence among the underclass say they are most disturbed by the number of young people getting caught up in these crimes at an earlier age. Twenty-three percent of the 61,500 people who live in North Lawndale are ages 10 to 19.

Judge Whitaker, who oversees Calendar 9 in Juvenile Court, said he has been threatened by teenage gang members and spat at by other youngsters as he sat on the bench. The number of times that boys appear before him on gun-related charges is increasing, Whitaker said.

"These children reflect the brutal conditions of the environment they are raised in," Whitaker said. "Through health problems and their environment, they have the stamp of the ghetto on them by the time they begin school."

In the six months that ended Sept. 30, Calendar 9 had the highest rate of delinquency findings of any Juvenile Court branch in Chicago. It also made the greatest number of commitments to state and county juvenile penal facilities. The bulk of the offenses involved attacks.

Claudia Semeniuk, a public defender assigned to Whitaker's courtroom, noted: "We have probation officers coming in and saying, 'Your Honor, the minor is deceased.' Later we find out he has been shot to death."

Judges, prosecutors and attorneys who work with juvenile offenders say they have observed an alarming attitude among many of the young defendants—that the mistake was not in committing the crime but in getting caught.

"They don't think they're doing anything wrong," said Jeff Friedlieb, a Chicago Police Department youth officer assigned to North Lawndale. "The problem is that somebody complained. And they will tell you: 'All I did was take his money and knock him down. Can't I just give the money back?' "

R. Eugene Pincham, a veteran jurist who spent 6½ years on the Criminal Court bench before stepping up to the Illinois Appellate Court, thinks one way to stem the rising tide of youthful violence in the underclass is to make sure children growing up in ghetto areas understand the legal consequences of crime at an early age.

"These particular offenders have not been mentally conditioned to punishment," Pincham said. "They don't hear punishment. They don't see punishment. In fact, it is fortunate that the intellect of the criminal offender is what it is, because if he were a little smarter, you'd really have chaos."

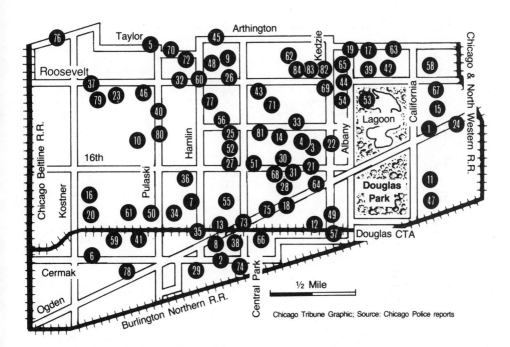

Chicago Tribune Graphic; Source: Chicago Police reports

Murder in North Lawndale
A homicide rate more than 6 times the national average

1983

1 **Lorenzo Coley**, 27, found stabbed Jan. 13 at 8:30 p.m. in his apartment in 2700 block of W. Ogden.

2 **Douglas Moore**, 18, found stabbed Jan. 16 at 1:15 p.m. in 3700 block of W. Cermak.

3,4 **Patricia Lanigan**, 21, and **Leon Billings**, 21, found stabbed Jan. 16 at 5 p.m. in her apartment in 1500 block of S. Sawyer.

5 **Bernice Tyler**, 57, shot Feb. 13 at 1 p.m. after she resisted 2 teens who tried to snatch her purse at Taylor-Pulaski corner.

6 **Carey Epkins**, 26, a deaf mute, shot March 5 in 4300 block of W. Cermak by gang members who mistook his hand gestures for those of a rival gang.

7 **Donna Roberts**, 24, found stabbed March 17 at 5:30 p.m. in her apartment in 1800 block of S. Avers.

8 **Eugene Kimbel**, 19, shot by rival gang members April 15 at 5:50 p.m. in 3700 block of W. Cermak.

9 **Sherman Lilton**, 25, found stabbed April 25 at 9 a.m. in his apartment in 3600 block of W. Grenshaw.

10 **Randy Smith**, 22, beaten to death April 30 about 4 a.m. in gangway in 1500 block of S. Karlov.

11 **Efren Godinez**, 16, shot in alley May 2 at 4:30 p.m. in 2700 block of W. 18th.

12 Fred Elkins, 47, found stabbed May 18 at 6 a.m. in basement of building where he lived in 1900 block of S. Sawyer.

13 Ray Johnson, 29, shot May 16 about midnight in yard in 1800 block of S. Lawndale.

14 Anthony Miller, 17, shot May 19 at 10:40 p.m. in 3300 block of W. 15th.

15 Leon Armstrong, 28, shot May 31 about midnight in 1300 block of S. Washtenaw.

16 Robert Redmond, 29, shot June 18 at 5 p.m. in 1800 block of S. Kildare; he dies 3 days later.

17 Robert Baber, 31, shot June 26 at 5:20 p.m. in 1100 block of S. Whipple in gang-related shooting; he dies 2 days later.

18 Anthony Bucciferro, 54, a W. Chicago truckdriver, shot July 2 about 11 a.m. as he made a delivery in 3400 block of W. Ogden.

19 Fred Jones, 42, stabbed Aug. 13 at 1:40 a.m. in his apartment in 1100 block of S. Albany.

20 Keith Perkins, 21, shot Aug. 13 in apartment hall in 4300 block of W. 19th.

21 Edgar Thomas, 19, shot Aug. 15 at 11:20 p.m. in 3200 block of W. 16th.

22 Charles Jackson, 36, a double amputee, beaten to death with his own wheelchair Aug. 24 at 3:20 a.m. in vacant lot in 1500 block of S. Kedzie.

23 Elvis Allen, 25, shot Sept. 3 about midnight in apartment in 1300 block of S. Tripp.

24 Graylin Moses, 21, shot Sept. 10 at 1:30 a.m. in 2600 block of W. Ogden.

25 Joyce Partridge, 31, shot in robbery attempt Sept. 11 at 3:30 a.m. while sitting with her boyfriend in his parked car near 1400 block of S. Millard.

26 Timothy Chapple, 27, shot Sept. 12 at 2 p.m. in alley in 3600 block of W. Grenshaw.

27 Allen Bates, 23, found stabbed Sept. 23 about 6 p.m. in vacant lot in 1500 block of S. Lawndale.

28 Charles House, 20, shot Sept. 29 at 11:20 a.m. in 1600 block of S. Homan alley.

29 Kenneth Price, 20, shot Oct. 3 about 9 p.m. in 2200 block of S. Avers.

30 Kevin Foster, 21, shot Oct. 5 about 9 p.m. at corner of W 16th and S. Homan.

31 Lionel Jones, 34, found shot Oct. 15 about 9 p.m. in vacant lot in 3300 block of W. 16th.

32 Gloria Mitchell, 24, stabbed Oct. 22 about 2 a.m. in front of her home in 1100 block of S. Springfield.

33 Raul Muguia, 23, shot Nov. 13 in 3300 block of W. Douglas.

34 Mary Stevens, 34, of Calumet Park, stabbed Dec. 4 about 10 a.m. in her car in 3900 block of W. 19th.

35 James Collins, 50, shot about midnight Dec. 18 in tavern in 3700 block of W. Ogden.

36 Jay Jackson, 46, found stabbed Dec. 20 at 9:30 p.m. in his apartment in 1600 block of S. Springfield.

37 Dorsey Dixon, 19, shot Dec. 29 at 8:40 p.m. in pool hall in 4200 block of W. Roosevelt.

1984

38 Roger Griffin, 26, stabbed Jan. 14 at 4 a.m. in gameroom he owned in 3600 block of W. Cermak; he dies 4 days later.

39 Harriet Price, 24, found stuffed in a plastic bag Jan. 14 at 2 p.m. under porch of apartment in 3000 block of W. Roosevelt.

40 Keith Jordan, 23, found beaten Jan. 22 at 6 a.m. in 1300 block of S. Pulaski.

41 Scott Pervie, 39, shot Feb. 13 at 3:20 a.m. in front of his home in 4100 block of W. 21st.

42 Jerry Fisher, 37, shot Feb. 26 at 4:40 p.m. in carwash during quarrel over pay phone at 3006 W. Roosevelt Rd.

43 Anderson Moses, 34, found shot March 10 about midnight in alley at 1227 S. Central Park Ave.

44 Matilda O'Neal, 50, beaten to death by her boyfriend March 25 at 11 p.m. in her apartment in 1100 block of S. Troy.

45 Luis Ashford, 26, shot on porch April 8 at 2:15 p.m. in 900 block of S. Independence.

46 James Pittman, 61, shot April 13 at 3:55 p.m. in his home in 1200 block of S. Komensky.

47 Marcissa Martinez, 26, shot April 19 about 1 p.m. in apartment in 2700 block of W. 18th.

48 Thomas Kitchen, 35, stabbed April 25 after midnight in parking lot at 3768 W. Roosevelt.

49 Oralia Velazquez, 25, shot on her way home from work by 2 teens May 30 about 9 p.m. on "L" platform, 1944 S. Kedzie.

50 Derrick Wallace, 15, shot June 9 about midnight in 3900 block of W. 19th.

51 Cleveland Brown, 31, shot July 7 at 3:20 a.m. after quarrel with group of friends in 3500 block of W. 16th.

52 Wilfred Smith, 26, stabbed July 12 after midnight in gangway at 1511 S. Lawndale.

53 William Perkins Jr., 19, shot July 18 about 10 p.m. in 1300 block of S. Sacramento.

54 Genella Profit, 32, shot July 16 at 1:40 a.m. in 3100 block of W. 15th; she dies 4 days later.

55 Christopher Franklin, 20, found stabbed Aug. 8 at 4:45 p.m. in vacant lot in 1800 block of S. Lawndale.

56 Troy Thomas, 18, 3722 W. Douglas Blvd., shot Aug. 22 at 2 a.m. in front of his home in 3700 block of W. Douglas.

57 Truely Hunter, 72, found beaten Aug. 22 at 6 p.m. near his home in 1800 block of S. Kedzie; he dies almost 2 months later.

58 Bernard Welch, 30, found shot Aug. 25 at 9:30 a.m. in lot at 1145 S. Fairfield.

59 Delshay Rolling, 24, found by her 2 children as they came home from school; she was stabbed 31 times Sept. 6 at 2:30 p.m. in her apartment in 4200 block of W. 21st.

60 Frank Davis, 31, shot Sept. 19 at 10:30 p.m. in apartment in 1200 block of S. Independence.

61 Winfield Johnson, 60, of Berwyn, shot Oct. 27 during robbery of his grocery store at 1945 S. Keeler Ave.

62 Oscar Holman, 25, shot Oct. 28 at 5:40 p.m. in 3300 block of W. Fillmore.

63 Larry Jackson, 28, shot Nov. 3 at 9:15 p.m. in house in 1100 block of S. Richmond.

64 Sam Stokley, 24, found beaten Nov. 25 at 5:30 a.m. in dumpster at 3219 W. Ogden.

65 Michael Wade, 28, found shot Nov. 27 at 5:40 p.m. in 1100 block of S. Troy alley.

66 Leroy Smith, 38, shot Nov. 2 at 9:30 p.m. in front of his home in 2100 block of S. Drake.

67 Donald Tankson, 37, assaulted Nov. 30 at 9:30 p.m. in apartment in 1300 block of S. Washtenaw; he dies 5 months later.

1985

68 Jerome Andrews, 50, of Peoria, beaten to death Jan 22 about 2 a.m. in 1600 block of S. Homan.

69 Donnell E. Pearson, 21, shot Feb. 3 at 11:30 p.m. in tavern at 1200 S. Troy Ave.

70 Richard Gay, 35, shot March 28 at 6:45 p.m. in Webster School, 4055 W. Arthington St.

71 Richard Wallace, 20, stabbed April 1 at 8:30 p.m. in 3500 block of W. 13th Place.

72 James Perry, 27, shot May 16 at 2:50 a.m. in basement in 3800 block of W. Fillmore.

73 Maria V. Martinez, 74, while on her way to Sportsman's Park with a friend, is accosted and pushed down a stairway by 2 teens May 29 at 8:25 p.m. on an 'L' platform at 1910 S. Central Park Ave.; she dies less than a month later.

74 Vincent Lynch, 23, shot July 6 at 11:30 p.m. in front of his home in 3600 block of W. Cermak; he dies 2 weeks later.

75 Bernard Hoskins, 28, shot June 2 at 2 a.m. in his car in 3500 block of W. Ogden; he dies 2½ weeks later.

76 Scott Gregerson, 34, found shot July 23 at 6 a.m. in his auto in parking lot of American Steel Container Corp., 4445 W. 5th Ave., where he was a truck driver.

77 Charles Farmer, 33, found shot Aug. 13 at 11:45 p.m. in 1200 block of S. Independence.

78 David Allison, 54, stabbed Aug. 15 at 8:40 p.m. in front of his home in 2200 block of S. Keeler.

79 Roy Lee Croft, 18, shot Aug. 15 at 5 a.m. in 1200 block of S. Kildare.

80 Andre Massie, 18, found shot Sept. 2 about midnight in 1400 block of S. Pulaski; his body is not identified for 3 days.

81 Benjamin Cook, 73, stabbed Sept. 11 at 7 p.m. in his apartment in 1500 block of S. Drake.

82,83,84 Tony, 3, Stephen 2, and Shaun Stokes, 1, die in house fire allegedly set by their father Sept. 13 about 3 p.m. in 1200 block of S. Kedzie.

Parole system putting crime back on the streets

Unskilled ex-cons fall back into a destructive lifestyle

T he first time Edward Williams was on parole, he committed murder two months after leaving prison.

Williams and an 11-year-old boy were stealing tires from the lot of an auto supply store. The youngster was tossing the tires over a fence when a worker ran out of the store and grabbed him.

"He catches him and tucks him under his arm like a sack of potatoes," Williams recalls. "In my mind I was thinking, 'I hate all white people.' I turned around and blew the man away."

Eleven years later, Williams, 33, is out on parole again, one of 95 ex-convicts on the caseload of parole agent Oliver Gilbert. Most live in North Lawndale.

In six years with the Illinois Department of Corrections, Gilbert has been there when ex-convicts like Williams were released from prison and sent back to the streets where they had first turned to crime.

"A lot of times their only option is to fall back into the same patterns of criminal activity that sent them to prison in the first place," explains Gilbert, who says he has had to arrest hundreds of parole violators.

Left: Parole agent Oliver Gilbert pauses in a North Lawndale apartment while looking for a parolee.

According to Illinois corrections officials, about 40 percent of the more than 18,000 people now in prison have been there before.

Many ex-convicts who manage to remain out of prison slip into wasted lives, passing time on street corners or in vacant lots, getting high on drugs or alcohol, living off public aid.

Either way, they are a financial drain on society.

It costs about $16,000 a year to keep one convict locked up in an Illinois prison. Despite this large expenditure, most parolees are released unprepared to lead productive lives.

They go in—and come out—uneducated, without the skills or discipline needed to hold a job. On parole they have additional handicaps: prison records plus whatever psychological scars remain after dehumanizing treatment behind bars.

Gilbert, 37, who grew up in North Lawndale when it was a much less troubled neighborhood, estimates that only 1 percent of his parolees have jobs waiting for them when they get out of prison. After long searches, some succeed in finding work, but in many cases they can't hold on to them.

Officials of the Safer Foundation, which helps ex-convicts find employment, estimate that about 6,000 parolees in Illinois seek their assistance each year. They say they are able to find work for about 2,400.

After a month, only 60 percent of those who get jobs are still working. After three months the figure drops to 30 percent, or about 720 of the original 6,000.

Beset by serious economic and social problems, underclass communities across the country have little to offer ex-convicts, who often end up adding to the malaise.

An unemployed parolee is just one more flawed role model for children growing up in shattered families, attending ineffective schools and seeing crime and violence all around them.

About 9,360 ex-convicts are on parole in Illinois. About 4 percent of them, around 400, live in North Lawndale, though the 61,500 residents there represent just one-half of 1 percent of the state's population.

About 165 of North Lawndale's parolees live in K-Town, a narrow, square-mile strip on the neighborhood's western edge where most of the street names begin with K. One in every 85 residents there is on parole.

The growing number of teenagers and young adults committing serious crimes in ghettos is reflected in Gilbert's caseload. The ex-convicts being assigned to him today are much younger than the ones he worked with when he first became a parole agent.

"The situation is getting worse," Gilbert says. "A lot of men on my caseload are very, very young. They don't have any skills, they're hard to train, and they're committing crimes at a younger age."

The average age of ex-offenders contacting the Safer Foundation also is dropping, officials there say, from 25 a decade ago to 21 today.

Gilbert believes that underclass ex-convicts need "intensive deprogramming" if they are to move away from the self-destructive lifestyles they have been raised in. Parole officers try to change basic attitudes, but their individual efforts are no match for the negative influences that permeate poor black communities, he says.

"It's an inescapable fact of life in North Lawndale that eventually you'll become a victim or an offender," Gilbert notes. "A casual dice game on the corner can lead to a robbery or a murder, and the robber later becomes a victim in another dice game down the road. It's a vicious cycle."

For much of his life, Edward Williams has been either a criminal or a convict.

"I stuck up so many people I can't even count," he says. "It had to be more than a hundred. Most of them right around here."

He started stealing cars when he was 12. He and his friends took joy rides through North Side neighborhoods, where "we could always find someone with $100, $150 to stick up," he remembers.

At 14 he joined a street gang and broke into his first house. At 16, already a heroin addict, he was arrested four times. Convicted twice for armed robbery, he served six months in the Cook County Jail.

"If I had never gone to jail, I probably would have ended up getting killed," Williams says. "We were young and wild on the streets. We thought we were doing what was smart, what was slick."

Out of jail, Williams went right back to crime. At 17, during a robbery attempt, he shot a man with a sawed-off shotgun stolen from a preacher's house. This time he was sent to prison with a six-year sentence.

Released on parole after five years in Stateville Correctional Center, it wasn't long before Williams stole more guns and began using LSD regularly.

"I came back with the attitude that the whole world owed me something," he recalls. "I was feeling hate."

What he describes as the "diabolic mentality" he developed on the streets and in prison led to the killing outside the auto supply shop on June 28, 1974.

Back in Stateville with a 14- to 17-year sentence, Williams was a troublemaker and a gang general who spent much of his time in segregation. Nevertheless, he was released on parole after slightly more than nine years. That was in February, 1983.

For the next year or so he tried to make a better life for himself. He enrolled in an electronics course, found a steady girlfriend and started attending church.

He seemed so determined to make a success out of his parole that he was even allowed to live with his girlfriend in Iowa for a while, though he had to keep in frequent telephone contact with his parole agent.

After six months there Williams grew restless, and he and his girlfriend came back to North Lawndale, where he slowly began to drift.

He found a job as a price reporter for the Chicago Board Options Exchange but decided he would rather be a welder and enrolled in a vocational training program. Gilbert helped him find a job as an apprentice welder in Arlington Heights, but he was fired after a week for not showing up. Williams says his car broke down but concedes that he never called the company to explain why he would be absent.

He quit a job as a groundskeeper at the Glenview Naval Air Station after two weeks. "It was hard," he explains. "I'm not used to doing manual work."

On a recent visit to the first-floor flat that Williams shares with his mother, Gilbert gets more bad news. Williams has quit his latest job with a trucking company.

"I told him he made a stupid move by quitting," Williams' mother says. "Now he don't do nothing but sleep. He acts nervous all the time. Oh, he gets up every day and looks at the paper. I just say you don't get nothing by looking in the paper."

Later, a disappointed Gilbert confesses that he feels guilty about the way things are turning out for Williams.

"I thought I had prepared him." he says. "I thought he was job-ready. I was really dumb."

Gilbert parks his car in front of the red-brick building where Ronald Coleman is supposed to be living with his mother, Lillie.

In June, Coleman was released from Centralia Correctional Center after serving 11 months of a two-year sentence for theft and possession of a stolen motor vehicle.

Coleman, who dropped out of high school as a sophomore, has never worked and doesn't have a Social Security card. As soon as he got out of prison, he started drawing general assistance payments.

As a recent parolee, Coleman is expected to meet with his parole agent three times a month. Parolees who have been out of prison longer and who have stayed out of trouble are required to see parole agents less often, anywhere from twice a month to once every three months.

Gilbert last saw Coleman on Sept. 16. The 20-year-old had cried while Gilbert scolded him for stealing money for drugs from his mother's purse. Gilbert should have seen Coleman at least three times since this encounter.

A week ago Coleman's mother called Gilbert and said she thinks he is selling drugs. She also believes that he is snatching purses while riding a bicycle.

Today she tells Gilbert she thinks her son needs stricter supervision. She wants him either sent back to prison, moved to a halfway house or put under psychiatric care.

"I do all I can for him," she explains during this visit. "Things he do just don't make sense."

She complains that her son's time in prison, where he had a television and a record player in his cell, did little to steer him from crime. In many ways his life in Centralia was better than at home, she explains. "It didn't teach him anything. He don't mind going back," she says.

Gilbert, who has tried to interest Coleman in several vocational training programs, has concluded that the young man is beyond help.

"I thought I had gotten through to him," the parole agent

says. "I've tried to give him the benefit of the doubt, but Ronald has rejected all of my efforts. I have no other choice but to ask that a warrant be issued for his arrest."

Gilbert's next call is at the apartment where Johnny Poole, alias Michael Poole, John Clay and Lawrence Roberts, is supposed to be living with his wife.

Poole has missed several appointments at Gilbert's office, the last time because he was in a hospital being treated for a leg wound suffered in a fight.

Gilbert thinks Poole, who was paroled in May, 1984, after serving five years in the Joliet Correctional Center, is selling drugs. "I think that's how he supports himself," he says.

"Is Johnny Poole here?" he asks the tall young woman who answers the door.

"No," she says, looking puzzled. "He's in and out."

"My name is Oliver Gilbert. I'm his parole officer. I can't seem to get hold of him. If you see him, can you give him a message to contact me as soon as possible? It's really important."

Poole's wife appears stunned. "He's still on parole?" she asks. "I just saw him last night. He just told me he got an early discharge because he was doing so good. We even had a celebration.

"He's such a convincing liar."

As Gilbert drives around North Lawndale, he scans the streets for negligent parolees or someone to relay this oft-repeated message: "Tell him I'm looking for him."

Behind the wheel of his beat-up Chevy Malibu, Gilbert peers into vacant lots and liquor stores, where he sometimes finds four or five parolees together.

The area has deteriorated sharply in the years since Gilbert was a boy here. "The memories are good, for the most part," he says, "but I have a lot of negative feelings about the neighborhood now. A lot of the people are just like the vacant lots. They're without hope."

On his rounds, Gilbert carries a .357 Magnum, which he says he has never had to fire. "We don't go in like storm troopers," he explains.

"I like to rely on the grapevine instead of acting like a law enforcement type. If you can communicate with the people, you can accomplish anything. You can even get a guy arrested."

The easygoing Gilbert is considered almost a friend by many people in the community. They bum cigarettes from him and wave to him when they see him. His attitude is so relaxed that dope peddlers have offered him drugs.

Occasionally he finds himself in difficult situations. Two men once tried to rob him. "In this community, if you can make change for $20," he explains, "you're going to get robbed of $20."

The most difficult aspect of his job, Gilbert says, is having a parolee rearrested and sent back to prison.

"The hardest part is writing that report after you've put so much work into a person, pooled so many resources, spent many, many hours trying to deprogram him, deinstitutionalize him, and then you have to add that he's under new criminal charges and back in an institution," he explains.

"That's a rather bitter pill for the parole officer to swallow."

Addicts slip out the back door of reality

Where so many have lost hope, drug trade flourishes

S mile, Ivory!" Officer Patrick O'Donovan yells as he eases his unmarked police car past the intersection of 16th Street and Kedzie Avenue.

"Ain't nothin' to smile about," answers Ivory, one of hundreds of drug addicts living in North Lawndale, whiling away their days in the vacant lots or on the street corners of the West Side neighborhood.

"You ain't in jail," Maureen Doyle, O'Donovan's partner, chimes in. "That's something to smile about."

"Don't jinx me like that!" Ivory complains as the police car moves away.

Two blocks farther, the car slows down again as it passes the building at 3410 W. 16th St., which a large sign identifies as John's Video Game Room.

But the storefront operation, with bars protecting the windows and a wary lookout posted at the front door, is known throughout North Lawndale as something else.

"It's a drug house," O'Donovan says. It is one of more than 100 in the neighborhood, police believe, through which about two dozen major dealers dispense such drugs as heroin,

Left: A North Lawndale storefront calls itself "John's Video Game Room," but it's known in the neighborhood as something else. "It's a drug house," says police officer Patrick O'Donovan.

cocaine, codeine, amphetamines, barbiturates, hashish, marijuana and PCP, an animal tranquilizer.

In this economically depressed area, where three of five adults do not have jobs and more than half the residents are on public aid, drugs are widely used as an escape mechanism.

They are a staple of North Lawndale's underground economy. Police estimate that residents spend about $1.5 million on narcotics each year. Most of that money comes from outside the community—from welfare payments or crime.

Wherever the underclass lives, drugs are pervasive, contributing to the social decay. Sgt. Robert Thorne of the police narcotics unit estimates that almost a third of North Lawndale's unemployed residents use drugs regularly as do 10 percent of the working residents.

Most of the violent crime that plagues places like North Lawndale is committed by people seeking money for narcotics or acting under their influence.

As a rule, street gangs control the drug trade, and gang leaders who make impressive profits from it become role models for underclass boys, most of whom have little or no relationships with their fathers.

Very little of the money earned from drugs filters down to lower-level gang members, but many boys, some of them not yet in their teens, are lured into gangs by the illusion of easy money. They become "mules," delivering drugs for big-time dealers.

Also, drug use among the underclass exacts a heavy toll from the rest of society. Drug users from North Lawndale and other poor black areas frequently commit crimes in wealthier neighborhoods to support their habits.

Law enforcement experts believe that citywide, as much as 80 percent of all street and property crime, including hold-ups, purse snatchings and burglaries, are committed by drug addicts.

"Drugs and crime are interrelated and inseparable," noted Patrick Healey, executive director of the Chicago Crime Commission. "You see it time and again, a drug addict arrested in a series of armed robberies or burglaries."

In a single night, Healey said, a drug addict from a ghetto might commit six or seven robberies in a nonghetto area.

"If they break into a garage in North Lawndale, they may

find only a case of empty bottles," said Lt. William Callaghan of the police narcotics unit. "Homes in North Lawndale aren't as good picking. They go out south or up north. They go out of the neighborhood."

"Naw, ain't nothin' happening," says the man perched on a stool just inside the shadowy doorway at John's Video Game Room, his hands waving a visitor away. "I just called him and he said he'd be here in 30 minutes . . . but I don't know."

"He" drives up several times a day, bringing "bags"—small quantities of heroin wrapped in foil—that sell for $10 to $20 apiece, police say. He brings only a few at a time, ready to flush them down the toilet at the rear of the arcade if the police appear.

The game room is just one of several drug houses along a six-block stretch of 16th Street, according to police who patrol this neighborhood.

"That's a walking bag," says Lt. Clemente Robles, the Marquette District commander, as he drives through the neighborhood. A walking bag, he explains, is a dealer who carries drugs to his customers instead of waiting for them at a fixed location.

Drug dealing in North Lawndale can be extremely lucrative, according to police. The least ambitious of the major pushers make $700 to $1,000 a week after expenses, according to Thorne.

Some dealers earn considerably more. During his heyday in the late 1970s, Charles "C.W." Wilson reportedly took in about $50,000 a week. "In Lawndale today, there are three or four dealers who average about $500 to $700 a day," Thorne said.

One of the smaller dealers operates out of John's Video Game Room, which makes a pretense at authenticity in its outer room, a small, dark chamber where the walls are lined with warped wood paneling and the floor is covered with a filthy carpet. There is a Donkey Kong game, along with four other coin-operated machines.

The pretense ends at the flowered curtain that covers the door leading to the inner room, which addicts call the shooting gallery.

In this narrow room with a worn sofa, addicts inject drugs day and night. Two small windows in the wall allow those in the shooting gallery to keep an eye on the front room.

A Doberman pinscher is chained to the back door.

Off to the side of the shooting gallery is a cramped, foul-smelling toilet with boards tacked across its window. Cobwebs are woven around the light cord. Just outside the bathroom door, a black-and-white television sits on an upturned pail.

It was in this bathroom that 30-year-old Johnny Calvin Russell died of an overdose one hot night in June. When the Fire Department ambulance arrived, Russell's body was sprawled next to a syringe and a rubber hose.

Russell was a familiar type among the underclass: An ex-convict who had failed to lead a productive life after being released from prison.

Seven years earlier, Russell had been convicted of armed robbery after he used a gun to steal $32 from a young newsboy in the early morning hours. He spent the next three years in prison, at a cost to society of about $48,000.

Out on parole, he was arrested again—this time for shooting a man. He was returned to prison, but only for a month. He was released again in December, 1982.

On the last night of his troubled life, Russell stumbled into a tavern on 16th Street and Homan Avenue. His eyelids were drooping as he leaned over the counter and mumbled to the bartender that he was "so high—as high as I ever want to be."

According to the autopsy report, Russell had been drinking liquor and codeine syrup. In the next half-hour, he stumbled down 16th Street and into John's Video Game Room. In the back room, he gave himself two lethal injections of morphine.

"I was glad it happened this way instead of him killing someone or someone killing him," Russell's brother, Ronald, recently said. "Glad he didn't have to worry anymore about being broke, or wanting a drink, or wanting his drugs."

Joe Mack has been luckier than Johnny Calvin Russell—at least so far. Now 42 and a janitor in the Methadone Clinic at 4010 W. Madison St., Mack says he used hard drugs for about a decade.

"When you back away from drugs, your body is clean but your mind could go either way," he said. "I have flashbacks. They come and go, but I just block it out.

"Basically what is happening in Lawndale is people are escaping reality."

In North Lawndale, Thorne observed, "you have only a few

block clubs and a few active community groups. There are not many in the community who would go up against drug operations because of fear of reprisal."

Since January, Thorne said, the narcotics unit has conducted 30 raids on known "drug houses" in North Lawndale. Evidence was confiscated in 15 of those raids, and 19 people were arrested.

Police recovered 113.3 grams of PCP; 228.2 grams of cocaine, and 42.7 grams of heroin—with a total street value of $101,926—along with eight handguns and $5,128 cash. One hundred grams is equal to .22 pounds.

Thorne says his unit has raided John's Video Game Room twice in the last six months. The first raid was in June, shortly before Russell died. The second was in October in reaction to an inquiry from The Tribune.

In both cases, Thorne said, an informant made a purchase, but when a warrant was obtained and the raid was conducted, no narcotics were found and no one was arrested.

"You may hit the place 10 times but never catch anyone with anything," Thorne explained.

James Grooms, 65, who is listed with his wife as owner of the building housing the arcade, said he was unaware of the raids.

"All I know is they running a game room there," said Grooms, a retired auto mechanic who has lived in North Lawndale since 1950. He said the monthly rent on the arcade is $150.

"If any raids were made down there, it was when I wasn't down there during the day," he said. "All I know is they found a pistol down there on one of the guys."

Did he know someone had died of a drug overdose in the bathroom?

"No. That's the first time I heard of this."

Did he know Johnny Calvin Russell?

"Calvin? I know Calvin. I didn't know what happened to him. I haven't seen him. I use to see him around there all the time, every day. He was good friends with the guys there in the game room."

According to Thorne, there are two starkly different types of drug dealers within North Lawndale's underclass. One is the professional. "The good dope dealer will have more stolen goods in his house than a small store." The second is the "hustler," described as one who "tosses dope," a street term for selling small amounts.

Both types will employ young boys as runners. Police recently caught a 7-year-old delivering drugs for his mother.

"There's no limit on what pushers can make," said 'Silk,' a 36-year-old former dealer now being treated in a methadone program. "It can run into the thousands. I've known some who made as much as $10,000 a week."

Silk said he was 21 when he started "dealing with people on the street, being around the wrong people and seeing how much money they made." In eight years, he said, he made about $100,000.

His habit cost him $300 a day, Silk said. "Most women who get hooked become whores," he said. "If they ain't working for a pimp, they're working for that drug habit.

"I stopped because there was too much danger. People started getting wild, complaining about the drugs. People trying to rob you. And the police were around all the time knocking your door down.

"Drug dealing is very dangerous," he said, reflecting on his experience. "I've had my life threatened by people in the street quite a few times. It went as far as to have shootouts . . . a couple of times."

He added that most of the people he knew when he started selling are now "dead or locked up."

Being arrested "quite a few times" never stopped him, he said. "You learn from arrest how to get around the police, what not to do. . . . Sometimes you just make payoffs.

"I'd pay several policemen each week. You know, different ones would come by. You just give them a package—it varied, between $300 and $500 a week—and they divided it up however they wanted to."

A major police scandal unfolded in North Lawndale in 1981. Ten officers, nine of them plainclothes investigators from the Marquette District, were convicted of taking payoffs from drug dealers to overlook their illicit operations.

C.W. Wilson testified that he regularly paid off police in North Lawndale so his multimillion-dollar curbside operation just off 16th Street could thrive. Before he was finally arrested by other police, he had become a rich man with luxury cars, expensive jewelry and a pack of Dobermans to guard his fortresslike home on South Christiana Avenue.

Though the imprisonment of Wilson and of the 10 policemen put a visible dent in some of the big-time operations in North Lawndale, police observe that it has had little impact on the volume of sales.

Over the last few weeks, police said, a war has been going on in the neighborhood, with two midlevel peddlers vying for the position of "narcotics king." It was sparked, according to O'Donovan and Doyle, when police concentrated on one of the prime dealers, arresting his runners and confiscating his money and drugs. They tried to arrest the dealer but never had much luck.

"We would stop him in his Cadillac," O'Donovan recalled. "He was always nice and polite. He was a neat dresser and he always wore a bulletproof vest."

III

FINANCIAL
INCENTIVES

Even money can't seem to cure poverty

Despite programs, gap between rich and poor widens

Federal help for the poorest has an eager but melancholy history; over the last 20 years, aid programs were known as much for their largesse as for their failure.

One sore characteristic of those multibillion-dollar programs was that they either passed over or were ineffectual in touching the new underclass, a feared and troubled group in the inner cities.

It is now fashionable to believe that the programs actually helped create an urban black underclass by making people dependent on welfare while they remained grounded in ghetto crime and hopelessness.

The history of real successes in the Great Society of Lyndon Johnson and others has been blurred by the current conservative enthusiasm. In the debate over policy today, not much middle ground is left: Either the solution is to return to those enormous outlays of federal funds or to scrap the entire system.

Despite some isolated attempts to encourage new housing-voucher or job programs, the dominant mood is against further outlays, at least on the national level.

Clearly, no one is confident enough to guarantee a solution for

Left: A poor youth in North Lawndale: "In the war on poverty," President Reagan has said, "poverty won."

erasing poverty or for containing the underclass that infects the cities, victimizing black and white residents and causing unconscionable public expense.

Efforts to help the jobless and poor have been exhaustive and exhausting to the country: $60 billion was spent in the 11 years of the Comprehensive Employment and Training Act [CETA] alone.

President Johnson made this bold pronouncement in his 1967 State of the Union message: "This administration today, here and now, declares unconditional war on poverty in America."

"In the war on poverty," said President Reagan, summing up the nation's feeling last January, "poverty won."

One of his aides, Patrick Buchanan, White House director of communications, crowed recently that the drop in poverty—the first in a decade, down 1.8 million people, to 33.7 million—showed "that American capitalism, and not the welfare state, is the best means for bringing people out of poverty."

Data from the Bureau of the Census, however, also show an income gap greater now than at any time since the bureau started collecting information in 1947. The poorest 40 percent of the nation received 15.7 percent of the national income in 1984, while the top 40 percent received 67.3 percent. The bureau also reported that the number of families with incomes below $5,000, the poorest of the poor, has grown faster than the poverty rate in general.

"We've got to find new ways to generate wealth," said Atlanta Mayor Andrew Young, a former United Nations ambassador and civil rights leader.

The smokestack industries and the other sources of manual-labor jobs that were the way out of the ghetto for most minority groups, Irish or Polish or Italian, have largely disappeared from the cities.

Though Young said he has seen the successes of the Great Society, he thinks more must be done in the areas of family planning and economics, because "there is an income gap widening between blacks and whites in the country."

The trend in the last decade, with last year as the exception, is not promising:

In 1960 nearly 40 million people, or 22 percent of Americans, were considered poor. By 1969 that figure was reduced to 24 million, or 12 percent of the population. There was little improvement during the 1970s, and from 1978 to 1983 the number climbed steadily, adding 10.8 million people.

Recessions and the failure of benefits to keep up with double-digit inflation accounted for much of that, but there still is debate on the future of the current recovery and on a second decline in poverty figures.

The entire underclass may represent only 1 to 3 percent of the population, but its existence is a lightning rod for social consciousness.

Sar Levitan of George Washington University describes members of the underclass as being those who "most frequently are poorly educated, aged, black, female, or reside in an inner city. Afflicted with serious behavioral problems, they become trapped in a cycle of poverty and welfare dependency that poses one of the most troubling and complex problems in social welfare policy."

Levitan believes that without cash benefits, 25 percent of all American families would be in poverty. "The impact of federal aid to the poor is evident; nonetheless, the nation's increasing affluence makes the deprivation of those who remain poor both more noticeable and more poignant."

Several aid efforts actually deal with the underclass. One involves a $1 billion five-year project to create a housing-voucher system in 20 cities and states. Its goal is to replace virtually all other federally assisted housing programs, which now cost $10 billion annually, and to help the chronically unemployed move where the jobs are. A side effect would reduce federal aid to restoring cities.

On the other end of the scale is a tiny effort in Fairfax County, Va., one of Washington's and the nation's wealthiest suburbs, where there is a demonstration project to help 14 families get out of chronic welfare dependency by getting them jobs.

The local government is being assisted in Project Self-Sufficiency by the American Enterprise Institute, a conservative think tank in the capital.

Though the term "workfare" has been largely discredited, there is a new program in California called the Employment Preparation Program aimed at welfare receivers not caring for children younger than 6.

Some call it involuntary servitude, but it is clearly the wave of the future for a society soured on welfare programs.

Martin Anderson, a domestic-affairs adviser for President Reagan during his first term, in a speech last year defended Reagan's policies on welfare and also chastised the Census

Bureau and other poverty researchers for using imprecise data.

"As we have gradually lost track of the true nature and extent of poverty in the United States," said Anderson, now at the Hoover Institution at Stanford University, "we have also begun to slide away from a clear idea of who should be eligible for social-welfare benefits."

In the book that made Charles Murray one of the most quoted men in Washington, "Losing Ground—American Social Policy 1950-80," he recommended "scrapping the entire federal welfare and income-support structure for working-aged persons, including AFDC [Aid to Families with Dependent Children], Medicaid, Food Stamps, Unemployment Insurance, Worker's Compensation, subsidized housing, disability insurance, and the rest."

Murray's arguments reflect the homespun traditionalism now popular in Washington. It takes solace in attitudes shared by Benjamin Franklin. "The best way of doing good to the poor," he once said, "is not making them easy in poverty, but leading or driving them out of it."

Alexis de Tocqueville's 1835 Memoir on Pauperism also gives comfort to antiwelfare thinking: "Any measure which establishes legal charity on a permanent basis and gives it an administrative form thereby creates an idle and lazy class."

The Reagan administration has relied more on the belief that "a rising tide lifts all ships" than on programs for the poor or the urban underclass.

The Center on Budget and Policy Priorities, an advocacy group in Washington, asserted that over the four fiscal years 1982-85, programs for people with low incomes were cut more than twice as much as other social programs.

Part of the problem is that society has changed. When the ADC program [Now AFDC] was enacted along with Social Security 50 years ago, 88 percent of the families getting aid were those in which the fathers had died. In March, 1983, more than 88 percent of the children in the program had able-bodied fathers who were not living at home; 47 percent of those children were illegitimate.

The Children's Defense Fund reported that in 1950 only 18 percent of black infants were born out of wedlock; by 1982, the figure was 55 percent.

Another problem: 27 states do not offer AFDC to unemployed two-parent families, and states are not allowed to help needy two-parent families in which parents have jobs.

The Congressional Research Service expressed it this way: "Over the years, there has been concern that concentration of AFDC benefits on fatherless families, and the program's exclusion of needy families with full-time jobs, may have inadvertently encouraged family break-up and unwed parenthood."

M. Carl Holman of the National Urban Coalition is worried that the public has already written off the underclass and that "racism is much, much more dangerous than before. . . . You used to be able to blame the Bull Conners. Now you've got people who are apologists for doing nothing. They are sophisticated and make it more palatable. There is a kind of cynicism that gets people to accept this as a natural economic phenomenon."

The flaws of past programs have been seized as an opportunity.

"They rejected all the assumptions of the Great Society and, once [they are] rejected, they don't have to feel guilty about them," said Levitan. He also admits that liberals "never sat down to get a good inventory and have the fortitude to say it didn't work. . . . We got tired of expansion of the welfare system."

Stuart Eizenstat, domestic-policy adviser to President Jimmy Carter who has since become a Democratic "voice in exile" in Reagan's Washington, admits that liberals and Democrats failed to review and revamp and consolidate social programs while the country was getting fed up with their growing cost.

Reagan articulated the conservative mood, he said, and "there was already a predisposition to believe we were wasting their tax dollars." Eizenstat, who was a junior member of Johnson's White House, added, "No success could measure up to the rhetoric of Johnson's time."

William Julius Wilson of the University of Chicago has blamed the declining liberal influence on several factors, among them fear of speaking directly to the problems in the city.

"One approach is to avoid describing any behavior that might be construed as unflattering or stigmatizing to ghetto residents, either because of a fear of providing fuel for racists' arguments or because of a concern of being charged with 'racism' or 'blaming the victim,' " Wilson said in a lecture last May.

Wilson's aim is to help the liberal view revive. He said: "I am fearful of the rise of conservative perceptions. I think they ignore some of the broader problems in society that have impact, such as economics."

Eleanor Holmes Norton, former chairman of the Equal Employment Opportunity Commission during the Carter administration and now a professor at the Georgetown University Law Center, is equally blunt.

She complained that the black family is deteriorating under enormous pressure and that the nation is unwilling to deal with it.

"Our country essentially has no strategy" for competing globally for the manufacturing jobs that once built the middle class in American cities and now are in short supply for those living there.

"The people who are caught are the people with the least preference, and they turn out to be . . . black men."

The National Urban League's director of research, James McGhee, recently wrote in a report that the Jobs Training Partnership Act [JTPA] and the Job Corps are underfunded:

"It remains a mystery as to why the economic benefits of massive support programs for farmers, dairy producers and tobacco growers, for example, are so obvious, while the long-term economic benefits of effective jobs programs are not. . . . The rationale for the bailout of the Chrysler Corp. by the federal government, for example, would apply equally well to the bailout of hundreds of thousands of black families."

Norton also points out that all the present job emphasis is on recently laid-off workers and not on those who have never held a job, the chronically unemployed.

"You won't get the same kind of success rate" in making them employable, she said, but those are the people government should assist.

Anthony Downs of the Brookings Institution, writing in "The New Urban Reality" about the future of industrial cities like Chicago, said: "Unfortunately, the conservative belief that more vigorous private economic growth can solve city problems is false.

"City unemployment and poverty rates were very high in the late 1960s, especially among minorities, even when overall unemployment rates were as low as 3 percent [it was around 7 percent in September]. Most of the reduction in urban-poverty populations since 1959 has resulted from larger government transfer payments and in-kind services, not from greater private prosperity." Nor will the "trickle-down" theory work, he said; it must be direct benefits.

Concern for the black underclass in the cities now focuses on two major areas, economics and family structure.

Even the U.S. Catholic bishops are getting involved; the first draft of their pastoral letter on the economy goes beyond traditional rights and calls for "the formation of a new cultural consensus that all persons really do have rights in the economic sphere and that society has a moral obligation . . . to ensure that no one among us is hungry, homeless, unemployed, or otherwise denied what is necessary to live with dignity."

Washington's Joint Center for Political Studies said in its "Policy Framework for Racial Justice" that "family reinforcement constitutes the single most important action the nation can take toward the elimination of black poverty and related social problems."

Others have been equally forthright.

In a recent article, Norton cited Dr. Martin Luther King Jr.'s statements in the 1960s about the "alarming" statistics on "the rate of illegitimacy." She said he described the black family as being "fragile, deprived and often psychopathic."

She said the fact that more than 55 percent of all black children are born illegitimate is "a natural catastrophe in our midst—a threat to the future of blacks without equal."

U.S. Sen. Daniel Patrick Moynihan [D., N.Y.] echoed Dr. King's words, calling the black family structure "a tangle of pathology."

Andrew Young, who was one of Dr. King's aides, said he has been concerned since he was a young preacher in the South about young blacks being unable to control their birth rate so they could break out of the poverty cycle.

For the last 20 years Moynihan has proposed a national family policy that would change the tax codes and require other federal legislation to help stabilize families.

He said such a policy is needed not only for the underclass itself but for the dire problems of which the underclass is only the most visible victim. "Twenty years ago I picked up a few vibes on my radar that said a storm was coming," he said. "Well, the storm came—an earthquake, seismic, let's say."

Despite his early warnings in 1965 about deterioration of the black family, Moynihan—who was severely criticized as being racist then for sounding that alarm—said the breakdown of family structure in the nation, among all classes and races, is "a huge social change that we barely anticipated."

The poverty that creates and distorts family problems appears to be as entrenched as the underclass. Said Moynihan:

"If you are under 6 years old in the United States, you are six times more likely to be poor than if you are over age 65. We are the first industrial nation in the world in which children are the poorest age group."

In his 1982 State of the Union address, President Reagan said he had inherited a system in which "available resources are going not to the needy but to the greedy."

"The Reagan administration . . . has by contrast made the shortcomings of other administrations seem minor," declared John Jacob, head of the National Urban League.

Norton seconded that. "History is going to hold it culpable in the worst way," she said. "It doesn't deal with the underclass. This administration has abandoned entirely the underclass and created the opposite of a 'safety net.' "

Levitan and Clifford M. Johnson, in "Beyond the Safety Net," write: "Not since the inauguration of Franklin Roosevelt's New Deal half a century ago have political views regarding government's role in promoting social welfare been so polarized."

This is a national dilemma. A National Agenda for the Eighties, a respected but little-noted report made at the end of the Carter presidency, spoke of an "ambivalent attitude" among Americans, who simultaneously wanted overall reductions in the scope of government and the expansion, or at least maintenance, of every program from social welfare to national defense.

On taking office, Reagan dismantled many of the systems and programs built during the reign of the Democratic Party. Downs, of the Brookings Institution, says the party developed those programs partly in response to urban rioting in the 1960s and partly because it needed big-city votes.

Since then, he said, large chunks of the population have moved to the South and West, the baby-boom generation has aged and economic growth has slowed—and all this has made the nation more conservative.

Some poverty workers have responded to that change, and the resulting polarization, in innovative ways, first developing their own programs and then seeking federal and local support by appealing to the current ideology.

"Focus: Hope" in metropolitan Detroit is a civil-rights organization that not only helps feed inner-city families but also trains chronically unemployed young men as machinists because it recognized a severe shortage of tool-and-die makers.

"This organization is opportunistic as hell," said Rev. William

Cunningham, a Catholic priest who has headed Focus: Hope since 1968. Though the civil-rights group is apolitical, he said, we "never had any real sympathy with the Democratic administrations which look at the problem and covered it with compassion. That's a typically liberal response. What we want is not compassion; the people want justice. . . .

"With Republicans, forget that kind of compassion, show them the economics. With Democrats, show them the terrible suffering, the problems of children. With Republicans, show them that dollar for dollar it's cheaper to do it this way."

Marion Wright Edelman, president of the Children's Defense Fund, is supporting proposals that would cost $14 billion if enacted, which is more than unlikely.

She said, however, that both liberals and conservatives see the sense in spending $600 for prenatal care rather than $1,000 a day for intensive-care nursing for a premature baby.

The climate for spending is as cool as the national deficit is deep. Congress has held off the heaviest cuts proposed by the administration, but beyond that the mood is for more local solutions.

As Martha Hill, of the University of Michigan's Institute for Social Research, summed it up: "There does seem to be more of a climate for people to be responsible for themselves."

Still, there are few initiatives for the underclass plaguing American cities. It is resistant to do-gooder schemes, contemptuous of social planning and virulent in attracting and ruining young lives.

There is also the danger of infection, a growth that already debilitates the cities.

Berneita Holsey sees all the family and related problems in her work as coordinator at a jobs-training program in Baltimore. She said that unless the federal government is more involved and does something to change the economics of the underclass, "you'll wind up having more street people and more crime, and the government will have an answer to that: We'll build more prisons."

Checks bring basics
and a dead-end emptiness

'It's like running in quicksand'

At 19, Freddie Hopkins is the mother of two daughters, Ranetta, 2, and Ransheka, 1. She would like a son.

"Then I get my tubes tied," she explains.

Freddie Hopkins has never been married. The father of her daughters is a 21-year-old who, she believes, has fathered at least eight other children in their North Lawndale neighborhood.

Hopkins met the young man three years ago when he came to visit her younger brother. "He just kept comin' over," she recalls. "He would take me where I wanted to go. He had a car. We went to stores, to drive-ins. He was nice. He didn't give me no hassle."

Hopkins was taking birth control pills, but she still became pregnant. "Didn't feel nothin'," she says. "Everybody else I knew was havin' babies, so I just went along."

The young man was elated. "He say: 'Freddie! You pregnant with my baby?' And I say, 'No, I not.' I just didn't want to believe it. He put his head to my belly and listened, and he say, 'Man, I done got me a son.' "

When the girl was born, Hopkins' grandmother named her Ranetta. "I couldn't think of no name," Hopkins explains.

Left: In North Lawndale, a teenage girl learns early that if she has a baby, the welfare check will be there to help her. Seventy percent of the births in the community are illegitimate.

The father kept coming around. "He bring Pampers," Hopkins says. "He came around every day. He be proud of his baby, except he was hurt because it wasn't no boy."

Freddie Hopkins had been a student at Marshall High School. When her daughter was born, she dropped out. Freddie Hopkins had been raised on public aid. Now, with a child to support, she applied for her own case number.

In the welfare culture, Freddie Hopkins had become a woman. She was getting her own check.

The check is American society come to the ghetto, teaching lessons that are hard to ignore. It feeds and clothes the body, but drains the soul of drive and pride. It mocks commitment, planning and work.

The check pays the rent and the doctor, and it helps— barely—to keep body and soul together. The money is not much. A mother with one child receives $250 a month under the Aid to Families with Dependent Children [AFDC] program in Illinois and $147 in food stamps—a total of $397.

Still, the check is enough—if the recipient doubles up with a mother or a sister or an aunt in an overpriced apartment in a dilapidated building in a crumbling neighborhood; and if she can put up with rats and bugs, the heat in summer and the cold in winter and the bathtub that doesn't work; and if she can put up with the drunks next door and the street gang members hanging around outside; and if she and her children don't eat too well.

But there is much more that the check brings.

It brings dependency, passivity and listlessness. An atmosphere of emptiness and alienation in which marriage is rare and sex is simply something to do. A dead-end existence in which the rite of passage to adulthood occurs when an unmarried teenage girl gives birth and gets her own public aid case number.

The check relieves the need to take control of one's life, to get a job, to get ahead. It pays for babies to be born and fed, but drives families apart or keeps them from forming. It creates men who live off the checks of women, men known as welfare pimps, and women who permit them to do so.

The check asks for nothing. It pays for failure.

Freddie Hopkins may not have wanted to have a baby. But

she knew from her short lifetime of experience that, if she had a baby, the check would be there to help her.

The young man who twice made her pregnant never had to worry about marrying her and taking responsibility for his daughters. He knew, from his short lifetime of experience, that the check would be there to support them.

Freddie Hopkins may not have a job or a high school education or any real prospects in life. But she knows that she can get by anyway. The check will keep coming, month after month. If she has the son she wants, the check, slightly bigger, will go on helping her.

Freddie Hopkins is cushioned by the check. That's what the check was designed to do.

But Freddie Hopkins is also trapped by the check. And that is a perversion of its purpose.

Instead of helping underclass people improve their lives, the check has done much to suck them deeper and deeper into the mire of poverty, illegitimacy, ignorance and boredom.

Despite middle-class stereotypes, living on the check is neither easy nor fun.

"We find that public aid is not something they jump on; they use it because they need it," says Philip Matute, director of Family Focus, a program for teenage mothers in North Lawndale.

"People recognize public aid as a support mechanism, but maybe it's really a banana peel for them to slip on."

The check, says Donald Green, a caseworker with the Illinois Department of Public Aid, "is a debilitating, emotion-eating thing. After a while, you don't want to do any better.

"It's like running in quicksand."

Green, who was born and raised on the West Side and who still lives there, says, "People learn to live down to welfare standards. The girls often ask, 'Who do I got to ask for this or that?' Not 'What do I do?' but 'Who should I ask?' They don't know how to think for themselves.

"Sometimes it's funny, but more often than not, it's heart-breaking."

At one time in her life, Sarah Madlock would have been embarrassed to be living on welfare.

"Our parents told us never to rely on aid, even if there's

nothing else," she says. "The peoples in the South really don't rely on aid. One reason is our pride."

But in 1959, she moved out of the South, up from Batesville, Miss., to the West Side of Chicago. She was 18 and brought with her a 4-month-old son, Glenn.

She got a job in a laundry and was paid $1 an hour to fold linen. Eleven months later, she was laid off. Over the next eight years, she held a string of jobs. She was a hat-packer and a waitress, and for five years, she worked at an electric company until it moved to west suburban Schiller Park.

In 1968, after the birth of her third child, she went on welfare, and she has been on it ever since. In the intervening years, she has given birth to three children. She has never married.

Now, at 44, she is living in North Lawndale, in a five-room apartment with three of her six children. Also living with her is David, the 1-year-old son of her unmarried 18-year-old daughter.

Madlock has difficulty remembering why or how she started on welfare 17 years ago.

"I could have . . . You wind up . . . I was laid off . . . I don't know. It's a long story," she says.

"It wasn't no hard decision. That was your only thing to do. My young peoples was small. A lot of the jobs went to the suburbs. If you didn't find something downtown. . . ."

But life on the check, she says, is a struggle. "If you don't know how to manage your money, it's hard," she says.

"It's easier in the summertime. The kids eat less in the summer. We can kind of make it. In the winter, you got the heating bill and the light bill and the phone bill. In the winter, some peoples can't make it."

The check doesn't teach people how to budget their money. It doesn't teach them how to find adequate housing or how to get a good job or a decent education.

It does teach some clear lessons: Don't work or you'll lose the check. Don't marry or you'll lose the check.

Illinois, unlike many other states, does not make marriage an immediate disqualification for AFDC, though many recipients think it does.

A married woman can receive AFDC in Illinois and 25 other states, but only as long as her husband is unemployed. An unmarried woman can keep her grant if she weds, but only if her new husband is unemployed.

In 1983, the last year for which statistics are available, only 287,000 of the 3.7 million families on AFDC nationwide—7.7 percent—had two parents in the home. In Illinois, only 16,180 of 242,632 families—6.7 percent—did.

Strong indications of the effect of the check on the underclass can be found in a survey of 2,000 black men between the ages of 16 and 24 that was conducted in 1979-80 in Chicago, Boston and Philadelphia by the National Bureau of Economic Research. The results were outlined this summer by Richard B. Freeman and Harry J. Holzer in The Public Interest, a social science magazine.

"Youths from welfare homes, with the same family income and other attributes as those from nonwelfare homes, do far worse in the job market," Freeman and Holzer wrote. "Youths living in public housing projects do less well than youths living in private housing."

In other words, growing up in a welfare family tends to weaken in many underclass people the drive to get a job and the ability to keep one.

● ● ●

Benjamin Jones Jr., 22, has been living in North Lawndale since 1970. Six years ago, he joined a street gang. Four years ago, he was kicked out of Farragut High School for fighting.

For a year, he stayed at home, mostly sleeping and watching television. When he went out, he says, he sweet-talked girls into giving him money from their welfare checks. "You always got to be thinking when you're talking," he explains. "Don't give her time to think."

Finally, his mother, Lorine, who has worked at Curtiss Candy as a candy wrapper for 20 years, got fed up with him and ordered him to start paying rent.

So Jones went looking for work. He filled out six applications, then stopped.

"You got to have qualifications," he says. "You have to be a master in this and that. They never call you back. When they didn't call, I said, 'Hey, forget this.' "

So he went on the check. Each month, he receives $154 in general assistance and $79 in food stamps. He gives the food stamps and $25 to his mother. The rest, he says, he spends on clothes.

His father lives elsewhere in North Lawndale. Asked what his father does for a living, Jones responds, "Same thing as I do. He's on G.A."

The check dominates an underclass neighborhood, as these facts about North Lawndale indicate:

- One of every two people is on welfare.
- Three of every five potential workers are unemployed.
- At least two of every five families are headed by women.
- Seven of every 10 births are illegitimate.
- One of every two mothers is 21 or younger, and one of every seven is 17 or younger.

The statistics about families headed by women, in particular teenagers, are especially worrisome because, in the American economy, female-headed households earn significantly less money than households of couples, and black female-headed households do even worse.

Last year, the median family income of black households headed by women was $8,648, just over half the income of a similar white family, according to U.S. Census data, analyzed by Andrew Brimmer, a black economist who was on the Federal Reserve Board.

In contrast, the median family income of the households of black couples was $23,418, more than three-quarters of the income of a similar white family.

What this means is that a black family that is headed by a woman is likely to have an income that is only a third of what it would be if it was a two-adult family. In fact, nationally, one of every two black families headed by women is living in poverty.

In addition to the emotional support that marriage can bring, there are strong economic reasons for black women to marry.

Yet in the underclass, fewer and fewer are doing so.

● ● ●

"Marry? Nothin' but problems," says Freddie Hopkins.

"I ain't ready to settle down. I ain't going to get married. I got at least 10 more years left of fresh air."

Marriage, Hopkins explains, has nothing to do with having babies or starting a family. It means you settle down and "don't have no fun."

Will she marry the father of her daughters?

"You kidding?" she says. "What I need him for? He bad news."

● ● ●

It is one of the more unfortunate facts of underclass life that many of the young men available for marriage are "bad news" from the standpoint of unemployment, crime and family violence.

Using employment as the measure of marriageability, studies directed by William Julius Wilson, head of the sociology department at the University of Chicago, have found that in the North Central states, including Illinois, there are only 49 marriageable black males, ages 20-24, for every 100 black females in that age group. For whites, the ratio is 70 marriageable men for every 100 women. Similar ratios were found for other parts of the nation.

In other words, for every marriageable black man in his early 20s in America, there are two black women.

Among the underclass, where unemployment is often more than 50 percent, the situation is much worse. "The perception," says Sara McLanahan, a sociologist with the University of Wisconsin's Poverty Institute, "is that there is nothing to be gained by marriage.

"The young black man has no future—at least not the men who are available. If you look at an 18- or 19-year-old father who has no job, no chance at a job and no education, [not marrying] may even be a rational choice.

"In fact, if these women married the fathers, they would all still be poor."

Some men recognize this ruefully. Alfred Lewis, a 25-year-old North Lawndale man on general assistance, and his girlfriend have one child and a second on the way, but they are not planning marriage. Lewis explains, "I can't see me saying, 'I love you and be my wife,' when I ain't got no job and I'm on aid and she's on aid. What can we do?"

But there are also men who take advantage of the situation, men known throughout the inner city as "welfare pimps."

"They have a woman here, and another there," says Hattie Williams, a longtime activist in the Oakland neighborhood on the South Side. "Two or three women they keep barefoot and pregnant so they can survive with $50 a month or so from each of them."

"My God," says a middle-class black woman who works at a West Side housing project, "they are all over the place. They know the day the check comes and they wait outside the currency exchange. If a woman doesn't give them money, she's beaten.

"One guy here, he got two sisters pregnant. They each have several children by him. And he gets money from both of them."

In the world of the check, there is little for teenage girls to look forward to.

Living in apartments where the television is often blaring throughout the day, living in families in which affection is often only rarely given, living with a parent who has few if any parenting skills, these teenage girls are bored and lonely, and often starved for tenderness.

"Sex is something to do," says Hannah Meara, a sociologist and past president of Healthy Mothers and Babies, a maternal health advocacy group based in Chicago.

"It's something they think everybody does. For the girls, it's often a pitiful attempt to get the nurturance they've never gotten at home."

The result, all too frequently, is a pregnancy, a birth and a new welfare mother.

Eleanor is 15. She has a 1-year-old daughter, Levetta, and a second baby due in December. She receives $250 a month in AFDC and will get an additional $91 when the second child is born.

When she was 12, she would have sex with her boyfriend and then run out onto the sidewalk to jump rope with the boy's younger sister.

Eleanor is sitting in an arm chair. The apartment is cool, but Levetta is wearing only a short-sleeve T-shirt and a wet disposable diaper.

The baby sits beside a dustpan and pats the dirt. A bottle half-filled with formula is on the floor near a television set. A fly is on the nipple.

When Eleanor was 11, her mother gave her birth control pills but failed to explain how to use them.

"I had friends who told me to take them once a day, but they never told me, if I missed a day, I'd come up pregnant," she says.

In addition, taking the pills seemed to make her sick. She tried five brands. "But I still got sick."

So she stopped the pills. And she got pregnant.

Levetta was born Oct. 24, 1984. A few months later, Eleanor met John, now a 16-year-old junior at Kennedy High School. A short time later, she was pregnant again.

"Got pregnant 'bout June," says Eleanor.

"Shoot!" John says. "It was 'bout the first day I met you."

Will Eleanor and John marry?

"I say yes. He say no," Eleanor answers.

"I say maybe," says John, adding, "I ain't going to be married at an early age."

"He don't want to get married until he's 25," Eleanor explains. "Who's going to wait that long? Not me. By the time he's 25, I won't be around. I'll be married."

"To who?" asks John.

"Somebody," Eleanor says. "I don't know who."

Eleanor says she has flunked two grades but can't remember which. She is enrolled in an 8th-grade class at Theolene Simpson Alternative School for Pregnant Girls. Her attendance is spotty. Some days, she stays home to watch the soaps. On others, she plays cards at a friend's home.

Nonetheless, Eleanor says she wants to go to college some day and become a 1st-grade teacher.

"If I go to school and get my education and get a good job, I can buy my children whatever they want," she explains. "I wants to go to teacher-training school and then college-training school."

For now, though, she is waiting to give birth.

"It okay," she explains. "I take care of my babies. I get my check."

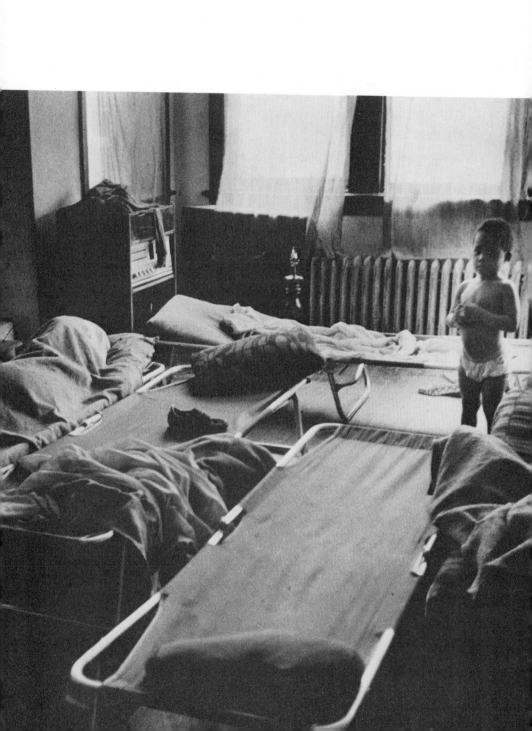

Welfare warfare: The victim is the family

System filled with disincentives to a stable home life

W elfare, as it is structured now, has become the National Complaint.

Critics retell stories of "welfare queens," those rare but celebrated ladies who rip off the system to buy mink coats and pearly slippers.

On the other side, advocates complain that support payments are too low out of political meanness and expediency. It is a program, they insist, that pits whites against blacks, rich against poor, men against women and the aged against the young.

The most serious accusations against the welfare system—specifically, against the largest program, Aid to Families with Dependent Children [AFDC]—are that it encourages the break-up of the black urban family and the rise of teenage pregnancy and illegitimacy.

Welfare nurtures in the cities a black underclass, destructive to itself and to others, headed by single women who are dependent and whose children begin to fail in American society from the moment of birth, according to urban social scientists who have begun to study the problem. While AFDC is feeding

Left: A 2-year-old wanders in a room full of cots in an inner-city apartment. The 11 people living there are supported mainly by welfare checks.

children, it also is feeding a small and apparently permanent underground economy that supports a drug culture and crime.

Researchers have been pointing out the link between the underclass, the high rate of black male unemployment and how AFDC and its rules lead to the matriarchal black family and the "feminization" of poverty.

"It is still true in this society that a man's worth is determined by his ability to earn money," wrote James McGhee of the National Urban League in this year's "Report on the State of Black America."

"And long-term unemployment has a devastating effect on others' opinion of the male and on the male's opinion of himself," the report says.

The portrait of the urban black underclass, as reported by members of The Tribune staff, shows how AFDC has failed to keep pace with inflation and with social changes in the culture of America.

It is a system swathed in myths and resentment. It galls those who contribute to it and humiliates those who receive it. People are outraged at the antics of a flamboyant welfare queen like Linda Taylor, suspected of using 100 aliases in 12 states, but they fail to listen to the far more haunting life of Chicago's Shirley Williams, whose family has known nothing but generations of public assistance.

"The issue of welfare is the issue of dependence," said Sen. Daniel Moynihan [D., N.Y.] more than a decade ago. He said dependence "is an incomplete state in life; normal in the child, abnormal in the adult."

Across the nation, AFDC supports 7.2 million children in 3½ million families. In Illinois, 490,000 children are on AFDC, two-thirds of them in Cook County. Though the state has a program to include unemployed fathers, the vast majority [88 percent] of AFDC families in Illinois are missing fathers in the home.

Even if a couple wanted to live together, there is an "economic disincentive to marriage," says John Bouman of the Legal Assistance Foundation of Chicago. Generally, an able-bodied father in the home disqualifies a family from certain welfare benefits.

"Poverty is now inextricably associated with family structure," said Moynihan, who is promoting legislation on the family that would amend AFDC and the tax code. "Half of all poor persons live in female-headed households." For black children in such homes where the mother is single, younger than 30 and not a high school graduate, the poverty rate is 92.8 percent.

AFDC is budgeted nationwide at $14.5 billion in cash payments this year. Federal and state governments share the cost almost equally. The administrative cost of the welfare bureaucracy is an additional $1.8 billion.

Unlike Social Security payments, which have grown with cost-of-living increases, AFDC payments have lost about 36 percent of their purchasing power in the last decade. In Illinois the loss is closer to 50 percent, according to Jerome Stermer, a former executive director of the Legislative Advisory Committee on Public Aid and now a welfare advocate.

The state's public aid budget has nearly doubled since 1977, administrative costs are up 130 percent, payments to doctors and other providers are up 86 percent—but cash payments to welfare recipients have increased only 33 percent.

A national study, not yet published by the Center on Social Welfare Policy and Law, shows Illinois ranks fifth-highest in terms of how much money a family needs to maintain a minimum standard of living set by the state. But Illinois is 26th in the benefits it disburses.

The numbers fly across the welfare debate on ideological wings. Though the combined federal and state amount is less than 1 percent of the total federal budget, AFDC is the most common field on which liberals and conservatives battle.

"As we have gradually lost track of the true nature and extent of poverty in the United States," said Martin Anderson, a former Reagan adviser, to the Urban Institute, "we have also begun to slide away from a clear idea of who should be eligible for social welfare benefits."

"The concept of failure of the program is a myth perpetrated to penalize the poor," countered James Weill of the Children's Defense Fund, an advocacy group in Washington. "Why is it that the smallest programs for the needy are the most targeted when it comes to the budget?"

Nonetheless, welfare is a barometer of political change in society.

"The days of the dole in our country are numbered," President Lyndon Johnson declared in 1964 while signing the Economic Opportunity Act. AFDC eligibility rules were expanded by the administration in 1967 as part of Johnson's Great Society program and by the Supreme Court in the following two years.

The first budget of the Reagan administration, in 1981, by comparison, lopped 442,000 people off the AFDC roles and dropped 209,000 from the federal food-stamp program.

"We let AFDC become a program that permitted able-bodied adults to choose welfare over work," Jo Anne B. Ross, associate commissioner for family assistance, told a congressional subcommittee last July in the administration's continuing effort to redirect welfare goals. While welfare helped sustain children, she said, "We were far less successful in fostering financial independence and promoting work efforts."

Welfare also reflects social change across the United States: The sympathy once granted welfare mothers who stay home with their children has diminished in recent years as other, more middle-class mothers put their own children in day-care centers and head off to work.

Efforts to reform AFDC seem common sense to one side and brutal to the other. It is not always a rational debate. Some insist that all on welfare get jobs, apparently forgetting that most are young mothers with children under 6 years old and that there is a 7 percent national unemployment rate [8 percent in Chicago], meaning that many American workers with far more developed skills cannot find work.

People also believe AFDC rewards and encourages women to bear more illegitimate children, but federal statistics show that the number of welfare families is steadily declining and that the size of the average welfare family is declining to two children a family, although the inner-city mother who has many children has become a stereotype despite the national averages. Nearly 70 percent have only one or two children.

Others assert that welfare lures people out of Southern low-benefit states into Northern states, where the cities are more dangerous but the benefits higher. The Center on Social Welfare

Policy and Law has documented the fact that the poor are migrating in the same direction as the general population—out of the Northeast and Midwestern states and into the Southwestern and Sun Belt states, where welfare benefits are generally lower but jobs may be more available. Despite that data, a residue of the impoverished remains trapped in the inner cities.

Some critics want a clean break with past efforts rather than an effort to unknot the programs that have evolved.

Charles Murray, a political scientist favored in conservative circles for his scathing attack on all welfare programs, said liberals like "luxuriating on the moral high ground" by seeking more money for welfare and food stamps.

But there is strong evidence suggesting that "the amount of malnutrition attributable to ignorance or poverty-and-ignorance is overwhelmingly greater than that caused simply by poverty," according to Murray.

Murray's supporters say that means that no matter how much money is thrown at the welfare programs, the problems are more fundamental, perhaps ingrained in a portion of society that knows nothing else.

"If there were no welfare programs tomorrow, I don't believe the underclass would disappear," said Gregory Coler, director of the Illinois Department of Public Aid, which administers the $891.3 million program.

"It's a question of to what degree does a program encourage or discourage dependence. . . . What would characterize most people in the underclass is an attitude of despair. They don't believe they have the capability to become independent."

"The only thing that can stop the cycle of the underclass is intervention," said Sister Antoinette Bergen, whose Sisters of Charity run Marillac House, a settlement agency at 2822 W. Jackson Blvd. in Chicago, "and that takes a human being, not a check. Intervention is what we believe in, but every month more and more are coming to our door."

Some reflect the national statistics. Others are more in keeping with the stereotype of the urban welfare mother. Shirley Williams got pregnant in the 6th grade, when she was

"14 going on 15," and she stayed in her mother's home until she turned 18 years old.

"Then they took me off my mom's [aid] and put me on my own."

She is now 29, unmarried, and has had eight children. "I thought about having a family and kids," Miss Williams said evenly, recalling dreams.

"I thought I'd have a husband. And I'd be a housewife and stay home and take care of the kids. Like it's supposed to be. But it didn't work out that way."

Her youngest five children, including a 2-year-old daughter, now have been "placed" by the Illinois Department of Children and Family Services because, she said, a relative was "fooling around" with them. When the sisters at Marillac House found Shirley Williams, she was in a bleak apartment where electricity was poached from an outside line, and extension cords, despite the children, ran waist-high from room to room.

The torch of the underclass had been passed from one generation to another. Williams' mother had 18 children of her own and lives on welfare. Thirteen are still alive today. Between Shirley Williams and her four sisters, who are also on AFDC, they have a total of 33 children getting aid.

"I don't know nothing about work," Williams said. "All I know is housework and baby-sitting."

As McGhee of the National Urban League said bluntly in his report: "Among black families whose resources usually are scarce already, divorce or long-term separation spells economic disaster. . . . Unfortunately, many black parents, especially those who are still teenagers, lack the knowledge and skills that are necessary to be good parents."

The number of AFDC recipients who pass on their welfare role from mother to daughter is in hot dispute. Researchers at the University of Michigan and in separate studies at Harvard believe generational welfare dependency is statistically small.

Most spells of poverty, they claim, last less than two years, though there are a number who never leave the welfare system. Illinois figures show most families are on AFDC for less than 5 years, but those staying 5 to 9 years were 17 percent of the total and those on 10 years or longer were 12 percent.

Welfare cheating is the biggest and strangest misconception.

The all-time welfare queen was probably Dorothy Woods of Pasadena, Calif., who lived in an 18-room mansion. Formerly of Chicago, she drove a Rolls-Royce and five other luxury cars. She was 40 when she pleaded guilty two years ago to welfare fraud totaling $377,500. The mother of 6 had made 12 welfare claims under false names, claiming 49 children.

Federal and local programs have studied abuse, fraud and overpayments and reached varying findings about their extent, ranging from 2.7 percent to 8 percent of any particular welfare program. The high end is usually the overpayment category, which means the state was in error. Sen. John Heinz [R., Pa.] introduced a bill this summer to provide more computer matching of welfare rolls to prevent incorrect payments.

The League of Women Voters in Illinois published results of a six-month study that showed 3.5 percent of recipients misrepresented their status.

That is in contrast to the results of the Grace Commission's study of government waste and found, according to staffer John Grabowski, which found that in any government program approximately 10 percent is wasted or spent inefficiently.

Welfare fraud, said Illinois' Coler, represents a "much less significant dollar amount than that perpetrated by providers. That's where the big bucks are."

Last spring a Waukegan physician, Eugene Tapia, and 17 other people pleaded guilty to federal mail-fraud charges arising from a scheme to defraud the state of nearly $20 million by submitting bills for codeine-based cough syrup and other controlled substances they were dispensing illegally.

In 1977, the inspector general of the AFDC agency estimated that 2.7 percent of the budget was lost to client fraud. A year earlier, the same inspector general's report estimated that fraud and abuse by doctors, clinics and other providers of Medicaid was three times that amount.

"This program [AFDC] has evolved over a long period of time," said Coler. "People's attitudes and perceptions of its purpose have changed pretty dramatically. . . . But there has been no major overhaul of a basic system designed some 30 years ago."

The American system goes back more than 70 years. It is a modern reflection of the English Poor Law of 1601, which provided aid either in the home or in a poorhouse or almshouse.

In the 19th Century, religious organizations took care of needy children and state boards of charity placed them in institutions. The radical change came after President Theodore Roosevelt's White House Conference on Dependent Children in 1909 recommended helping children by giving financial aid directly to their mothers.

"No child should be deprived of his family by reason of poverty alone," the conference declared.

The program at the time was directed almost entirely to widows. Missouri was the first to enact a Widows Pension Law in 1911, and Illinois followed. By 1935, when AFDC was created as part of the Social Security Act, only two states did not have such plans.

One of the current arguments, made by Anderson and Murray and others, urges that control of welfare be handed over to the states. Weill of the Children's Defense Fund believes that effort is insincere and asked why no one proposes turning over Social Security payments to state control.

The history of the widows' pension funds is also an argument against such a move. Federal studies at the time it was established showed that state aid programs were underfunded, arbitrary and discriminatory. One study showed that most families deemed to be "fit" were white, and another, in 1922, revealed that mothers and children in 25 percent of the programs got smaller benefits if they were Italian, Mexican or Czechoslovakian.

The latest figures from the Bureau of the Census show that in 1983, 43.5 percent of all AFDC families were black, 41.8 percent were white, 12.2 percent were Hispanic and American Indians, and the rest Asians.

Society also has changed from the years of the Great Depression, when 88 percent of AFDC recipients were widows.

The majority of recipients later became separated and divorced women, and since 1981 the leading cause for eligibility has been unwed parentage rather than marital break-up.

If there is little sympathy toward teenage pregnancy and

illegitimacy, a working paper of the Ford Foundation recognized that "Americans remain ambivalent about whether women with young children should be required to work."

Government, both state and federal, is also ambivalent. It neither quivers with liberal sympathy nor withholds with conservative righteousness. It seems, rather, to display an excess of both, adding individuals to the welfare rolls by liberally applying standards, but, in a conservative mode, giving them less money than they need.

Welfare, according to its critics, fails in five areas:

● It does not reach most two-parent families who need aid. Twenty-six states have an AFDC-UP program [the UP stands for unemployed parent, usually male], but nationwide it accounts for only 287,000 families out of 3.7 million; in Illinois, in 1983, only 16,180 out of 242,632.

● The benefits are too low for families really to participate or expand their roles in society. The AFDC payments and related benefits are not only below the state's own standard for "minimum living" but also short of the federal poverty levels. Currently a family of four on AFDC in Illinois receives $385 a month in AFDC, the equivalent of $219 in food stamps and an $18 federal energy credit.

That falls 16 percent short of the state minimum standard of living and 30 percent below the federal poverty line. Public assistance is the sole reported income of 93 percent of welfare recipients.

"The main issue still has to deal with inadequacy of the grants," said Betty Williams of United Charities of Chicago. "There just is not enough money to help a family take care of basic needs. Somewhere along the line, the thinking became if we gave them less than enough it would encourage the poor to go out and work. . . . Unemployment is at critical levels. What else is left? Crime is probably the only alternative."

● There is no widespread affirmative work program. Anything smacking of "workfare" has been scorned by liberals as punitive, though the Reagan administration now is behind a bill in Congress that would mandate work programs in every state, to be initiated over a three-year period.

"Most workfare programs have very little potential to get

people into the job mainstream,'' said Weill of the Children's Defense Fund. "It's a scattershot approach. It doesn't create any self-sufficiency but just says we'll make you work for the minimum wage."

But California Gov. George Deukmejian recently signed into law a work program for welfare parents with children over 6. It is expected to reach 32 percent of that state's recipients. Democrats and Republicans supported it because the state agreed to spend $134 million a year for a new child-care program for both welfare and nonwelfare families. It will spend an additional $36 million for state-run child-care centers in abandoned schools and other buildings.

● There is a need for more health insurance to cover those on the margins of poverty. For instance, a welfare mother who went to work at a General Motors Corp. plant in Michigan discovered, when several of her children became sick, that she was financially better off back on welfare. She quit and returned to dependence.

● Again, those on the margins of poverty have a proportionately greater tax burden, and that may encourage many to remain on welfare. Once a person on AFDC moves into a job, for example, he or she faces taxes that may cut her income to less than welfare provided. Moynihan's bill on family security would increase and index the Earned Income Tax Credit and reauthorize and increase the Targeted Job Tax Credit. It would also reduce the tax burden of low-income, single-parent households.

There are other directions in which society needs to look to reassess the AFDC and welfare predicament, say critics and social thinkers who have studied the problem. There must be greater interest in child support by fathers absent from the home.

Eugene Smolensky of the University of Wisconsin's Institute for Research on Poverty compiled these figures: Only 59 percent of eligibile women now receive child-support awards from the courts. Nearly 90 percent of unmarried women, and half of those who are separated, receive no award. Only 49 percent of the children received the full amount due them. Twenty-eight percent received nothing.

Coler, the state welfare chief, asserts that 90 percent of AFDC families could get off the rolls if child-support laws were enforced.

The father of seven of Shirley Williams' eight children is paying the state some child support under a new state program aimed at enforcing child-support payments, she said, but she has no intention of marrying him.

"Too many rules," she said, displaying spirit in her voice. "He tells you what to do, but when you tell him what to do, he's gone do his own thing. I don't like that. I don't need that. I can take care of myself."

Williams seems confident about that, but can she in reality change her life?

"I can't do nothing," she insisted on a recent autumn day when the nuns had bused her and others downtown to demonstrate for the Illinois Campaign for Family Stability.

Williams huddled inside a yellow parka, her hands stuffed her pockets. "Somebody out of this family should have made something of themselves," she said, summing up family history in the sunshine of the city streets.

A social worker's losing battle to help hopeless

Caring and courage are musts—for $13,000 a year

C arolyn is 24, pregnant and the mother of three children. She does not know how to spell her 2-year-old son's name.
"C-A . . . V . . . A-L . . . E," she tries.

"C . . . A-R-O . . . E-L-E," she ventures again.

Then she shrugs: "My mother named him."

Carolyn has been a welfare mother for six years. She seldom sees anyone from the outside world—no one except the landlord, who stops by once a month to collect his rent, and Lovie Griffin.

Griffin is a social worker. She is black. She works for Marillac House, a social agency run by the Daughters of Charity, an order of Catholic nuns. And she is one of the few social workers in the impoverished North Lawndale neighborhood who leave their offices and make daily confrontations with the homes of the black underclass.

"Carolyn. Carolyn."

Griffin is standing on the sidewalk, hands on her hips and eyes fixed on a closed third-floor window.

"CAR-o-lyn."

Left: Social worker Lovie Griffin leaving a client: "To do this kind of work . . . you have to honestly care about these families."

At 10 in the morning, Griffin stands alone. She wants to make sure that Carolyn is home before she ventures inside the building. There is no front door, and it is dark at the bottom of the stairs.

For a good eight minutes, Griffin paces, waiting. Then suddenly, she turns on her heels and tosses her head back as she fires off a command.

"CAROLYN!"

A face finally appears at the window. Griffin hurries into the shadows, past the empty beer cans and a disposable diaper and up three flights of stairs worn so thin that they give a little with each step.

It is not easy to reach Carolyn.

"She's in there," says Carolyn's mother, gesturing toward a small room. "Whooo boy," she adds, laughing, as Griffin walks past. "That girl's gonna get it now!"

Carolyn is sitting on top of a twin-bed frame piled high with three mattresses but no box spring. Her two small boys, Roger and Carvelle, are climbing over each other on a miniature chair, taking turns taunting their baby sister, Tammy, with a piece of peanut butter candy.

Carolyn ignores them, her attention on the two television sets at the corner of the room, one of which picked up only the picture, the other only the sound. Both are tuned to a rerun of "The Big Valley."

"What happened to the appointment?" Griffin asks from the doorway.

Carolyn stares blankly at the screen.

"You are 6 months pregnant with another baby, and you haven't been to the doctor. Carolyn, why didn't you go?"

There is no reply.

"What is the problem, Carolyn?" Griffin demands, situating herself between Carolyn and the televisions.

"I was going to go."

"What happened?"

"I don't know."

Griffin glares.

"Didn't have nobody to watch my kids," Carolyn finally offers, removing a barrette from her hair and twisting her bangs.

"You know that is no excuse. You can take them with you."

"Uh, oh," offers Carolyn's mother, who appears to consider the discussion a form of entertainment. Carolyn and her mother begin to laugh.

"Am I laughing?" Griffin snaps, angry eyes flashing first at the mother and then back to Carolyn. "We are talking about a little baby, an unborn child. Carolyn, what were you doing that was so important that you couldn't go to the clinic?"

"Watched TV."

Exhaling, Griffin pauses a moment to gain her composure, then walks over to the bed and sits next to Carolyn, blinking back tears. Beside her is a grown woman of 24, old enough to do things for herself, old enough to run a household, old enough to have three small children and another on the way. Yet Griffin sometimes feels as if she is dealing with a disobedient child.

"Carolyn, you better eat something, for the baby."

"I'm not hungry."

"Then at least get up off the bed and get your kids some breakfast. It's not good for them to eat that candy in the morning."

"They eat like that all the time."

Griffin brings herself to her feet. "I'm going to make you another appointment, and you are going to go. And if you don't go, I am going to come and get you and take you there. Do you understand me?"

Carolyn stares at the TV.

"Carolyn?"

"Uhm hmm."

Griffin turns and walks out of the apartment, down the three flights of stairs and out onto the sidewalk, where she looks back up at the window.

"Sometimes," she whispers, still fighting the tears, "I think I care more about that baby than she does."

In many respects, Carolyn typifies the difficulty this country has in coming to grips with its urban underclass, a group of people who live in seemingly permanent poverty and for whom there is little hope that their prospects will improve. She is not motivated to improve her lifestyle. She does not plan for the future of her children.

The underclass in Chicago and other major cities is comprised of people who largely depend on welfare, crime or an underground economy for their sustenance. It includes people who have not worked for years and others who may never hold a job because they lack the education and necessary skills. The underclass is primarily black.

For her efforts to overcome the barriers and reach a handful of people like Carolyn, Griffin is paid $13,000 a year. It is a salary that makes a statement.

"To do this kind of work with the situation in these homes as critical as it is today, you have to honestly care about these families," Griffin said.

"You have to go out into the community and find the families, because they are not going to come to you. They are not always the easiest of people to work with; it takes a lot of energy. What is sad to me is that there are not enough of us, black or white, who really seem to care."

Griffin works with 63 clients on the West Side, about half of whom live in North Lawndale. She found them by canvassing the neighborhood and knocking on doors. Much of her time is spent teaching the basics of child-rearing to young women ill-equipped to become mothers. Days may be invested in getting just one pregnant woman to a clinic for a prenatal check-up.

Her first client in North Lawndale was an 18-year-old woman with four youngsters ranging in age from 4 months to 3 years. They lived in a small, dirty apartment without a refrigerator or beds and they used milk crates for tables and chairs. The woman kept baby bottles in the kitchen sink with cold water running on them to keep the formula from spoiling.

Today, Griffin's clients include a 15-year-old girl who is expecting her second baby and a 23-year-old woman who has had two infants die shortly after birth.

Griffin oftens finds situations in which basic mothering and housekeeping skills need to be taught. She makes trips to the laundromat to show young mothers how to separate laundry and wash clothes. She tries to teach them how to budget welfare money. She makes a point of cuddling infants in front of their mothers, hoping to show the kind of contact needed to nurture a child properly.

Three of her young clients have offered to give Griffin their babies.

At 40, Griffin, the mother of nine children, is a robust woman with an easy smile. She attributes her commitment to helping others to her deeply religious feelings and to the strength she gained by overcoming problems in her own life over the years.

One of 14 brothers and sisters, she spent her childhood in Pickens, Miss., reared by her maternal grandparents. When she was 16, she dropped out of high school and entered a marriage arranged by her grandmother.

"It was a generational kind of thing," Griffin said. "Back then, in the country, you did what you were told. My grandmother told me what to do. I didn't want to marry him, but I had to."

In May, 1967, while visiting a cousin in Chicago, she was offered a job at a neighborhood discount store. She left her husband and moved with her children to the West Side.

She supported her family with a series of jobs, including clerk, waitress and assembly line worker. One of her children is a New York teacher. The rest either work or still are in school.

When she was laid off from a job five years ago, Griffin said, she lived for a while on unemployment benefits, then went on welfare for about a year. But she used her time on aid to decide that she wanted something more out of her life. She went back to school and earned her high school equivalency certificate. Today she is studying child development at the National College of Education, where she expects to receive her degree in May.

Griffin eventually found a job as an outreach worker with a community resource agency and with the Illinois Department

of Children and Family Services. Her work did not go unnotic-
ed. Late last year, Kathryn Hallagan, who directs the Marillac
program for pregnant women and teens, asked Griffin to join
her agency. At Marillac, Griffin oversees a program for women
of childbearing age that is funded by the Chicago Department
of Health.

When she began canvassing North Lawndale, Griffin said, she
had no idea of the problems she would find behind almost every
door.

"I had read about it, I had heard about it, but my thoughts
when I saw it were, 'My God, I didn't know it was this bad,' "
she said.

Working in North Lawndale has made her aware of a
troubling situation: Though some American blacks have
achieved much in the last two decades, others have fallen
hopelessly behind. It is Griffin's feeling that part of the
responsibility for helping these least fortunate people must be
assumed by better-off blacks.

"When black people achieve certain goals, they don't see the
problem any more," Griffin said. "They perceive it differently.
Then they move out. I don't think there are enough of us who
are committed. My goal is to give something back to the people
who need it."

The extent to which some of the family environments have
deteriorated is not an easy thing for Griffin to see. It makes her
wonder why more committed professionals are not making
forays into the community, knocking on doors instead of
waiting for people to come to them.

"It is very difficult for a black person to see what is going on
in these families," Griffin observed. "It breaks my heart, but
what burns me up is the fact that no social workers seem to be
going out into this community. Something is very wrong. I
always ask myself, 'Am I the only one going into these
homes?' "

Over the last decade, a number of public and private agencies
that serve the urban poor have undergone something of a
change in roles. For example, the Illinois Department of Public

Aid, the one agency that has an impact on the lives of almost every person in the black underclass in Chicago, no longer sends caseworkers into homes on a routine basis to look for fraud or to assess living conditions.

Department spokeswomen Sandra Lynn said routine visits were discontinued in February, 1984, after officials decided the department could function just as well by determining clients' eligibility by asking them to mail in forms and then tracking their cases by computer.

Today, the only time a caseworker is required to visit the home of a welfare recipient is to verify the address of an applicant or to respond to reports of emergencies, such as child abuse.

Though the population of North Lawndale has dropped by more than 30,000 in the last decade, the percentage of the people living there on welfare has increased by more than 45 percent. Today, almost 32,000 people receive some form of government assistance, which will total more than $139 million funneled to this community this year.

"Just the other day," Griffin said, "I was on the telephone with a welfare caseworker from the Ogden office, which is in North Lawndale. I was asking him about a situation involving one of my clients. He said, 'Lady, I don't go out into the neighborhood.' I said, 'Beg pardon?' and he said, 'I don't go out into the neighborhood.' "

What Griffin found in Carolyn was fairly typical of what she has discovered in families of the black underclass.

Carolyn, her children and her mother were living in a small room that they rented from a cousin. None of the children had had their immunizations. Carolyn, who had dropped out of high school in her junior year around the time her brother Bobby was killed in an arson, was on welfare. So was her mother.

It took two canceled appointments to get Carolyn and the children to the doctor, and hours of discussions over why Carolyn couldn't go. No clean clothes; no soap to wash them; no way to get there. Griffin eventually escorted Carolyn to the clinic. She talked with Carolyn about the importance of birth control, and the young woman was given pills. Four months later, Griffin was shocked to discover that Carolyn was pregnant.

"Them pills make me sick," was Carolyn's explanation. She had taken them for only a week.

Carolyn said she has had only one job in her life, at a candy store on 13th Street when she was 16. She became pregnant a year later and had her first baby by caesarean section when she was 18. Two months later, she went on public aid.

Today, six years after receiving her first check, there is nothing to suggest that she aspires to ever break away from welfare. She is not even motivated enough to fill out the paperwork necessary to receive the full amount of welfare money to which she is entitled. She never has made the effort to get her youngest child listed as a dependent on the rolls.

The Department of Public Aid tries to collect child support from the fathers of children on welfare. Because Carolyn has repeatedly refused to identify Carvelle's father, a man she said is working at a K mart, public aid is deducting $25 a month from her check. Carvelle's father asked her not to give his name, and she is honoring the request, Carolyn said.

She and her children live on $490 a month in cash and food stamps.

Two months after the conversation about going to the clinic, Griffin tracked down Carolyn at a relative's home two blocks away. The cousin they had been staying with had been evicted for not paying rent.

"Why didn't you call me when you got put out?" Griffin asked.

"I forgot the number," Carolyn explained.

Carolyn said she does not plan for her children's future. "I never think about it," she said. She does not appear to be looking forward to the birth of her fourth child. "Really, I didn't want no more kids. They a lot of trouble." She and Griffin have discussed birth control again, and Carolyn said she has decided to become sterilized after this baby is born.

Griffin is not entirely optimistic about the successes she can have with a woman like Carolyn. One of her biggest concerns is the impact that Carolyn's lifestyle has on her children. "Sometimes I find myself thinking that if I just had this big house with a big back yard, I would bring all of these little children home and give them all the love I had," Griffin said.

But Lovie Griffin is only one social worker, and Carolyn is only one woman who needs her help.

"There have to be hundreds, if not thousands, of young women out there just like her," Griffin said. "You tell me, who is going to care enough to help them?"

Another child is born without a fighting chance

High infant-mortality rate comes with the territory

Roosevelt McGee was born in a toilet.

His mother, Rosemary Gordon, was only seven months pregnant at the time.

She remembers feeling labor pains that morning, Nov. 11, 1984, shortly after she awoke. But she did not tell anyone. She went about her normal routine, she explains, because she and her mother had planned a shopping trip that day. She ate breakfast. She dressed.

"Then I went to the bathroom, and as I stood up, he just slid out."

Roosevelt McGee was a tiny infant, weighing slightly more than two pounds, so small that he fit comfortably in just one of his mother's hands. When he started to cry, Gordon recalls, she looked up to find her mother standing in the bathroom doorway—gasping, with her hand up over her mouth.

"Girl!" the mother said. "You done had the baby in the bathroom!"

The next few minutes were frantic. Gordon handed the baby to her mother. Then the two women walked slowly into the living room. They feared that the baby was dead.

Left: Rosemary Gordon, 25, has given birth to four children. One died at the age of 4 months.

"My mother said he wasn't breathing," Gordon remembers. "She thought he was dead. I told her to, and she spanked him on the butt, and he started crying again."

A friend of the family who had been in the apartment ran to the corner and flagged a passing police car. Then he telephoned an ambulance. One of Gordon's three young children peeked out of a room to watch what was going on. The policeman came to the doorway and stood there watching. Finally, they heard sirens.

When the ambulance arrived, the baby was barely alive. A paramedic cut and tied the umbilical cord, then cleaned mucus from the baby's nose and mouth.

"She said it wasn't breathing," Gordon remembers.

She watched as the paramedic put an oxygen mask over the baby's face, then waited tensely until there was a response.

"We've got a winner here!" the paramedic shouted.

Four months later, Roosevelt McGee died.

He spent most of his brief life in Children's Memorial Hospital, receiving intensive medical care. His mother was allowed to take him home on March 8 of this year. He was home for only five days before he died.

He was Rosemary Gordon's fourth child. She is 25.

The cause of death listed by the medical examiner's office was bronchial pneumonia. But the reasons this baby died go beyond precise medical terms.

Infant mortality—the death of a child during the first year of life—is a serious and worsening problem in the neighborhoods of the black underclass, linked to the social and economic problems there that sometimes seem to defy solution.

Poverty, segregation, disintegrating family structures, poor education, substandard living conditions, and indifference toward medical care all contribute to the infant mortality problem in underclass communities.

Roosevelt McGee was born into an underclass family in Chicago's North Lawndale neighborhood, an impoverished area on the city's West Side that is 97 percent black. While the infant mortality rate has been declining in Chicago and nationwide over the last four years, it continues to climb in North Lawndale and has reached critical proportions there.

Though North Lawndale's population has declined by more than 30,000 during the last decade, and is still believed to be shrinking, the infant mortality rate there has increased from 17.5 deaths per 1,000 live births in 1980 to 28.2 deaths per thousand in 1984.

In 1984, the infant death rate in North Lawndale was 72 percent greater than the rate for the city as a whole, which was 16.4 deaths per thousand live births. It was nearly three times as high as the national rate of 10.6 per thousand that year.

The high infant mortality rate in poor black neighborhoods helps explain why the rate for blacks in this city is twice as high as it is for whites, although the infant death rate among blacks overall has fallen here from 24.9 in 1983 to 22.5 last year.

The role played by home and community conditions in the infant mortality crisis in poor black areas is underscored by a second set of statistics that measures the death of infants between the ages of 28 days and one year. This category largely excludes children who were born too frail to survive birth or who could not be kept alive right after birth by heroic medical efforts.

The 1983 figures for postneonatal deaths, the most recent available, show that the rate of such deaths in North Lawndale is 37 percent higher than in the rest of the city.

Recently there have been calls for approaches to the infant mortality problem that go beyond purely medical steps and deal with the problem in a socioeconomic and environmental context. Last month, Mayor Harold Washington and state health officials targeted North Lawndale as one of the city's 19 high risk areas in need of more effective programs for women of childbearing age.

The failure to stem the growth in the infant mortality rate in communities like North Lawndale has some public health experts worried that the decline in the infant death rate nationwide may be about to level off.

In February, the Public Health Service reported that the infant mortality rate appeared to be stabilizing at an all-time low of 10.6 per thousand, after declining steadily from a level of 24.7 per thousand in 1965. Cutbacks in federal spending on health care for mothers, children and pregnant women during the Reagan years are being blamed by some health experts and political figures.

The funding of such programs has also become a political issue in Illinois. This year, Republican Gov. James Thompson used his veto power to cut about $5 million out of Democratic proposals designed to deal with infant mortality. After much criticism of his veto, Thompson announced his own proposals, which call for spending of some $47 million on the problem over the next two years.

But the group that may need such services most desperately, women in the black underclass like Rosemary Gordon, may not be the type of people who are motivated enough to seek out or take part in such programs.

The short life and death of Roosevelt McGee illustrate how difficult it will be to come to grips with the infant mortality problem in underclass areas like North Lawndale.

Rosemary Gordon was raised in North Lawndale, the oldest of four children whose father died when she was 8. She was raised, at various times in her youth, by each of her grandmothers.

When she was 17, Gordon dropped out of high school, pregnant with her first child, a girl she named Samaria, who is now 8. Shortly after Samaria was born, Gordon joined her mother and maternal grandmother on the welfare rolls. Two more children followed—Antwoin, now 3, and Laketa, now 1.

All of Gordon's children have been low-birthweight babies, a pregnancy risk that is higher for black women, particularly among those who do not have adequate prenatal care.

According to Gordon, all of her children have the same father, a man who has been married to someone else for eight years. "As long as he helps me out with the kids, that's all right," she says. "He helps me out the best he can. I'm not ready to get married right now."

Gordon attributes the birth of her first three children to the fact that she did not take birth control pills according to schedule. At the time she became pregnant with Roosevelt, she adds, she was no longer taking any birth control measures.

When she realized she was expecting, she says, she investigated the idea of an abortion.

"The doctors said I was too far gone," she explains. "But I never went to the doctor. I talked to them on the phone. Well, I really didn't talk to him, my mother did."

Then in the next breath, she reconsiders the thought: "I really don't believe in having an abortion. The devil gave me that idea. My mother didn't kill me, so I wasn't going to kill my babies either."

Gordon did not take care of herself during her pregnancy with Roosevelt. She did not go to a doctor. She cannot articulate the reason why. She just shakes her head.

"I didn't take none of them iron pills, neither," she explains.

She said she did not eat well. She smoked. Her medical record at the hospital showed she told the doctors she smoked marijuana.

Roosevelt McGee did fairly well for such a tiny baby in his four months at Children's Hospital. In due time he was weaned off the mechanical ventilator that he depended on for breathing. He gained weight.

He was put on medication, including a drug that helps counteract episodes of sleep apnea, which can result in Sudden Infant Death Syndrome, and a diuretic to prevent fluid build-up in the lungs.

But during those four months, Gordon never got around to going to the public aid office to get his name added as a dependent on her Medicaid card, the only way to cover the baby's medical expenses, prescriptions and care.

"My mother was always on me to take care of my business," she explains.

The night before her baby was released, Gordon stayed with him for 24 hours, sleeping on a sofa beside his incubator. She watched the nurses hold him and feed him, and she asked questions.

More than $130,000 had been invested in the baby by the time he was sent home. It was a cool March day when he was released. According to Gordon, she went out and bought Pampers and a few pieces of clothing for him that morning. The child's father drove her to Children's and took both of them home.

Roosevelt weighed 8.8 pounds.

Home for this infant was a dingy three-room apartment in the basement of a building with inadequate heat. Though there were exposed radiator pipes running along the ceiling for steam heat, Rosemary said that it was still so chilly that each room needed its own small portable electric heater. Still, the arrangement was not efficient. "It was cool," Gordon says.

Five children and four adults lived in the three small rooms. Roosevelt slept with his mother on a small bed. He did not have a crib.

Rosemary Gordon did not fully comprehend how vulnerable her baby was when he came home. She did not understand that because of his severe prematurity, his lungs would be susceptible to respiratory problems and changing temperatures in her home.

She knows that the medications the doctors prescribed for the baby were "important" but she never fully understood what the medicine was for. She says she was given four different prescriptions, but she can remember filling only two of them in the five days the baby was home. Because she did not have his name on her medical card, she says, she had to go from relative to relative, scraping together the $5 it took to get partial amounts of each prescription filled.

Whether she followed the instructions on the medicine is an unknown. She cannot say.

But what Rosemary Gordon does remember is how strange her baby seemed to be acting the night before he died.

One moment, she said, he would laugh and want to play. Then he seemed tired and sleepy. He started to look ill.

"I called the hospital and they told me to give him his bottle, and if he took it, he was all right," she says. "He took his bottle, but still didn't look right to me, but he started playing and laughing to himself."

He went to sleep.

"When I woke him up to give him his next feeding, he didn't look okay, but I had already called the hospital. He looked like he couldn't keep his eyes open. I sat there with him, and he started playing and laughing to himself so I thought he was all right."

Throughout the night, she says, she watched television and stayed up with an eye on Roosevelt, watching as he drifted in and out of sleep. Then, at about 6 a.m., when he seemed to be resting soundly, she closed her eyes.

"When I woke, I looked over to see if he was wet. His body was cold. I could tell . . ." She stops for a moment and wipes tears from her eyes. Her voice breaks.

"I could tell my baby was dead."

When the paramedics came to take the lifeless infant, Rosemary Gordon refused to let her baby go. Her boyfriend had to pry her hands away from the child.

Roosevelt's funeral was held on March 18, three days after his mother's 25th birthday.

"At least it was a real casket," she says, "not one of them public aid boxes."

On a shelf in her living room sits a bottle of red medicine that a doctor prescribed for Roosevelt. Only a bit of it is gone.

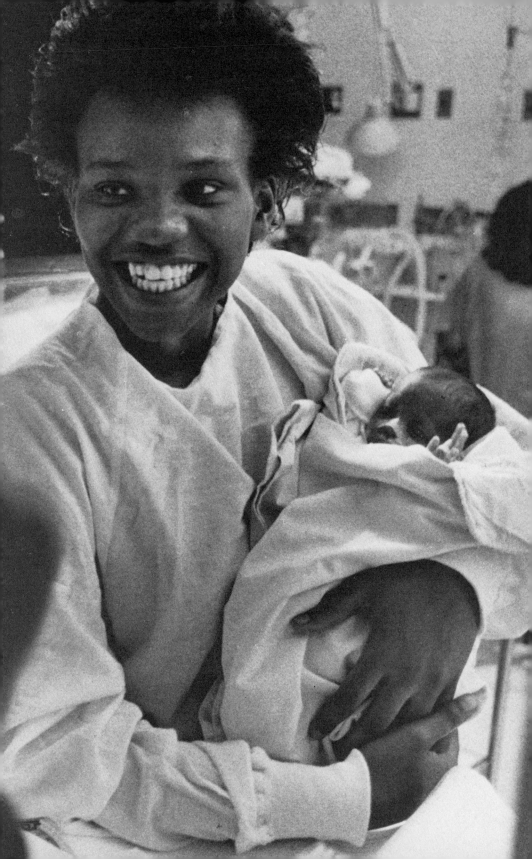

In the delivery room, poverty cycle starts again

Little chance to advance when 'babies have babies'

Iris Moore is chewing bubble gum and singing along with a song on the radio as she sits beside a tiny incubator in the intensive care nursery at Mt. Sinai Hospital, where sick babies are hooked up to tubes and wires and machines that help them breathe.

One of the infants belongs to her.

At 17, Iris is the oldest of five children in her family. Her mother is on welfare and her father unemployed. Dr. Ann West, a second-year resident at Mt. Sinai, remembers the sinking feeling that came over her when she delivered Iris' baby at about 11 p.m. July 21.

"I felt sad," West recalls. "You don't know how babies like this will do."

The baby, named Tina, was born too soon, 15 weeks premature. She weighed only 710 grams, slightly more than a pound and a half. Premature deliveries are often the result of adolescent pregnancies and are all too common at Mt. Sinai, a teaching hospital in the impoverished West Side neighborhood of North Lawndale, where on any given day, the medical world confronts the consequences of lives mired in the black underclass.

Left: Iris Moore, 17, shows off her baby, Tina, inside the intensive care nursery at Mt. Sinai Hospital. Born 15 months premature, Tina was hospitalized for 2½ months.

From the moment Tina Moore was born, her future was in jeopardy.

She depended on a whoosh of oxygen from a tube just so she could take her first breath. Medical complications resulting from her prematurity may leave her with respiratory difficulties, a susceptibility to Sudden Infant Death Syndrome and learning disabilities that might not be revealed until she is ready for school.

But she is vulnerable to much more.

Unless someone or something intervenes during the little girl's life, there is good reason to believe that Tina Moore will be condemned to repeat the same vicious cycle that took hold of her mother, her grandmother and her great-grandmother, by having a baby during—or perhaps even before—her teens.

The striking number of teenage girls having babies is a priority health concern in Chicago and across the nation, for the children born to these mothers are often premature and growth retarded and can suffer a number of devastating complications at or shortly after birth that can compromise the quality of their life.

But the impact of adolescents having babies has consequences far beyond the medical ones in communities of the black underclass. Once the cycle takes hold and a young girl has a child, her ability to improve her economic or social condition and pull herself out into a more productive segment of society is limited. Often, she drops out of school, has no job skills and falls into the welfare trap for support.

In monetary terms, Tina Moore has already been an expensive baby. The price of the heroic medical efforts employed to salvage her life had surpassed $120,000 by the time she was released from the hospital Sunday.

As she and thousands of youngsters like her grow up in environments that have little to offer in the way of nurturing, educating and inspiring, there can only be additional costs.

Tina Moore will live in North Lawndale, a neighborhood that has been culturally, spiritually and physically devastated by years of segregation, lost jobs and crumbling housing structures. As a community, North Lawndale represents the harsh challenge cities face in trying to solve the problems of what seems to have become a permanent underclass consisting largely of poor blacks.

Home for this baby will be on the drafty first floor of a building that her family inherited from a relative. Its value is questionable. There is no gas for heat or cooking; the service was cut off because of an outstanding $2,000 bill. A makeshift propane tank heats one room.

Iris, the child's mother, dropped out of Collins High School after attending only one day of her junior year. She has never had a job. Like her mother and her grandmother, she has signed up with the Illinois Department of Public Aid for benefits under the Aid to Families with Dependent Children program. She expects her first check this month.

At home one morning last week, Iris was watching a television rerun when asked whether she had any plans to go back to school, perhaps by finding a baby-sitter.

"I don't have anything to wear," she answered while combing her hair. "I'm not going to go up there looking like a bum. No way."

Figures from the Illinois Department of Public Health show that of the 1,492 births in North Lawndale in 1984, 33 percent were to women age 19 or younger. Fifteen percent were to girls 17 and below. One was to a girl who was 12.

Citywide, only 19 percent of the total 53,906 births were to women 19 or younger.

Dr. Norbert Gleischer, chairman of the department of obstetrics and gynecology at Mt. Sinai, said about half of the babies born to teenagers there are premature, are small for their gestational age or have physical difficulties complicated by alcohol or drug use by the mother.

In 1983, 96 percent of the babies born to teenage girls in North Lawndale were illegitimate. Figures for 1984 are not yet available.

Though she had miscarried once, a year before, Iris had her first baby just as her mother had done—at age 17. Iris has long since broken up with her child's father, an unemployed youth three years older who, she said, impressed her by "talking nice" and driving a big car.

Iris confided that she had hoped to get pregnant. "I wanted my boo-boo," she explained. "I wanted a little thing to love."

Teenagers are often labeled by physicians as "at risk" of delivering low birth weight or premature children because of adolescent lifestyles and their lack of understanding of how an infant needs to be nurtured in the womb. Iris admitted that she probably did not think enough about her baby when it was growing. Unlike many pregnant teens, Iris did go to doctors for prenatal care, but she saw a doctor only three times and missed one appointment. She told doctors that she smoked, sometimes a pack a day, that she did not eat well and that she once fell.

She almost lost her baby. She went into premature labor 11 days before Tina was born. After determining that the fetus weighed just 600 grams, which meant it would almost certainly die if delivered, doctors were able to stop the contractions with drugs. They admitted Iris into the hospital for bed rest, hoping to buy her baby time. When she went into labor a second time, birth could not be forestalled.

For the first six weeks, Tina Moore was among the most critically ill babies in the high-risk nursery, frail with saggy skin and tiny hands the size of a quarter. Her weight at birth was just over the threshold at which modern medicine can keep a child alive. For a month and a half, she depended for breath on a hose hooked up to a ventilator, from which perfectly measured and precisely timed bursts of oxygen were pumped into her lungs.

As she fought for life, the baby developed a severe case of respiratory distress syndrome, typical in premature infants, plus pneumonia and anemia. She underwent 10 blood transfusions.

Teenage girls also are not always mature or educated enough to assume the role of parents, a fact that can have devastating consequences on a child's prospects. A teenager's ability to nurture a premature infant is also of concern, for this kind of baby is often irritable, prone to childhood illness and more demanding of attention than a full-term child.

Iris was discharged two days after delivering her baby, and she returned to visit her child only sporadically. She once went 10 days without visiting, the nursing log shows, at which point a nurse phoned her at home and tried to explain the importance of bonding in the early weeks of a baby's life, particularly with such a sick infant.

"As a society, we pin a lot of hope on our children," observed Carin Ellis, one of the nurses who cared for Tina Moore in her most critical times. "We like to think of them as the future of the community and of the country at large. But when I see these babies, when I think about all that is involved, I get very, very scared."

It is difficult to tell whether Iris truly understands what obstacles her baby has had to overcome. "It doesn't weigh enough," she explained one day. She seems unaware of any of the complications the baby may face later. Iris has not bought her baby any clothes, and she said it will not have a crib.

This year a study assessing the economic impact of teenage pregnancies disclosed that adolescent pregnancies in Illinois cost taxpayers about $835 million a year, an average of about $200 for every taxpaying household. The study, conducted by a group called Project Life and headed by James O'Connor, chairman of Commonwealth Edison Co., was one of the first to address the economic impact of teenage pregnancies.

Economics is a point that cannot be overlooked. Tina Moore's medical fee of more than $120,000 could bring a working-class family to its knees, for private insurance carriers have begun to put caps on what they will pay on many hospital bills.

But Iris will not be responsible for paying for her infant's care. She has no concept of what the bill will be. "Maybe about $1,000," she estimated. "I don't know. I don't get the bill."

The bill won't go to her family, either. Her mother, Juliana Smith, supports herself and her four other children on public aid allotments of $505 a month plus $298 in food stamps. Her father, Willie Moore, is unemployed, unable to read or write. Both parents, who are 35, say they were terribly upset to find their oldest daughter pregnant, because they had been hoping she would continue her education and escape their desperate financial situation. Both insist that they will do nothing to contribute to the support of the child.

"I'm not even going to buy Pampers," Willie Moore said.

Tina Moore's bill will be reimbursed in part by the Illinois Department of Public Aid, which was estimated by the Project Life study to spend $145 million a year in medical benefits for 24,000 newborns born to teenage mothers.

Public aid, which pays for deliveries and some birth control methods, will reimburse the hospital and medical professionals for only a fixed portion of their bills. Mt. Sinai officials estimated that they expect to be reimbursed for only one-third of their portion of Iris and Tina Moore's bill.

"Our red ink as we care for our infant intensive-care population belongs to everyone," observed Ruth Rothstein, president of Mt. Sinai.

"Many of the so-called costs of health care are not health costs at all," she said. "They're the price we are paying for unresolved social problems, the costs of social neglect. They are the effects of substandard housing, poverty and ignorance."

IV
EDUCATION

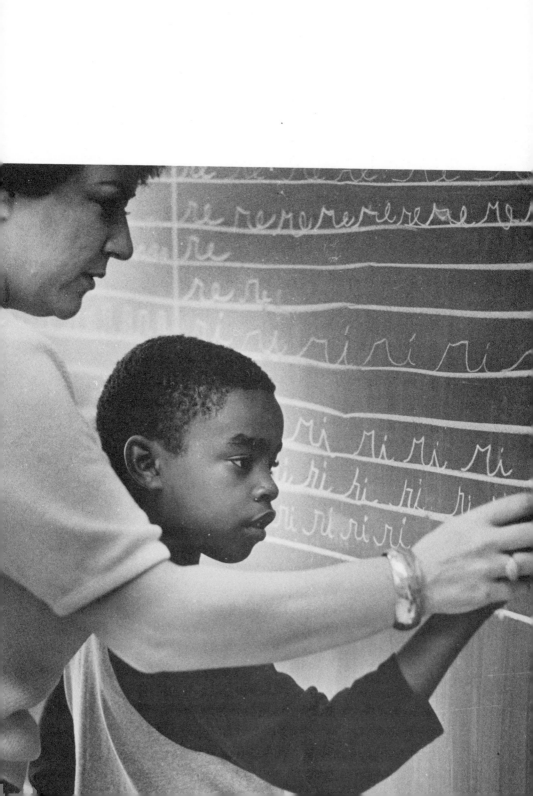

Schools outclassed
in a battle with failure

Problem of ignorance exacting huge toll
on society

When Earl Massel looks at the poor black teenagers in his social studies classes at Flower Vocational High School on the West Side, he is depressed.

"The majority of these students will become failures in life," Massel says. "Many are not going to graduate. Some will get married, have children, get menial jobs. A few will make it.

"Teacher morale is terrible. Teachers complain that the students are dumb. They can't read, and they can't write. And things are getting worse all the time."

Welcome to Chicago's inner-city schools.

These are the schools in which the children of Chicago's underclass are supposed to discover the beauty of knowledge and the joy of learning, the places where they are supposed to obtain the skills they need for a successful life.

But much too often, the children of the underclass leave these inner-city public schools not imbued with learning but shackled by an ignorance that will handicap them severely all their lives.

That ignorance will be passed on to their offspring, and it will exact a huge toll on the rest of society.

Left: For many children, inner-city public schools have become training grounds for failure instead of avenues to success.

Free public education, long seen as the ladder for climbing out of poverty, prejudice and deprivation, is failing in Chicago and in other big U.S. cities.

For many children, inner-city public schools have become training grounds in failure, boot camps where their membership in the underclass is solidified.

The people of the underclass are the poor, the unemployed and the undereducated of Chicago and elsewhere. Many are products of unstable families, and many are resigned to a life on welfare or a life of crime. A high proportion are black.

As the underclass grows, so do the problems that its members and the rest of society must face. Crime increases. The pool of well-prepared workers, needed by business and industry, shrinks. And the financial dead weight that the underclass represents becomes even more of a drain on the American economy.

"You know that an awful lot of kids are going to oblivion," says Sandor Postol, longtime principal of Einstein Elementary School, 3830 S. Cottage Grove Ave., in the midst of the Ida B. Wells public housing project. "It's hard to deal with."

Cold, hard numbers tell the story:

● Of the 29,942 students who entered Chicago public high schools in 1978 and didn't transfer to another school system, 12,804, or nearly 43 percent, dropped out before graduation, according to a study by the Chicago Panel on Public School Finances. Nationally the dropout rate is only 27 percent.

Much more startling, however, are the dropout rates the study found in inner-city schools. At two West Side high schools, Crane, at 2245 W. Jackson Blvd., and Austin, at 231 N. Pine Ave., the dropout rate was 62 percent. That means nearly two of every three 1978 freshmen left those schools before graduation. The rate routinely was 50 percent and higher at other underclass high schools.

● Of the 34,880 freshmen who entered Chicago public high schools in 1983, 75 percent were reading at a level below the national average, according to a study by Designs for Change, a nonprofit education research group.

Again, as bad as that finding is, the numbers for inner-city schools were much worse. At Orr High School, 730 N. Pulaski Rd., for example, 96 percent of the freshmen were reading below the national average; the figure was 90 percent or more at 16 other high schools, according to the study. Only 5 of the city's 64 public high schools had reading proficiency above the national average.

● Of the 32,338 freshmen who finished the 1983-84 school year, 12,590, nearly 39 percent, failed two or more courses, according to the Chicago Board of Education.

At Farragut High School, 2349 S. Christiana Ave., in the South Lawndale neighborhood, 70 percent of the freshmen failed at least two courses. At Du Sable High School, 4934 S. Wabash Ave., the rate was 67 percent. Most other inner-city schools had failure rates of 50 percent or more.

● During the 1984-85 school year, 2,937 pregnancies among Chicago public school students were reported by school nurses. At Harper High School, 6520 S. Wood Ave., in the Englewood neighborhood, 150 of the 600 female students are mothers. Each year about 200 of the 900 girls at Du Sable give birth.

"As long as our education system is locked into the pattern of not teaching children to read, companies that are here are going to relocate or hire kids from the suburbs, and new companies will not locate here," says Don Moore, executive director of Designs for Change.

The situation is not unique to Chicago. Across the nation, the children of low-income families, in particular poor black families, are being shortchanged in public schools.

A U.S. Census Bureau study, for example, showed that blacks were much more likely to drop out of high school than whites, especially if they came from low-income families. Only 25 percent of white high school students drop out, compared with 39 percent of black students. Among low-income black students, the national dropout rate is 57 percent.

"Our schools are discarding too many young people; our society is losing too much potential," asserts a report issued in 1985 by the National Coalition of Advocates for Students. "It is a waste we cannot afford and must refuse to tolerate."

Despite the ugly numbers, little public outcry has been heard.

"It's very difficult to understand why the general community of Chicago, particularly the business community, has not been absolutely outraged by the performance of the Chicago public schools, if for no other reason than self-interest," says Michael

Bakalis, former Illinois superintendent of public instruction and now dean of the school of education at Loyola University.

"Everyone reads the latest headlines and bemoans it, but no one is energized to make any changes. I can only conclude they've given up."

It has become easy for much of the white middle class and the black middle class to give up on Chicago's public schools, because increasingly the children of such families are being educated in private or suburban schools.

Today, more than 82 percent of the children in Chicago's schools are black or Hispanic, and nearly 70 percent of the public school students, almost 300,000 children, are from families living in poverty, according to the school board.

Whites make up 49.6 percent of the city's population but only 14.7 percent of the public school enrollment. At the present rate, there will be more Asians, American Indians and Pacific Islanders in the school system than whites by the year 2000.

What this means politically is that those with money, jobs and influence have little incentive to improve the schools: Their children are not affected.

"You have an aging middle-class population whose children are out of school or in private schools, and they don't care," says Roger Fox, research director of the Chicago Urban League.

In 1962 the situation was much different. In that year the Chicago public school system was predominantly white and predominantly middle class. Its black students were segregated on the Near West and South Sides.

That was the year a move to desegregate the school system started, and white flight began from the public schools and from the city.

Unquestionably, racial prejudice played a large role in the efforts by whites to keep blacks out of their schools and in their decisions later to transfer their children to private schools or move their families to the suburbs.

Over the last two decades, black children attending previously all-white schools were often greeted by hoots and shouts and threats from sign-carrying parents.

Yet, mixed in with such prejudice were the legitimate fears of whites and middle-class blacks who worried about their children's safety and education.

In part, it was the result of a self-fulfilling prophecy.

As more and more whites and middle-class blacks fled the school system, the influence of underclass children increased. Undisciplined and ill-prepared by parents for school, such children set a tone that led more middle-class families to leave.

When the school board, seemingly more interested in politics and union negotiations, did little to reverse the trend, the exodus accelerated.

Many parents who pulled their kids out were afraid of the crime and violence that continue to increase in the schools despite the $8.2 million the school board spends each year for security.

In addition to driving out middle-class students, gang violence in the schools forced many underclass students to drop out, according to a legislative study.

To combat crime and violence, students at some schools are required to check with security officers when they enter the building and surrender any clothing that might represent a gang affiliation.

All this has added to the image of the public schools as places where fear is commonplace and learning is scarce.

The public schools are often seen as "reserves for the poor," former Supt. Bakalis says. "As they continue to take on that tone, everybody wants to avoid them like the plague."

Mabel Moore, who has taught in the inner city for 24 years, notes: "So many whites and blacks think we're teaching an animal species. We're teaching human beings."

Statistics from the Illinois State Board of Education indicate that financially, at least, the city's public schools are doing as well as, if not better than, those in the suburbs.

During the 1982-83 school year, Chicago spent $3,574 per pupil. That was about $9 more than the average per-pupil spending in suburban school districts in Cook County and about $300 more than the averages in Du Page and Lake Counties.

Yet, teachers and other school officials argue that inner-city children are much more difficult to teach because of the underclass environment from which they come.

At Einstein Elementary School, for example, nearly all the 630 students come from four public housing project buildings near the school.

"A kid has to work out in his mind how he's going to get down the elevator or down the stairs and across the play lot without having to pay off someone or fight someone," says Postol, the Einstein principal. "Over the years, I've had a kid killed about every year."

Jerry Schwartz, a science teacher at Flower Vocational High School, 3545 W. Fulton Blvd., characterizes his students as "educationally indigent" and says:

"These kids are lacking food, affection, any kind of positive image. They get no positive reinforcement at home. They are from welfare families and families of half-brothers and half-sisters."

And the children often receive little parental supervision.

"Sometimes they will be tired in class because they did not receive enough rest the night before," says Maureen Beard, a 6th-grade teacher at Einstein.

"The children are on their own a lot. They make the decision of when they're going to come in and when they're going to bed.

"Some of them need so much more attention than others. Some of them have a need to sit near you. They act like they don't understand when they actually do. They just need attention."

Because of the way segregation in Chicago has isolated the underclass in highly concentrated enclaves of poverty and unemployment, inner-city students often have little concept of the rest of society.

"There is very little realistic future planning," says Denise Williams, a social worker at Tubman Alternative School, 4607 S. Greenwood Ave. "I've had several tell me, 'I want to be a lawyer.' They're getting D's in school. They have no conception of what it takes."

At Flower, Nancy Barrett, chairwoman of the home economics department, says: "I have to instill the work ethic. I have to teach them that it's important to wash dishes. They have to unlearn what they have learned at home."

The greatest obstacle to education, however, is that many students have little incentive to learn. They see no future reward in the form of a good job, or any job at all. They know as well as anyone that unemployment among Chicago blacks is epidemic. It averaged 23 percent last year, more than double the 1979 figure.

Because of the high degree of racial and economic segregation in Chicago, underclass children and teenagers know of few success stories, black or white.

"In an underclass situation, you don't have any aspirations," says Chicago School Supt. Manford Byrd Jr. "There is ample evidence, to them at least, that no matter what they do, their lot has been determined."

To overcome such environmental handicaps, bold programs have been proposed in recent weeks, but they carry hefty price tags.

One idea, suggested in August by Los Angeles Mayor Tom Bradley, is for underclass children to be taken out of their homes and placed in boarding schools to break "this whole cycle of failure."

The willingness of Bradley, one of the nation's most prominent black officials, to suggest such a radical proposal indicates the growing seriousness of the problem of underclass education. Yet, he was quick to note that his city would be unable to administer such a costly and, most likely, controversial program.

Another suggestion, proposed on Sept. 23 by a task force appointed by U.S. Sen. Paul Simon [D., Ill.] to suggest improvements in Chicago's public schools, is to have preschool classes, possibly mandatory, for all 3- and 4-year-olds in the city by 1988.

"An awful lot of these kids don't come to school school-ready because they don't have the home environment they should have," says William Blakey, a Simon aide.

Still another proposal is to issue tuition vouchers to parents so they can enroll their children in private schools, which, in the inner city, are generally Roman Catholic institutions.

"In so many neighborhoods the only place for a poor black kid to get a decent education is the Catholic school," says John McDermott, a longtime civil rights activist and now urban affairs director for Illinois Bell Telephone Co.

Unfortunately most inner-city Catholic schools charge tuition that is difficult, if not impossible, for underclass families to pay.

Private schools are attractive to parents, whether poor or rich, because many feel that the failure of poor children to learn is the fault of public school officials.

"The vast majority of students can learn to read and do math if they're taught properly," says Don Moore of Designs for Change.

Under a 1977 school board policy aimed at promoting desegregation, magnet schools for the best students in the system were established throughout Chicago.

But Moore notes that those schools, in effect, became "a private school system that's being operated in the public schools," leaving underclass students of lower academic ability even more isolated in inner-city schools.

In addition, the sheer size of major metropolitan school systems is often cited as aggravating the problems of underclass children.

"A system so big results in a lack of accountability," says Bakalis. "If money's wasted, who gets blamed or who's fired? If kids drop out or don't learn, who gets blamed or who's fired?"

Bureaucratic inertia also makes change much more difficult to accomplish.

"The system was geared to teach children from stable families," says McDermott. "It has never adapted to deal with really deprived kids."

More subtle but also more pernicious for underclass students is the tendency of middle-class teachers to expect them to do poorly.

"From the minute they walk into school, many low-income students get the message that society does not really care about their education, that schools expect little from them," notes the report by the National Coalition of Advocates for Students.

Concern about such lowered expectations has sparked a four-year investigation by the U.S. Justice Department into whether school districts are discriminating against low-income and minority students by downgrading their curriculums to ensure that such students graduate.

The moving force behind the investigation is William Bradford Reynolds, the associate U.S. attorney general for civil rights.

Reynolds, who has waged an all-out battle in the public and private sectors against the use of hiring and promotion quotas to correct past discrimination, believes that if minority students get educational opportunities equal to those of whites, they do not need to be helped by employment quotas.

Much of the talk, however, about the educational problems of the underclass is beside the point, according to Gary Orfield, a University of Chicago political scientist:

"Lots of people want to blame the poor black mothers, the schools, the welfare system. But the white middle class does not want to blame the white middle class.

"We set up the structure to keep all those people separate from us and to allocate to them the least resources.

"We are not responsible for that individually, but we are part of the system that, right now at least, is working for us, and we don't really want to change it."

Poverty and crime hold education hostage

Schools lose their place as traditional stepping-stone

In a kindergarten classroom at Julia Lathrop School, a 5-year-old girl "punishes" her doll by shoving an iron into its face. A boy pretends to burn his doll with a cigarette.

Another boy jabs a pencil into a doll's arm and says he is "shooting up."

In the eight months that Janet Dvorak has been teaching at Lathrop, she has been shocked by some of her pupils. Last spring, when she talked about family life in the doll corner of her kindergarten classroom, children bashed dolls against the floor, poked out their eyes and ripped them apart.

This year, as a 1st-grade teacher, she has seen boys sniff glue and punch girls at the slightest provocation. She has heard children talk about gunfire, street gangs and "whuppings" at home.

"My daddy dead," one girl offers. "My cousin killed him with a knife."

Nearly two-thirds of Dvorak's pupils do not have fathers living with them.

"My daddy live in a basement," a boy says.

"They beat him with a baseball bat," a little girl explains.

Dvorak's pupils, all of them black, live in North Lawndale.

Left: Graffiti-covered windows compete with teacher Janet Dvorak for the attention of 1st graders. Many of her pupils have minimal preparation for learning.

For America's poor, public schools have traditionally been the stepping stone to a better life.

But as Dvorak has learned at Lathrop, inner-city schools today must cope with a growing number of children who lack even minimal preparation for learning and who enter school already burdened with staggering personal and social problems.

Underclass families are generally headed by women, many of whom begin to have babies while in their early teens. Children growing up in communities like North Lawndale encounter drug pushers and street gangs on their way to school.

Compared with the general population, more underclass youngsters are born prematurely or with birth ailments that limit their ability to learn and to adhere to school routines.

Public schools, which are geared to teach children from more stable backgrounds, have not adjusted to this type of pupil. Low reading scores and high dropout rates in urban schools, due largely to the influx of children from underclass families, underscore the inadequacy of existing efforts.

In Chicago nearly 70 percent of public school students come from families living in poverty. Not all of the poor or all welfare dependents or the products of shattered families fall into the underclass. Despite their economic circumstances, many are from stable homes.

But their educations—and their futures—are compromised by the problems caused by their less fortunate classmates.

More than 43 percent of the students who enter Chicago public high schools drop out before graduating, according to a study by the Chicago Panel on Public School Finances. Of the 34,880 freshmen who entered Chicago's public high schools in 1983, 75 percent were reading below the national average.

Underclass children are largely responsible for the discipline problems that disrupt so many inner-city classrooms. As they grow, they cause much of the violence and crime that have driven middle-class youngsters out of the system and made it difficult to recruit the most qualified teachers.

Despite spending $3,574 per pupil—higher than the average outlay in suburban districts—Chicago's public schools have not found a way to keep underclass children from dropping out in their teens, lacking job skills and destined for lives of dependency, crime and prison that exact a heavy toll on the rest of society.

"Even though we have been developing special programs for minority and poverty students for years, we are really still geared to educate well-behaved, motivated students, not those with significant problems," according to Robert Crain, an expert on school problems at Johns Hopkins University.

"If we were to really build a school system for very poor students, we would probably restructure it from top to bottom."

The burden that the growing underclass imposes on inner-city schools can be seen in the daily life of Lathrop School. After only eight months in the classroom, Dvorak is losing hope that she can make much of a difference.

"I try to do the best I can," she explains, tears welling in her eyes, "but sometimes I go home and I feel like a loser."

Across from Lathrop School, 1440 S. Christiana Ave., teenage boys and men loiter on front stoops, sharing bottles of cheap liquor. They whistle at young mothers walking their children to class past burned-out buildings, through vacant lots and around abandoned cars.

Street gangs have spray-painted graffiti and nicknames such as "Slick" across the west wall and windows of the three-story building. No one at the school challenges the gangs by washing off the graffiti.

Many of the school's windows are broken or boarded. There are no hoops on the basketball court and no swings on the playground, only the skeleton of a rusted jungle gym.

Each morning, janitors sweep up broken glass left on the playground from the night before so children will not cut themselves on their way inside.

Two years ago, recess was abolished to reduce the number of accidents and avoid confrontations with dangerous people who wandered onto the playground, according to Principal Georgia Hudson.

Hudson has been at Lathrop for 10 years, 1½ as principal. Last year she was tough on gang members, running out and chasing them away if they got too close to the building.

Recently, however, she has learned to coexist with them. When a teacher's car is stolen, Hudson has found, she can usually "get the word out and have the car back by the afternoon."

Hudson says it is difficult to get substitute teachers to come to her school once they realize what kind of neighborhood it is in. "When they see the building and the neighborhood," she explains, "they just keep on driving. You can't even get a taxi to bring you here."

In the area immediately surrounding Lathrop, there have been 6 murders in the last year, 246 serious assaults, 19 rapes or attempted rapes, 174 robberies, 206 burglaries, 131 car thefts and 553 other crimes. Fear of violence keeps some teachers from venturing into the neighborhood to contact parents who won't come to school.

"I don't especially feel safe going out into this community," says Karen Rooks, who teaches a combined 5th and 6th grade class.

All of Lathrop's 601 pupils are black. Of those, 592 qualify for the free breakfast and lunch program. Hudson estimates that 90 percent of her pupils live in female-headed households.

"Our children usually have a series of fathers. This week it's one guy, next month it's someone else," Hudson said. "Sometimes the children get confused. They might say, 'That was my other father.' "

The lack of male role models in the home is not compensated for in the school, where only 4 of 31 teachers are males. Throughout the Chicago school system, about 27 percent of the teachers are men.

Until a year ago, Lathrop had no Parent-Teacher Association. After 21 years without a library, work has just begun on one. Books actually sprouted mold as they lay abandoned in the lunchroom.

"The kids don't even notice how bad things are around here because it's part of their environment," says Hudson. "I had a kid describe a park in an essay once. He wrote that a park is a place to find beer bottles, wine bottles and lots of broken glass."

Lathrop's reading scores rank it among the 10 worst schools in the system, but children continue to be routinely promoted from one grade to the next. Last year, only 5 percent of Lathrop's pupils were left back. According to Hudson, flunking simply adds another negative to a life filled with frustration.

"Failing doesn't improve motivation," Hudson explains. "Most of the kids come in feeling defeated." Maybe it's a mistake not to flunk them, she concedes, "but if we err, I feel we should err on the side of the child."

While even superior teachers would have difficulty coping with youngsters like those at Lathrop, school board practices relegate the newest and least experienced teachers to inner-city schools. Teachers with seniority generally choose to transfer to safer, more effective schools.

New teachers are bounced from school to school. Janet Dvorak, for example, twice has been transferred in the middle of a school year.

Hudson blames the fact that Chicago has had five school superintendents in the last 10 years for some of the problems at Lathrop. Instability at the top has led to bad curriculum decisions. Program after program has been forced on her, she says, without regard to their educational value.

Lathrop received the second workbook in the recently discarded Mastery Reading Program months before the first arrived, Hudson says. She says school officials told her "it was all right to work backwards as long as the material was covered."

"Can the schools save these kids?" Hudson asks. "Probably not as they are structured now. If we could, we would. It's as simple as that."

From kindergarten to 8th grade, the obstacles interfering with education at Lathrop are considerable. Teachers blame parental indifference and the home lives of their pupils for their failure to achieve better results. Many pupils, they say, seem to be adjusting to a life of poverty.

There is no overall strategy for solving the problem. Solutions are largely left to individual teachers.

Odessa Foster teaches kindergarten. She complains that the children she sees on the very first day of school are hungry, unruly, loud and late. They don't know how to hold a pencil.

They don't even know their names.

"John," Foster calls out to demonstrate how far she needs to bring her class along.

"My name not John. It Malibu."

"No, that's your nickname. In school you're John."

"You see? Their parents call them 'Little Man,' 'Boo Boo,' everything but their real names," Foster explains.

"Most of the kids hear their first fairy tale in this room. Mother can't read to her children. In some cases, she isn't even speaking to them."

Karen Rooks has learned to expect that her 5th and 6th graders will not complete homework. Few families place a premium on the task, she explains. One day recently, only two of her 6th graders came to school with their homework done.

"This is ridiculous," Rooks lectures. "How do you expect to pass tests if you don't do your assignments?"

She tells her 5th graders to open their geography books. She takes a globe and talks about longitude and latitude and hemispheres. She gives an open-book test.

Question: Which hemispheres are separated by the equator?

A pupil answers: Indian Ocean.

Question: What lines measure distances north and south of the equator?

He tries again: Yellowstone.

In the 20 years that she has taught at Lathrop, Mary Wyble has watched the level of discipline decline. "The student of 20 years ago, his behavior was different," says Wyble, who now teaches 8th grade. "If you informed the student you were going to tell his parents, he'd straighten up. Today they pay no attention to that."

The problem, as she sees it, is babies having babies.

"We have a lot of young parents. They're children growing up with their children," she observes. "They treat their child as their equal."

Wyble spends the first two months of each school year drumming strict discipline into her pupils. She is what another Lathrop teacher described as "a tough mama."

"I'm strictly a rules-and-regulations person," Wyble says. "Even when they're walking to the lunchroom. I insist they think exactly where they should be standing."

For her pupils, going to lunch is a tedious lesson in discipline. Wyble marches her 30 pupils like wind-up soldiers, using the floor tiles along the corridors as guides. They fall in, three tiles apart, and wait for her to signal with a nod that they may move one-third of the way down the corridor.

Wyble marches alongside them. They stop. She passes the first person in the line, and it begins to move again—another third of the way down the hall. They move like this down three flights of stairs and into the lunchroom.

All of Wyble's pupils qualify for free lunch. Today it's a slice of pizza, half a canned peach, a spoonful of corn kernels and a half-pint of milk.

Most of the 8th graders wrinkle their noses at the pizza and leave it untouched on their plates. "It look like dog doo," one says.

During the first few weeks of this year, Wyble had to teach handwriting to nearly one-third of her pupils. Last year she bent the rules a little by allowing a 13-year-old to bring her baby to class so she could continue her education.

"We make a big thing about graduation around here," Wyble says. "It's the only cap and gown some of them are ever going to see."

Janet Dvorak, 24, was born and reared in the all-white suburb of North Riverside. She earned her degree at Blackburn University in Carlinville.

When she announced that she had accepted a teaching position in Chicago, her family was startled. "I wanted to join the Peace Corps," she laughs. "In a lot of ways, I feel like I did."

Her family and friends worry that she will someday be attacked. And, Dvorak confides, lately she startles easily if she hears a noise outside her classroom. She says she has written a will in which she asks her loved ones not to hate blacks if she should be murdered in North Lawndale.

Dvorak has wanted to be a teacher since she was in 7th grade. Lately she has her doubts. On most evenings after she gets home from school, she is too exhausted to do anything but eat dinner and go to bed.

"I know I won't last," she explains. "I can feel it right now. I won't have the energy to do this anymore."

On a recent afternoon, her class was in an uproar.

"Miss Dvorak! Miss Dvorak!" a 6-year-old wails. "Miss Dvorak! Timothy stole my pencil!"

Timothy punches the girl in the arm. The force knocks her back into her chair as classmates scurry about the room, indifferent to her cry or the latest assault by Timothy. It has happened too many times for them to take much notice.

They are absorbed in their efforts to wrestle magazines away from another boy. He was supposed to pass them out to everyone, but he's hoarding them instead, prompting the 28 children in Dvorak's classroom to jump from their seats and crowd around him as he holds the tattered magazines high above his head.

"Miss Dvorak!" the girl yells again. At the front of the room, Dvorak cannot hear her above the din.

The teacher is trying to ignore Timothy today, in keeping with her latest scheme to deal with the classroom bully. She has her hands full anyway, separating two boys who have been fighting over a pair of scissors. One of them is crying.

The girl gives up on Dvorak and chases Timothy. He darts across the room, yanking magazines off desks along the way.

Timothy is not supposed to be in Dvorak's classroom. But at

7, he has the learning ability of a 4-year-old. He is hyperactive and destructive.

Timothy lives with his great-aunt, Ella Nelson, who has cared for him since he was 6 months old. Nelson says Timothy's mother gave the child to her to rear after the mother's boyfriend threw him against a wall and broke his hip.

"The reason why I got him," Nelson explains, "first of all, his mother was a dope addict and she didn't take care of him."

Lately Nelson has taken to sitting next to Timothy in class, to help Dvorak keep him in his seat. "He's come a long ways," she says. "They can keep him down half a day now. They used to couldn't keep him in his seat at all."

Du Sable's students learn the laws of survival

When violence erupts around Du Sable High School, Dorothy Thomas, a streetwise 17-year-old junior, reacts with instincts honed in a lifetime soured by crime and acts of random violence.

"If there is a fight in third period, I'm gone at third period-and-a-half," said Thomas, who grew up in the Robert Taylor Homes public housing complex. "If they're shooting at Taylor, I lay low."

Thomas says she is not afraid, only realistic.

Brutality is a grim but unavoidable fact of life for teenagers who attend the South Side alma mater of Mayor Harold Washington, and it contributes to the 60 percent dropout rate there. Some youngsters are too frightened to continue attending; others join the street gangs that cause most of the trouble.

Du Sable, 4934 S. Wabash Ave., was one of 15 Chicago public high schools named by former school Supt. Ruth Love in 1984 as beset with intensive street gang activity. It is hampered by the problems that face many public high schools in America's underclass communities.

Most of Du Sable's 1,800 students live in the Chicago Housing

Authority's Taylor Homes, a two-mile State Street corridor that is one of the most concentrated pockets of poverty in the nation. Single-parent homes, usually headed by welfare-dependent mothers, are the norm.

"The problems of violence and poverty are overwhelming," Du Sable Principal Judy Steinhagen said in an interview late last spring. "These kids are not interested in much else but survival." Fear of gangs is so pervasive, the principal said, that "we always have kids who tell their mothers they can't come to school."

Steinhagen estimated that half of Du Sable's students overcome the physical and psychological burdens of their environment to find jobs and build stable lives, but half never make it.

"Don't Give Up Hope" coaxes a sign tacked to the wall behind her desk.

"It's a tough life to live," said Anthony Ranson, a senior who wore his red and white Du Sable football jersey home from practice on a recent cool afternoon.

"You do have to watch out for the bullets that fly. The ones in the gangs usually just drop out and hang out. And the ones that are afraid to come to school, you just don't know because you don't see them anymore."

Ranson and other Du Sable students said a crackdown has tightened school discipline since last year, when the school's full-time police officer said threats and minor assaults against teachers, in particular substitutes, occurred daily.

Four guns and dozens of knives, bats and other weapons were confiscated from students during the 1984-85 school year, according to Nate Blackwell, the police youth officer who has been assigned to Du Sable since 1961.

"Violence," Blackwell explained, "is a way of life here."

Allen Knox and Linda Carter, science teachers who completed their first year at Du Sable last June, expressed amazement at many students' passive acceptance of their harsh lives.

"I have students who try and students who, when they do come, all they do is draw gang signs on their papers," Carter said.

"There may not be that many success stories, but each one really is a blessing," Knox said. "That's one less individual who is going to end up leading a life of poverty and degradation."

hwestern Universit
Sheridan Roa
OOL OF EDUCATION
TEACHING PROFESSIONS
OMICS DEPARTMENT
SESSION OFFICE
ATION OFFICE

Escape is a struggle,
but some will pay the price

'Welfare wasn't anything to be proud of'

Derrick Williams was uncomfortable living on welfare. "I didn't like going to the store with food stamps," he says. "My mom used to send us to the corner store, and I thought it was kind of embarrassing standing in line and paying with food stamps."

But a decade ago, welfare was the only option for Williams, his mother and four sisters after his stepfather abandoned them.

For four years, the family lived on public aid in the Humboldt Park neighborhood, members of the urban black underclass, caught, like those around them, in the vise of poverty, unemployment and welfare.

For many members of the underclass, dependence on welfare has become a chronic condition. But the Williams family escaped this trap. And they are not alone.

Despite all of the obstacles, all of the messages of failure that pervade underclass life, many people manage to claw their way out. Many others are struggling to do so.

Success is elusive among the black underclass of Chicago and other American cities, where the depressing facts of life stack

Left: Family discipline and pride helped Audrey Williams rise from Humboldt Park's underclass to Northwestern University's senior class.

the deck against them—the widespread poverty, the lack of jobs, the violent crime, the poor schools, the many dropouts.

Yet there are many who refuse to give up.

If they can, they escape. They go to school, learn and graduate. They get jobs. They are not picky about where they start working. Then they are on their way—out of underclass life and, usually, out of underclass neighborhoods.

Such escape comes only after years of struggle. It is not easy. Yet in the culture of poverty that defines the underclass, the mere decision to fight, to try to escape, is itself a sort of triumph.

And there are those who, unable to escape, refuse to give in to the dead-end mentality that undermines their neighbors. Often, such people are parents who realize they must rely on welfare to raise their children.

But they strive to help the children rise above it.

Today, Derrick Williams is a 20-year-old junior majoring in business at the University of Illinois-Urbana, where his sister, Carroyl, 18, studies marketing. Another sister, Audrey, 21, is a senior majoring in industrial engineering at Northwestern University. Gwendolyn and Jacqueline, twin 15-year-olds, attend Roberto Clemente High School.

Their mother, who works as an accounting clerk at a bank, recently enrolled at Roosevelt University.

"When we were growing up," Audrey Williams says, "we thought my mom didn't care about us because she didn't let us do all the things our friends were doing. We had curfews. We had to do homework. We had to do chores before we could do anything else.

"When I was younger, I thought it was unfair. As I got older, I thought it was the best. I realized how right she had been.

"One time, I was talking to a friend. It was around the end of August before school started. I was saying how we had to go buy school supplies.

"She couldn't believe we were buying our own. She said she just went to the welfare office with her mother and told them they had run out of money and they needed some school supplies.

"I thought, 'Oh, boy, wait until I tell my mom.' But she got really upset with me. It was then that I realized welfare wasn't anything to be proud of."

Derrick Williams got his first job when he was 11.

"I worked for a guy who did construction work for the landlord of our building," he says. "I've been working ever since. I had lots of summer jobs. I was a bag boy and a cashier. I did construction work, and I worked in the Kraft factory.

"Several of my high school friends—I'd say the majority—didn't make it. Whenever I go home, I stop by and visit them.

"The difference was my mother. She wasn't very strict, but she made sure my education was first and foremost. When I was young, she put a big emphasis on going to school and doing your homework before you could go out and play.

"Apparently, most families don't do this."

Success among the underclass has its price. It requires constant vigilance against the allure of the streets. It requires setting standards and living up to them. It requires staying in school, doing homework, learning. It requires determination and drive and a belief that goals can be reached.

In every underclass neighborhood, there are many who pay the price. Many who, in the gloom of poverty, keep alive the flame of human decency. Right-living people who refuse to accept a life without responsibility, a life without commitment, a life without goodness.

Their lives may not be easy, but they are ennobled by the fight.

Carolyn Hurley, a 17-year-old senior at Farragut High School, plans to attend college and to major in business.

She lives with her mother, Bernice, in North Lawndale. But, she explains, she doesn't like the "normal" things of the neighborhood, and that causes problems.

"When girls see how I live and that I'm not sitting around getting high and having sex, they pick fights with me," she says. "When I tell them I'm a virgin and a Christian girl, they tell me, 'You can't hang out with us.'

"I don't go out around the house. The environment is not for me."

Carolyn's father was a working man. When he died in 1973, his wife went on public aid. Life was a struggle, and, Bernice Hurley says, it still is. Nonetheless, she worked to teach her children right from wrong. "We live in a corrupt area, but my children are not," she says.

With most of the five older children, now in their 20s and 30s, she was successful. But with Alfred, Carolyn's 29-year-old brother, she failed. "My son, Alfred, is the black sheep of the family," she says. "He's an alcoholic.

"One day, I heard a lot of noise outside. People in cars were blowing their horns. I looked out the window, and there Alfred was, lying in the middle of the street, saying, 'Give me some money for some wine and I'll move.' "

Hurley has high hopes for Carolyn, whom she calls her "princess," and Carolyn has high hopes for herself.

When she turns 18, she will be taken off her mother's public aid grant. After that, she says, public aid "won't see me no more."

The people of the underclass are not all cut from the same cloth, notes Thomas Cook, professor of psychology and urban affairs at Northwestern University.

"Some people drop out of school earlier than others," he explains. "Some don't look as hard for work as others. Some girls don't have babies, and others do.

"We know there are many people who want to get out and will pay for it. Many parents in the ghetto prefer to send their kids to Catholic schools instead of public schools because the discipline's better."

It is still unclear why some have the drive to resist the tide of the underclass, Cook says. But discipline is an essential element.

This is often best learned from parents—"parents teaching the kids self-discipline, teaching their kids that they have some control over their lives, teaching that the things the parents want for them are likely to happen, and pointing to people in the community who have done it," Cook notes.

"The parents set the patterns for kids and show them how to reach those standards," Cook says.

"The streets are very attractive. If your home life is bad, if the schools are bad, where else can you go? People escape if they have other alternatives more attractive than the streets—a good home life, an early job, a teacher who takes a special interest."

Self-discipline is also taught by example. It is important, Cook adds, for underclass children to have someone in their lives "holding a job, seeing them struggling to keep it, seeing them bringing money home, seeing that it takes effort to get up in the morning and take the bus."

Among the underclass, role models like these are rare. The

burden of teaching self-esteem and self-discipline often falls most heavily on the shoulders of a single mother.

And she gets little help. Inner-city schools frequently fail to strike the spark of character in underclass children, and the streets are filled with pushers, pimps and prostitutes, penny-ante hustlers, drug addicts and drunks—Pied Pipers of violence, self-loathing and failure.

Those who find their way out of the mire or who continue struggling to do so are, Cook says, "little heroes."

One who continues to struggle is Patricia Hunter, a 25-year-old mother of four, ranging in age from 4 to 10. For seven years, Hunter has been on welfare, but she doesn't like it—and doesn't plan to stay on it.

After she got pregnant the first time at 14, she managed to stay off public aid for three years by working seasonal jobs and getting help from her mother.

Then life in the underclass caught up with her. "I had just turned 18," she recalls. "I had two kids. I had just dropped out of school, and I had no income." She signed up for public aid.

Each month, Hunter says, she carefully shepherds her money to pay her bills. With the $239 in food stamps she receives, she shops at discount groceries. Of the $450 she receives in Aid to Families with Dependent Children, $225 goes for rent.

In the winter, her electric bills can be as high as $70 a month because she must supplement the gas heat in her apartment with space heaters. In many months, she has less than $70 left over.

"I feel confidence in myself that eventually I'll get off public aid; I want to be something," says Hunter, who is studying for her high school equivalency test.

It's important to get off welfare for the sake of her children, she says.

"If they just see me sittin' around on welfare, then they're going to get the idea that that's all right to do," she says. "One day, they may say, 'Mom gets by on public aid. If she's doing all right, then I can do it, too.' A lot of people look on it as an easy living.

"When I had my last child, I thought, 'This is not what I want to do for the rest of my life.' So instead of seeing it as another year on public aid, I see it as another year and my boy got older and I can go out and find a job."

"I often wonder," John H. Johnson says, "what would have

happened to me. I often think, 'Gee, I wonder how many guys are out there just like me who didn't get the same breaks.' "

Johnson is in his 11th-floor office in the Johnson Publishing Co. headquarters at 820 S. Michigan Ave., an office from which he has a clear view, above the traffic and street work below, of Grant Park and Lake Michigan.

At 67, Johnson, whose company publishes Ebony and Jet magazines, is unquestionably one black who has made it. He is listed again this year on the Forbes 400, the magazine's list of the richest people in America. His net worth of $160 million may be small change to some of the billionaires on the list, but it is enough to make him still the only black among the 400.

Yet Johnson, too, once was on welfare.

"I was on the welfare rolls in Chicago from 1933 to 1936," he says. "I was on the rolls because my mother and I had come to Chicago from the Deep South, Arkansas, and she couldn't get a job. And my stepfather couldn't get a job.

"WPA got me off welfare. They gave me and my father a sense of earning our keep.

"I got off welfare so I know that some people would get off if they had gainful employment. You've got to pay the money in order for people not to starve. Why not find creative ways to put them to work?"

It can be a major accomplishment just to live among underclass people without being dragged into their self-destructive lifestyle.

Elettie and Freddia Jones lived in North Lawndale for 28 years, raising five children and keeping them on the straight and narrow.

"I often said to myself, 'What's going on here?' You'd hear shots on the street, and we would find needles used for drugs in our back yard," says Elettie Jones, who worked first in construction and, for the last 13 years, for General Electric.

"Church was our main outing," his wife says. "There just wasn't anything else. No theaters or anything. Our kids brought a lot of other kids into the church with them, and they patterned themselves after us.

"We stayed home a lot. We played a lot of games. I think I bought every game Milton Bradley made."

Last February, the Joneses and their 12-year-old son, Brandon, moved out of North Lawndale and into a two-flat they had purchased in Austin.

"We moved to better ourselves," Freddia Jones says. "The neighborhood is in bad shape, and the people act like they just didn't care what went down. Everywhere you look there're vacant lots. Some people just seemed to give up and they have nothing.

"If you want something you have to keep striving."

Escaping the underclass often means cutting oneself off from friends and relatives.

Clarence Moreland and his three older brothers grew up in the Ida B. Wells public housing project on the South Side. All were members of a street gang there.

Claude, the eldest, died of cirrhosis of the liver. Robert was gunned down three years ago in a gang shooting. Donald is unemployed.

Clarence Moreland, 32, lives in the suburbs, works as a computer software engineer in the Loop and earns $40,000 a year. He escaped the underclass. His brothers didn't.

"I think the big difference," Moreland explains, "is who I identified with in my family. I identified more with my father's family, and they were very religious."

Nonetheless, Moreland joined a street gang when he was 10.

"Gang membership was pretty much mandatory back then," he recalls. "They didn't have to draft you. You sought them out for protection. My brothers were leaders. It was pretty much taken for granted that I'd join, too."

But he eventually left the gang and began studying engineering.

"I guess I got my ambition pretty much from my family," he says. "I was always considered the brightest, and so they were always saying that I was going to be a scientist.

"I guess I believed them."

V

JOBS

As jobs disappear,
what remains is despair

What created the underclass? The economy, mostly

The huge property, 53 acres of it, sprawls at 26th and California like an old battlefield, a weed-grown monument to an area's decline. International Harvester's McCormick and Tractor Works once stood there, and 14,000 workers made their livings in the factories.

By the late 1960s they were closed and torn down. A local group has been trying for years to persuade new industry to locate there, to re-create some of those long-lost jobs. So far, no takers.

Most of the workers who toiled in the Harvester plants are gone too. If new factories rose there, would the jobs go to the stunned and drifting people who make up much of the area's population now? Could they do the jobs? Would they even take them if offered?

The old Harvester site isn't Chicago's only economic ghost town. Drive west on the Eisenhower Expressway, out past the hospital complex, and look south. What you'll see is block after block of abandoned, gaping old factories. The West Side once lived off them. Residents now would be satisfied just to have the dangerous, fetid carcasses torn down.

Left: Passing the time on a North Lawndale street: Poorer blacks once held unskilled jobs, but those were the jobs that disappeared in the postwar era.

Or walk under the "L" along 63d Street in Woodlawn, down what used to be, after State Street, the second-busiest shopping street in Chicago. It's as much a ghost town as a Wild West set: Boards cover doors and windows, but the grime and decay only half cover the names of businesses that once thrived there—an A&P, a Hi-Lo, a Walgreens, the Kimbark Theater, the Empire Warehouse, the Pershing Hotel, the Southeast Chicago Bank.

In all these places, and hundreds more throughout Chicago, the overwhelming sensation is emptiness. Not so many years ago, these factories and stores throbbed with people, jobs, money, goods, life. Now, all are gone. What's left is, literally, nothing.

Many of the people who lived off this vanished economy have themselves vanished, gone from the city, often to other and better jobs in the suburbs or Sun Belt. Some made new lives in the industrial areas still churning elsewhere in Chicago.

But thousands, most of them black, are still here, as much the debris of the economic collapse as the echoing West Side factories, their lives as empty as the Harvester site or the stores on 63d Street. In the years since their jobs vanished, new generations have grown up to face an equally bleak economic future.

Many of the older workers have forgotten what a job was like; their few skills are rusted or obsolete. Young people have never known work, indeed may not know anyone with a full-time job.

This is the underclass. It does not include people recently employed who may work again, or people with still-useful skills, or people temporarily down on their luck. It does not include the human fallout from the demise of Wisconsin Steel or other factories closed in the last decade, although it someday might if nothing replaces them.

It does include those who haven't worked in years, or who may never work, the single teenage mothers and their children, the high school dropouts, the street-corner hustlers for whom an honest job is only a rumor.

It includes, in short, a class of people, in Chicago and elsewhere, who depend on welfare, drug dealing, pimping, prostitution, panhandling, robbery or under-the-table pay for occasional odd jobs for their sustenance and live as far outside the everyday economy of industry and commerce as so many Third Worlders bartering for their existence.

This didn't just happen. The poor have always been with us.

But the underclass, as a large and important phenomenon, is fairly recent. Something caused it, and there's a lively debate in government and academia over what it was.

Some, such as Washington policy analyst Charles Murray, say it is all the fault of government programs that made otherwise able-bodied people dependent on welfare. Some, such as Harvard professor Edward Banfield, describe a "lower-class individual" with so many "pathological" attitudes and habits that he cannot take advantage of what opportunities exist.

But many economists say there is no need for such political and sociological finger-pointing when a perfectly good economic reason exists: the departure or collapse of the segment of the economy that supported many of Chicago's blacks, including those least able to find new work.

"The economy was the major cause," says William Julius Wilson, head of the sociology department at the University of Chicago. In his book, "The Declining Significance of Race," he writes:

"The current problems of lower-class blacks are substantially related to fundamental structural changes in the economy. . . . As the black middle class rides on the wave of political and social changes, benefiting from the growth of employment opportunities in the growing corporate and government sectors of the economy, the black underclass falls behind the larger society in every conceivable respect."

The studies of economists and sociologists, both white and black, answer many questions about the underclass and the ghetto: If so many blacks escaped into the mainstream economy, why didn't the underclass? Why is the urban underclass mostly black, not white? Is the reason racial or political or economic?

The answers grow from the history of black migration to Chicago, especially during and after World War II.

The 1940 census, just before the war began, reported 277,730 blacks in Chicago, barely up from the 1930 figures. But the wartime defense industries needed workers, and, with many former workers off to war, the factories actively recruited Southern blacks, urging them to come North. The blacks responded by the trainload: Factory work, hard and ill-paid as it was, was better than plantation labor back home.

The wartime boom merged into the postwar boom. Pent-up

demand from the Depression and war fueled the great economic expansion. Both whites and blacks benefited; unemployment rates were about the same for both.

Chicago looked better and better to Southern blacks. By 1950 the city's black population was up to 492,265. By 1960 it had grown even faster, to 812,637, and by 1970, to 1,102,620. [It has since leveled off; it stood at 1,197,000 in 1980.]

Even more dramatic was the growing black percentage of Chicago's population. White population was about 3.1 million from 1930 to 1950. It fell to 2.7 million in 1960 as the suburbs expanded, and was down to 2.2 million by 1970 and 1.8 million by 1980. Blacks represented 8 percent of Chicago's population in 1940, 23 percent in 1960, 40 percent in 1980.

As the black migration grew, so did the ghetto. There was no integrated housing in the beginning; almost all blacks lived in the ghetto. And despite what many whites think, they were not all poor. Instead, black professionals, middle-class, skilled workers and unskilled laborers all lived in the ghetto, because housing discrimination kept them there.

Around 1960 a lot of new things began happening, almost none of them noticed at the time.

As the black migration to Chicago continued, the jobs that brought them here began disappearing. There were 1,384,154 private-sector jobs in Chicago in 1957. By 1977 this had fallen to 1,174,744. By 1983 it was down to 1,101,720, a fall of about 280,000 jobs from its peak.

Even this startling figure obscures the impact of the shift on the poorer black population. As Wilson points out, these people once were poor but not destitute, usually employed in menial jobs, acquainted with the world of work, mostly living in intact families. They were the "lower class" but not the "underclass"—a crucial difference.

They held unskilled jobs involving lifting or shoveling or carrying, in factories, in the steel mills, or on loading docks, or in the stockrooms of stores such as those along 63d Street. The jobs paid badly but were better than nothing.

It was precisely these jobs that disappeared fastest. The stockyards closed. So did the can manufacturers, many of the steel mills, the foundries and a myriad of other manufacturers in the city.

Many of the jobs went to the suburbs, lured by the easy

transportation created by the building of the expressways and eager to be nearer their white workers who were fleeing the city. Later, many went to the Sun Belt, in search of nonunion low wages. Pure racism—the desire to get out of an increasingly black city into the mostly white suburbs—undoubtedly played a role.

Chicago had 8,087 factories in 1970, the first year in which such a census was kept. By 1981 this was down to 6,127, a net loss of about 24 percent of all the city's factories, large and small.

The trend was relentless. In 1972, for instance, 4 factories moved from the suburbs into Chicago—and 40 moved out.

As the factories went, so did the stores, especially in the ghetto. Some closed because the lost factory jobs robbed the economy of the purchasing power—the paychecks—that kept them open. Others lasted until the riots of the late 1960s burned them out or sent their owners fleeing to the suburbs.

Somewhere in the process, the neighborhood banks closed, and this was the coup de grace. All through the South and West Sides, former banks stand vacant or have been converted into churches. Often, they were the only institutions willing to lend money locally. When they went, so did local mortgages and loans to local businesses.

Something else was happening at the same time: the civil rights movement.

Suddenly, the gates to the ghetto opened for those ready and able to leave. The social integration within the deepest ghetto ended. Many blacks, using their new civil rights, entered previously all-white businesses or moved into previously all-white neighborhoods. Wilson, in fact, notes that the civil rights movement, with its emphasis on admission to restaurants, universities, swimming pools and the polling booth, reflected the political and largely noneconomic interests of the middle class blacks who led it.

Working-class blacks, including the many skilled workers, kept their old jobs but used their solid paychecks to buy homes in new and better areas. [Too often, these areas quickly became all-black, under the pressure of block busting and panic peddling. Many of them are the solid black working-class neighborhoods that still grace Chicago.]

Blacks with a good education and skills moved more or less smoothly into the growing service and information economy. It was a time of unprecedented opportunities for blacks, and millions of them, in Chicago and elsewhere, seized them. But the poorest, the former lower class, were left behind, trapped by bad education, semiliteracy and lack of skills.

"As a result of the decentralization of American businesses, the movement from goods-producing to service-producing industries, and the clear manifestation of these changes in the expansion of the corporate sector and the government sector," Wilson writes, "a segmented labor market has developed resulting in vastly different mobility opportunities for different groups in the black population. . . . The relatively poorly trained blacks of the inner city, including the growing number of younger blacks emerging from inferior ghetto schools, find themselves locked in the low-wage sector."

In short, the same forces—the post-industrial economy and civil rights—that opened a new world to millions of blacks condemned other blacks to the underclass.

Why weren't poor whites seized by this process too? Some, of course, were. But Wilson argues that racial oppression kept all blacks down for a century and guaranteed that the lower-class blacks would be on the very bottom of society, uniquely unfit to join the mainstream economy. His point is that, while the underclass has its roots in past discrimination, it exists today not for racial but for economic reasons: It is in the ghetto because it's black, but it stays there because there are no jobs.

Of serious concern to some observers is whether the younger members of the underclass can ever be imbued with the work ethic that sustained previous generations of poor blacks. Some suspect that the black pride movement of the 1960s left many of these people with a disdain for the kind of menial, low-paying jobs at which their forebears historically toiled. If so many illegal aliens find jobs, it is argued, then so could many members of the black underclass—if they really wanted to work, not live off public aid.

No systematic study has addressed the question of a decline in the work ethic among poor urban blacks. "Anyone who makes such an assertion is doing so purely on the basis of intuition," Wilson says. "There is no data, no research."

The reasons for holding a low-paying job have largely been

eroded in the ghetto, Murray maintains. Economically, there are other alternatives, he explained, including welfare, family and the underground economy. Beyond that, holding down a menial but steady job—which once brought poor blacks a modicum of respect—today is more likely to result in scorn.

"It is much simpler than a decline of the work ethic," Murray says. "Both the status of holding a job and the need for money to live on have disappeared as reasons why anyone should sweep floors 8 hours a day, 40 hours a week."

Walter Williams, an economist and author of "The State Against Blacks," contends that the unemployment rate among illegal aliens is so low because they lack the legal and illegal support sytems that underclass blacks can fall back on. Unlike poor blacks, illegal aliens cannot drop out of the work force for a significant length of time.

Publicly funded jobs programs—intended to teach work habits and skills and ease the way into the work force for poor young blacks—have instead left many of them with unrealistic concepts about the workaday world, according to Murray.

"The experience of the jobs programs consisted of learning how not to fit into the labor market," he explains. "Many of the programs taught that when you go to a job, you don't want to work too hard or you'll make life difficult for others."

In job programs, many youngsters learned that "whether you work hard or not, you make the same amount of money," Murray says. "Kids are not dumb. They looked at that and said, 'That is the way the world works.' It taught youngsters it was all a great big con game."

The plight of the underclass seems to be self-generating. Job loss in the poorest neighborhoods continued unabated—from 35,304 in Garfield Park in 1972 to 20,886 in 1983, from 21,292 to 10,365 in Austin in the same period.

As factories leave, more factories think about leaving. As jobs disappear, crime grows, encouraging the few remaining businesses to flee. As the possibility of employment recedes, so do the reasons for staying in school: About 55 percent of Chicago schoolchildren drop out before their high school graduation, practically guaranteeing that they never will work.

The impact on black men and on black families has been particularly savage. The jobs that vanished were heavy-lifting jobs—men's jobs. The new jobs in the service economy often were clerical—usually women's jobs. Suddenly, women became the breadwinners. There may be no better reason for the break-up of black families and the explosion in the number of female-headed households.

The effect of this on black boys has been especially strong. Many are growing up not only without a father but without knowing a man who has a full-time job. If role models are important to youths, the present unemployment of black men teaches negative lessons that will echo down the generations.

Does welfare play no role in this? Actually, many economists think it does encourage some growth of the underclass by providing an alternative to work. But welfare payments fell, when inflation is taken into account, during the 1970s, when the underclass was growing, undermining the argument that the poor were better off on welfare than working.

It is assumed that the plight of the underclass is an economic burden not only to those caught in its cycle of poverty but to society as a whole—from the increased expenditures for police and welfare, to the loss in tax revenues, to the "opportunity cost" of lost investment. But amazingly, there has been almost no systematic research aimed at singling out the cost of this "poorest of the poor," partly because there are such differences over how big the underclass is and who belongs to it, partly because the issue is emotionally explosive, exposing potential researchers to charges of "racism."

"It's very complex and very touchy," says former University of Chicago professor John Kasarda, now at the University of North Carolina. "It's hard to secure the funding for this. And it's hard to ascribe the costs to a certain geographic or demographic group without knowing what would have happened if some other group had been there."

"It's about as slippery a concept that's come along," says Sheldon Danziger, head of the Poverty Institute at the University of Wisconsin. "There are literally zero scientific studies of what the underclass is, much less what it costs."

Costs of welfare, lost taxation and other statistics are seldom broken down for specific neighborhoods. Perhaps deliberately, they are lumped into larger areas, where the specific impact of the underclass can be hidden.

The Woodstock Institute, however, has computed the number and size of mortgages and home improvement loans by neighborhood in an attempt to chart economic activity in the housing market. The differences are dramatic.

In the blighted Grand Boulevard area, there were 61 such loans in 1983, including 12 conventional home mortgages and 46 home improvement loans, worth a total of $809,000. In South Shore, another black community but one blessed with a committed and energetic local bank, there were 310 loans in 1983, including 66 mortgages and 200 home improvement loans, worth a total of $8,051,000—10 times as much activity in an area with only a slightly higher population.

The future is bleak. Attempts to lure investment into underclass areas—through enterprise zones, tax breaks or other lures—have had marginal or no success. Self-help neighborhood programs, crippled by the lack of capital and home-grown managerial skills, have achieved little. The fact is that these areas and their people have the aura of economic disaster about them: No company wants to be there if it can be somewhere else.

Increasingly, they can be somewhere else. An economic recovery is underway in the Northern states, but the new, modern, high-tech-based companies that exemplify it are often small and mobile and are setting up shop in suburbs, around colleges, in small towns—almost everywhere except where the underclass is. Moreover, public transportation networks in Chicago and elsewhere seldom link the ghettos, where the underclass is, to the industrial parks where the jobs are.

Industrialists deny there is discrimination in these local decisions. They say they need clean sites near a well-educated population that has skills beyond those taught in ghetto schools. For what they need, they say, the ghetto is the wrong place to look.

A land of broken glass—
and broken promises of '68

Community's lack of core proves barrier
to rebirth

Cecil C. Butler arrived in North Lawndale in 1968, while the embers from the fires that destroyed much of the neighborhood's economy still glowed. He came with plans, dreams and the promise of a better life for people who had little to hope for.

The fires, set during the riots that followed the assassination of Rev. Martin Luther King, cooled 17 years ago. The dreams took longer to die. Some plans are still there, but they've been sharply scaled back.

"I don't think it's realistic to measure our accomplishments by our plans and expectations, in the context of general economic conditions," Butler said in the barren offices of his Pyramidwest Realty and Management Co. "I'm not happy with what's developed. But a failure? I'll leave that to other people to decide."

His immediate plans for himself and the community?

"My plans now are to survive."

Butler, 47, is an enigmatic, brooding man who combines shyness with charisma. He has stood at the center of attempts to bring North Lawndale back from its economic collapse and provide jobs, businesses, housing, tax income and the other benefits of a vibrant area.

Left: Like many of its families, the neighborhood of North Lawndale itself seems shattered by years of hardship.

But after 17 years, things are worse economically, not better: Unemployment is higher, housing is crumbling, industry has vanished, there are fewer stores. Many residents of North Lawndale now belong to the black underclass, mired in social misery and hopelessness.

The question—for Lawndale and for other underclass neighborhoods throughout the country—is why the promise of 1968 was not kept.

Butler has been surrounded by other players—from business and government and the neighborhood itself—who also tried to help and failed.

Did Butler make key mistakes? Was the situation hopeless from the start? Was racism the biggest stumbling block? Did the city abandon North Lawndale? Did private business doom it by moving out? Can North Lawndale swim against the ebbing tide of a declining city economy?

One crucial barrier to the rebirth of North Lawndale is an almost eerie lack of a core—the sort of communal history, or memory, or focus that cements most communities, from neighborhoods to nations. There is no written history of North Lawndale's last 20 years, no academic studies, no newspaper, no scribes composing an agreed version of the area's past and present.

Like so many of its families, the neighborhood itself seems shattered by years of hardship and failure, with nothing to hold it together.

Instead, there is a jumble of neighborhood groups, businesses and activists, none with the power to give North Lawndale a communal view of itself. Without this glue, the area has no base on which to build an economy.

"There's no existing community there thinking together, working together, trying to sweat something out," said one government official who has tried to funnel development funds to North Lawndale.

North Lawndale went from mostly white to mostly black in little more than a decade. When the whites left, so did their businesses, houses of worship—mostly synagogues—and the other institutions that help bind a neighborhood. Very little has taken their place.

"The disintegration of institutions is the tragedy of North Lawndale," agrees Rob Mier, the city's economic development commissioner. "When you lose your industrial base, you also lose your historical record."

Possibly nothing could be built on such a foundation. But many have tried.

The federal government's Model Cities program sought to focus housing and economic development money on needy neighborhoods, including North Lawndale. It achieved some housing rehabilitation and social programs, but fell far short of its promise.

According to Mier, then-Mayor Richard J. Daley insisted that City Hall, not the federal government, allocate Model Cities funds inside Chicago.

"Daley was a master of spreading the resources," Mier said, "and there was never enough that went to Lawndale to make a difference." Moreover, he said, the funds went largely for social measures—better housing, health and other programs intended to ease economic hardship—rather than for the economy itself.

In North Lawndale, Model Cities is seen as "a pacification program that was designed to give out a few more crumbs," in the words of Jesse Miller, director of the Lawndale Peoples Planning and Action Conference [LPPAC], a local political organization. "It never did any good."

The Pyramidwest Development Corp., one of the nation's few black-owned development companies, was something different. It was set up to guide North Lawndale's redevelopment, with shares bought by local residents. Butler, one of only two black graduates from the 1962 class of Northwestern University Law School, was hired to run it.

Since then, Pyramidwest and its subsidiaries have built some townhouses and opened a nursing home. But its main accomplishment was the founding of the Community Bank of Lawndale in 1977.

The previous North Lawndale banks fled as blacks flowed in—usually the death knell for a neighborhood. The establishment of the Community Bank, locally owned and black-owned, was a source of enormous pride and hope. Its mission was to do what the big Loop banks wouldn't do—risk money on investments in North Lawndale's economy.

The bank moved into a handsome new stone building, sticking out like a manicured thumb in the battered neighborhood. Butler was its chairman and president—until Oct. 18, when he quietly quit, in circumstances that are still unclear. Bank officials said he left "to devote more time to other ventures." Butler refused to explain the move.

Butler, using federal grant money, also bought a 53-acre site at 26th Street and California Boulevard, where the old International Harvester plant had stood, and a two-block stretch of vacant land in the heart of what had been the Roosevelt Road shopping strip before the riots burned it out.

The old Harvester site was renamed the Cal-West Industrial Park. The idea was to develop it for industry, creating jobs for North Lawndale. The Roosevelt Road strip was to become the Lawndale Plaza Shopping Center, a mall of small shops anchored by two big stores—a supermarket and a department store—to soak up the income from those industrial jobs.

In all, the federal government pumped $22 million into Pyramidwest projects. The Economic Development Administration [EDA] alone invested $3,674,000 in the Cal-West project for sewers and other infrastructure to make it attractive to industry. It put up another $1,167,000 for the shopping center, contingent on Butler finding some tenants.

The results: nearly zero.

Today, the Cal-West park stands empty, weed-grown, part of it used illegally as a dump. The planned shopping strip is also empty except for one woebegone house, the LPPAC headquarters.

The EDA gave up on the shopping strip last year, after 12 years of waiting, and took back its $1,167,000 grant.

Pyramidwest, in filings with the Securities and Exchange Commission, admits it owes at least $2,020,112 in taxes dating back seven years, including at least $1,087,203 in Cook County real estate taxes on the Cal-West park.

It has written down the carrying value of the park by 50 percent, from $10.7 million to $5.3 million, in preparation for seizure for back taxes, but holds out hope it can still be sold, even at "significant loss."

The state's attorney's office planned to go to court to start proceedings to seize the park. Butler refused to discuss this suit.

Various city and industrial officials who have dealt with Butler over the years say he had a chance to land an industrial laundry, warehouses or a county jail for the Cal-West park. All were turned down—the laundry because the 300 jobs it offered were low-wage and dead-end, the warehouses because they offered too few jobs, the jail because it had nothing to do with industry.

Butler also refused to construct buildings on speculation or write down land prices to lure industry to the site. One Chicago executive says he called Pyramidwest to inquire about a site for a new factory, "but they never even called back."

Butler says he doesn't remember the warehouse deals. The laundry "required a subsidy which we were determined not to give," he said, and the "people in the community opposed" the jail.

To suggestions that the bank—one of the three smallest in Chicago—could have done more to encourage deals, he replied: "It's unrealistic to expect a bank that size to finance the development of a whole economy."

Mier agrees that, "in that environment, I'd question whether any amount of strategizing could have affected the outcome."

But Don Kane, a city economic development official during the period, argues that Pyramidwest, as a black-owned development organization, was "swimming upstream to begin with." Butler's refusal to accept deals or to write down the land value ended up scaring investors away, he says.

` "There's no question about it," Kane said, "that this created a perception among the private sector and the city that they were very difficult to do business with, and ultimately people stopped coming to them."

The laundry jobs may indeed have been bad jobs, and the warehouses meager employers. But the question must be asked: Would they have been worse than nothing at all?

Edward Jeep, local administrator for the EDA, says he agreed with Butler at the time because the EDA grant was intended to create good, long-term jobs. But he concedes reluctantly now that "it could have been a mistake, the way things look."

No store offered to move into the shopping center. Without jobs, North Lawndale offered nothing for a retailer.

Butler contends that North Lawndale failed because the economy around it failed.

"This area has been subject to the same economic forces as Chicago, Illinois and the nation," he said. "But because we have less to work with, the effects are more pronounced. If you're not in a growth economic situation as a city or a state, how can a community in isolation do that?"

Jerry Kelly, director of the Lawndale Business and Local Development Corp., says there may have been too many rival organizations stirring the development pot.

"The idea of turf is an important factor," Kelly said. "That's been a problem on the West Side among community organizations. There have been rivalries over turf. This slows things up."

After years of trying, no one in North Lawndale seems to know what businesses want or how to get them.

To get business, Kelly says, North Lawndale must "have something to attract people who want to develop—but I don't think anybody knows what that is."

James Hadley, acting chief executive officer of the bank, says he is frustrated that North Lawndale—a prime location along the Eisenhower Expressway, just 10 minutes from the Loop—has so little going for it.

"I'm not sure why," he said, echoing the baffled resignation of Butler and Kelly. Community activist Sam Flowers agrees that "if I had the answer to that, I'd be a genius."

All are reluctant to blame Butler, or private companies, or the city, or the bad schools, or high crime. Instead, the people most intimately involved shrug their shoulders and shake their heads.

Most economic development experts agree that, at the least, a community must make businesses feel wanted. But one venerable group, the LPPAC and its leader, Jesse Miller, seem almost hostile to investment.

"We've got to decide who we don't want in our community," said Miller, who describes himself as "a product of the 1960s" and who wants to form a "community union" to screen investors.

"We have to protect the way of life of people in our community," Miller said. "Our economy must be controlled locally. People who come in here have to be stopped and made to sit down and talk. It's like going into a foreign country. You just don't go in and work your will."

There are only three big employers left in North Lawndale—Joseph T. Ryerson & Son, a steel company; Mt. Sinai Hospital; and a catalogue distribution center for Sears, Roebuck and Co. Of the three, Sears is the biggest, with 3,000 workers, and is right in the heart of North Lawndale. But community leaders who single out Ryerson and Mt. Sinai for praise mention Sears only as an afterthought.

"People think that Sears is so large that it can do more," Flowers explained, recalling that the company employed 10,000 people at its North Lawndale facility before it moved its world headquarters downtown. "Sears has helped in neighborhood organizations. But if it had really cared, if it had stood out front and said, 'Hey, we're going to turn North Lawndale around,' then it would have happened."

Ryerson and Mt. Sinai remain. But both are tucked into the eastern corner of North Lawndale, separated by Douglas Park from most of the community. This seems to have been enough to reduce their impact.

Both gave money and expertise to community organizations for years, without visible result. Now they are cosponsoring a project by the Neighborhood Housing Service to revitalize housing in their immediate neighborhood. Ryerson also is trying to help local schools.

"We were supporting 15 different programs," Ryerson president Jack Foster said. "We got to the end of the year and didn't see progress anywhere. So we're concentrating now, to have some impact that we can see."

Ruth Rothstein, president of Mt. Sinai, like many in a position to work with Butler, says he is so solitary and aloof that she has wearied of waiting for him to suggest projects.

"I haven't seen Cecil for years," she said. "We were never able to sit down with him and say that we have mutual problems and mutual desires. He wanted to do it all himself— but that's not good enough."

Mier adds that Butler has not called him since he took office at the start of the Washington administration.

Butler responds, "When I see something that merits my communication, I'll do it."

Rothstein sees a failure in North Lawndale by all sides— Butler, the city, the state and private business.

"I don't think there's been any real thought given by the city or state as to what to do with this area," she said. "In 20 years, nobody has said what this community should be. Nothing can be done unless the city commits its total resources to making it happen. I think the community would accept a plan now. They're as frustrated as I am.

"There has to be some hope, or it will get infinitely worse," she said. "I have to think that there's hope—jobs, social services, industry. This is perfectly valid. It can be done."

Futures of three men get junked in a vacant lot

Jobs a dim memory, with prospects even dimmer

This is the story of three men whose lives have come to rest in a vacant lot.

Not one of them is older than 34.

Slim Ty, Juice Man and Willie have been out of work for three years. But they still put in a good 14-hour day.

Every morning they wander to the same place, to a patch of gravel and weeds beside the only building left standing on this one-block stretch of Roosevelt Road between Karlov and Komensky Avenues. The rest of the block was ravaged in the riots of 1968 after the assassination of Rev. Martin Luther King.

Conveniently, a tavern and liquor store is on the first floor of the building. It opens at 7 a.m.

Their outdoor living room is a comfortable enough place. The first man there in the morning does a little housekeeping. He picks up the shards of glass from the night before and sets aright the old, yellow-plaid couch, turned over most evenings just in case it rains. From behind the building he retrieves the card table and sets it up on wobbly legs. One by one come the wooden school chairs that the men helped themselves to when their alma mater, Bryant Elementary School, closed its doors.

Left: A game of cards takes place in the vacant lot on Roosevelt Road in North Lawndale. For this group, life holds just two certainties: The vacant lot and the welfare check.

"I got 60 cent," Slim Ty announces, dropping it on the table. The others throw in whatever they have. Eyes light up as they realize they have just enough for a bottle of Canadian Mist. "Let's go get a taste," Slim Ty says. There is a well-worn path from the couch to the Longdale Lounge.

That is how the day begins. That is how the day passes. And that is how it ends.

These three able-bodied men are living out their lives in the urban wasteland of North Lawndale, an impoverished black ghetto on the city's West Side. Unemployment has become so rampant there that almost half of the residents older than 16 have dropped out of the job market, according to estimates by the Illinois Department of Labor. Almost 62,000 people live in North Lawndale, 42,000 of them older than 16. Jobholders total 17,500.

Neither Slim Ty nor Juice Man nor Willie looks seriously for work anymore.

There appear to be just two certainties in each of their lives: the vacant lot and the welfare check. Each lives on $233 a month in general assistance and food stamps.

Even if they were able to find work today, their histories suggest that they probably could not keep it.

Slim Ty, Juice Man and Willie have slipped into the urban underclass, a group of people cut off, perhaps permanently, from the mainstream of American life. People in this class live largely off welfare, crime or an underground economy. Many have not held full-time jobs for years, and their prospects for employment are bleak.

While these three men were in their teens and early adult years, the United States was swept by the civil rights and black pride movements, which brought about dramatic improvements in the lives of many American blacks.

But these movements failed to uplift other blacks—Slim Ty, Juice Man and Willie among them. Their lives have deteriorated over the years, and disillusionment has eaten up the hopes they once nurtured.

Tyrone Golar's friends call him "Slim Ty" because he is tall and lean, standing 6 feet but weighing only about 140 pounds. He smiles a toothless grin. He is 33.

He gets up early in the morning, between 6:30 and 7, and watches the morning news programs and his favorite TV evangelist before he heads out the front door, already fingering his pocket change to see how much more his friends will have to come up with for a $2.50 pint of Canadian Mist.

He describes a typical day in this manner: "I just walk down the street and get with the fellas and drink. That's it."

Golar lives a block from the lot, in a tidy bungalow with his grandmother, Ruth, a small, white-haired woman of 85. She reared him; he calls her "Ma." His mother still lives in the neighborhood, and he sees her from time to time. But he refuses to talk about her. "That's personal," he says.

"I believe in the Bible," he explains one morning in the bungalow's front room, where a big leather-bound Bible sits on a coffee table. His readings of the Bible have convinced him, he says, that the world will end before the year 2000. "In a sense, no one really has a future," he concludes.

"I don't think you're going to be here to find out what happens at the rate you're going," his grandmother snaps, huffing a bit as she turns away. "I don't think you even pick up the Bible."

Golar grew up in North Lawndale, and his gravitation toward the streets began in grade school, when he cut class to play dice games on the sidewalk. He was truant so often that in his early teens he spent two years in what he refers to as a "bad boys" school.

Back in North Lawndale, he started 9th grade at Marshall High School. But a few weeks later, at age 15, he stopped attending classes. "No reason," he explains, "just dropped out."

Menial jobs are all Golar has known. Mixing cement was his highest-paying work, at $5.25 an hour. He also has been a car washer, and a metal plate stacker at a West Side factory that closed "a hundred years ago," he jokes. "Must have been 1970."

He first went on welfare at 21. He also resorts to a variety of hustles to get by. In 1975, he was arrested for stealing a car and served six months in Cook County Jail. While there, he began to study for his high school equivalency certificate, he said, but was released before he completed the program.

"I wasn't going to go back to jail to get it," he says, laughing. "But I almost got it. I ain't no dummy."

Pulling an encyclopedia from a shelf in his grandmother's

apartment, he boasts: "I can read them dictionaries right here. It's all about mammals, birds and reptiles."

Golar says he'd like to find a full-time job. For now, the only work that comes his way is a few odd jobs here and there, he insists.

"You might move a refrigerator, mow a lawn. Anything except stealing. That's out. We don't play that game around here," he says, referring to himself and his friends at the vacant lot. "If you ain't got nothing in your pocket, you still don't steal. If you do, you through. You got to move."

Alcohol, Golar notes, has been the downfall for him—and for a number of his friends. "Do you know how many funerals I've been to this month?" he asks. "About seven. Some died from drinking, 'cause they didn't have nothing to do except drink, drink, drink."

Golar says he has suffered seizures and undergone treatment for alcoholism. His wife recently left him, taking his son, Terrell, who will be 2 in December. Every now and then, Golar says he phones to ask her to come back.

" 'You ain't taking care of us,' she says. When I call her now, she hangs up," he said. "I tell her I'm trying to do the best I can. When I get through giving my grandmother, my wife and my son money from my check, I don't have nothing. Not nothing.

"When I do manage to get some carfare together and go over and see my son, he jumps straight into my arms. I bought him a toy. A pull-string duck. He loved it."

Education can be a dangerous thing, as Ruben "Juice Man" McKenzie sees it. It can teach you that you don't have to do just any kind of work. A man with an education doesn't have to take just any kind of job.

"I don't want to be pushing no buttons," McKenzie says as he leans back on an old wooden school chair in the lot and looks at the cards in his hand. "I want to be communicating. I don't want to be standing under no machine metal pressing some bullshit all day."

McKenzie is 34, and he knows that the way he is living is not what his father had in mind all those years when he encouraged him to stay in school. For 25 years, McKenzie said, his father has driven a truck for the post office. Sometimes he drives the truck past the vacant lot and sees his son sitting on the sofa or leaning against the building. McKenzie says he hides his bottle behind his back until his father passes.

"He don't like me standing on the corner drinking," the son explains. "He tells me there's nothing wrong with my health. Get a job. My father don't understand me."

Growing up, McKenzie was an athletic boy, tall and skinny, a point guard on his junior high school basketball team. Because of his height, he could be a little intimidating, an asset he remembers came in handy whenever he and his friends shook down the white storeowners along Roosevelt Road.

It started out as a game, he recalled, sauntering into the businesses and trying to cow the owners. It graduated into full-scale extortion. "If we needed some boots, we took them," McKenzie says.

His nickname, he explains, was conferred upon him because of his success at this extortion hustle. "The white folks," McKenzie boasts, "they were afraid we'd whup their ass."

While part of McKenzie was at Marshall High School studying mathematics and biology, his favorite subjects, another part of him was drifting. He remembers cutting history class and gambling in the bathroom. He was caught shoplifting. When he was 18, he was arrested for robbing a man of "a watch, a ring and some chump change," he says. His parents refused to bail him out, trying to teach him a lesson. Eventually the charges were dropped, he says.

Unlike Golar, McKenzie stayed in school and graduated from Marshall. He went on to study child development at Chicago State University. The Chicago Board of Education confirms that for three years, between 1970 and 1973, he was a teacher's aide at Herzl, a North Lawndale elementary school. But he never finished college, and he gradually slipped out of the job market.

He says he has been on welfare since 1974.

"Mostly, it was stealing cars, some burglary and extorting from the stores," he admits. "I've spent time in jail for theft, armed robbery, burglary and disorderly conduct numerous times."

For eight years, he was addicted to heroin, he says. At one point, the habit cost him $165 every few days. He recites a litany of drugs that he says he has used frequently over the years, and he becomes animated as he describes the different highs the drugs produce. Now all he does is drink, he insists.

McKenzie says he is the father of five children, one by his wife, who left him four years ago, but he does not contribute to their support. He has seen the son by his wife only 10 times this year.

"Funny thing," he explains, "he only lives five blocks away."

Three years ago, McKenzie said, he took a menial job as an aide in a nursing home. He wheeled patients down the halls and changed their bedpans. He says he figured that if he stayed there long enough, he might have become a social worker.

Accused of drinking in the broom closet, he was fired after only 23 days, he says. He has not worked since.

When Willie Holmes gets up in the morning, he still puts on a nice shirt and a pair of dress pants. He does a few odd jobs around the house. He dreams.

"I always had my dream of being a truck driver," Holmes says. "I always played with toy trucks."

But then he sits in front of the television set, watching "Ryan's Hope." When the soap is over, he heads for the lot to join his friends. His afternoons are spent on the old yellow couch, sipping beer, playing cards, laughing at the jokes.

"I stay at home or come here to play cards and drink," Willie says, "because there is nothing else to do."

Until three years ago, Holmes had a good-paying job at a manufacturing company. When he got fired after a work place dispute, he says, he rounded up the carfare to go to the suburbs and fill out applications. But then the rejections came, and Holmes says he just got tired of trying. He is 32.

"Every time I go to a job interview, I have a negative attitude," he explains. "I'm wasting my time."

The second of eight children, Holmes learned about hard work from his father, John, a porter with the New York Central Railroad. He was close to his father, a man who bought him a gun when he was young and taught him how to hunt rabbits and raccoons.

In 1959, the father shot and killed a stranger who barged into the Holmes' house and made advances toward one of his daughters. He served 10 months in prison for this offense; his wife, Ethel Mae, was forced to go on welfare.

"It hurted me to go out there and wait in the car while my mother went in to see him," Willie Holmes recalls. "I couldn't understand why he was in there."

Holmes himself was sent to jail twice. When he was 16, he fired at a group of gang members with the .410 rifle his father had bought him. In 1980, while working as a bartender, he shot at a man who provoked a barroom dispute.

He dropped out of school in 10th grade, yet went on to get his high school equivalency degree. He has parked cars, tended bar, supervised a pool hall. He even decided to go into business for himself, painting and plastering neighborhood homes.

Once he enrolled in a truck-driving school but dropped out before finishing the six-week course.

He has never been able to hold jobs for long, he claims, because either the work moved out of the neighborhood or he lost his temper and was fired. He has been on welfare on and off since he was 18.

A few weeks ago, his wife and eight children left him. It's the end of the month, and money is scarce.

"I'm sitting up here broke, but I'm used to it now. I can't blame myself," he explains. "I'm trying." Then he takes another swallow of beer.

● ● ●

Slim Ty, Juice Man and Willie pass their days this way in the vacant lot on Roosevelt Road until winter approaches and the weather turns cold. Then they make a change.

They haul out a rusty trash can, stuff it with newspapers and light a fire.

Youths spin their wheels in the streets of despair

Idle young men vegetate, bitter and bonded in gangs

He likes to call himself "Shorty 20-Gauge." He thinks the name sounds tough.

He had it tattooed over his heart when he was 12, shortly after he joined the Black Gangster Disciples, the street gang that controls his North Lawndale neighborhood. His forearms are covered with gang tattoos—pitchforks, a six-pointed star, the word GANGSTERS.

He dropped out of Collins High School a year ago. He does not have a job. The only anchor in his life appears to be the corner of Karlov Avenue and 13th Street, where he and a handful of his fellow gang members spend most of their time.

"Every day be the same," says Shorty, now 17.

On his way to the corner, he sees his father's name scrawled in tribute in big orange letters in a hallway. A leader of a West Side street gang called the Egyptian Cobras, Shorty's father was 27 when he was shot and killed in a dispute with a heroin dealer.

Shorty was 8 at the time. "I remember he used to beat me and my mama," Shorty says. "But everybody miss they father."

Shorty, whose real name is Anthony Shumate, was born into

Left: Lawrence "Spin" Ivy and Anthony "Shorty 20-Gauge" Shumate cruise near the corner of Karlov Avenue and 13th Street.

the black urban underclass, and it seems quite unlikely he will ever escape. Raised by his mother on public assistance, in frequent trouble with the police, he says he has already fathered a child he has no intention of supporting.

He and idle young men like him—cast adrift, bitter and bonded in gangs—comprise perhaps the most menacing segment of the underclass.

Gangs of teenagers and young adults are responsible for much of the crime that occurs in the city and the nearby suburbs. The offenses range from random murders on inner city streets to well-planned property crimes in more affluent neighborhoods.

According to experts on gang activity in the Chicago area, the 110 street gangs known to be operating here maintain an underground economy that generates millions of dollars each year from drug dealing, auto theft, burglary, extortion, robbery, prostitution, gun sales and shoplifting.

As a rule, only high-ranking gang members earn sizable incomes from these illegal activities, the experts say. But these few individuals become role models for poor youths like Shorty and his friends, lending an aura of purpose and promise to gang life.

Violent and undisciplined teenagers create much of the havoc that disrupts inner-city high schools or plagues youngsters on their way to class. The Chicago public school system has identified 15 high schools as so beset with gang problems in their buildings or on surrounding streets that teaching and learning are seriously hampered.

Fear of gangs contributes to the dropout crisis in the city's public high schools, where 43 percent of the students stop attending before earning diplomas.

Teenagers like Shorty generally grow up to repeat the self-defeating social patterns of their parents—living on public aid, fathering neglected children and engaging in increasingly more serious crimes.

Those who do not end up in prison—at a cost of $16,000 a year to the taxpayers—are likely to become burned out on drugs or alcohol, spending aimless days on sidewalks or in vacant lots, getting by on food stamps and general assistance checks along with occasional crimes and street hustles.

Twice in his young, troubled life, Shorty has had employment. He kept neither job for more than a few months.

Three summers ago, under a federal jobs program, he was hired to sweep streets and assigned to a city sanitation crew that included two members of a rival gang.

From the first day, he says, the other youngsters threatened him and made him hate going to work. Eventually they beat him up and chased him from the job site. He never rejoined the crew.

In January, he joined the federal Job Corps and was sent to Dayton, Ohio, to learn welding. His behavior was disruptive there, Shorty admits. He started fights and was caught sneaking into a woman's room. In May, he was expelled from the program.

Of the child he fathered while in the Job Corps, Shorty says: "It make me feel proud to be a father. At least I got something in this world to carry on. I might die, but I got something."

He says he is not supporting the child "cause it ain't here with me." He hopes to have more children, he says, but he plans to never marry.

"I want to be a player," he explains, smiling. "I'll just spend the night. Just want to stick and move. Stick and move."

Approaching the corner of 13th and Karlov, Shorty smiles a little when he sees who is there.

A skinny youth called Chubby is waving a cigarette and talking about who the police want today for what offenses. Spin is adjusting the volume on his radio, as Shorty's best friend, Chicken, moves his arms and neck in a serpentlike dance.

David Holmes has his blond pit bull, Gangster Red, tied up to a street sign. The dog is growling and lunging as Holmes teases it with a plate of food.

Most of these young men have been in the Black Gangster Disciples for as long as Shorty has. Street gangs actively recruit young boys and assign them dangerous tasks because they know the law probably will treat them leniently if they are caught.

One of the gang chores performed by Shorty right after he joined the gang may have been responsible for the "20-Gauge" nickname. Though Shorty says he calls himself that for "no reason," his friends recall that he was once asked to deliever a 20-gauge shotgun to a gang member and stopped along the way to display it to his friends.

The lives of these young men are caught up in the oral history and mythology of the street. Day after day, they exchange the same stories of violence and sexual exploits. Much of what they say happened to them in the past cannot be easily sorted into fact or fiction because under Illinois law the records of juvenile offenders are kept secret.

But the tales they tell and the deeds they lay claim to give an insight into the ugliness and harshness of their lives.

At the corner of 13th and Karlov, they tell a story about Chubby and a 14-year-old boy named Junebug and a street fight several years ago. Those who claim to have been there say they heard a click and saw the knife and watched Chubby and Junebug dodge each other around a tree. Chubby thrust the knife, so the story goes, and the blade caught Junebug under the navel.

Chubby, the tale goes on, served six months in a juvenile-detention facility for the killing.

A 19-year-old known as Mr. Bus Driver owes his nickname to a story about a fight on a CTA bus involving Gangsters and some members of a rival gang.

As the boys on the corner tell the story, guns were drawn and the driver fled before the Gangsters finally managed to push all of their rivals out the back door of the bus. The story ends with Mr. Bus Driver sitting behind the wheel and flooring the accelerator.

The nickname supposedly became so widely used that the police heard of it and knew who to arrest for stealing the bus.

But, according to street lore, it is not only the police who know to come to the corner when they want somebody. A few weeks ago, a house down the street was burglarized, and a television and a pistol were taken. Word on the street was that Mr. Bus Driver had committed this crime too.

As a result, according to corner talk, the young man found himself on the receiving end of street justice: A group of neighborhood residents kidnaped him one night, determined to punish him for stealing from one of his own. They supposedly took him to a garage, held him down by tying a rope around his neck and scalded him with buckets of hot water.

Shorty and Chicken—a 16-year-old named Andre Moore—boast that they were picked up about a year ago for hitting a boy with a baseball bat and stealing his bike. When the case went to court, however, the teenagers claim, the victim told the judge that Shorty and Chicken were not the ones responsible.

Moore says he was expelled from school last year after being involved in a fight. As he explains it, he found himself surrounded in a hallway one afternoon by a group of rival gang members who looked as if they meant to assault him. Moore said he reached into his sock and pulled out a 12-inch hunting knife. According to Moore, school security guards grabbed him before he could stab anyone.

When the exchange on the corner is not about violence or crime, it is usually about sex.

Like his friend Shorty, Moore explains that he gives little thought to birth control when he has sex with women. "I want to be a bachelor," Moore explains, "I want to have maybe two kids. If you get married, the wife be taking everything if you get a divorce. I be knowing. I watch 'Divorce Court.' "

Shorty has similar ideas about marriage. "I ain't going to have no broad taking all my dust," he explains.

Sometimes Shorty says he hopes to have two sons. Other times he talks about a much larger brood. "I want a household full for when I get old and rolled at the tavern. I can get the kids to help me out."

Ronnie Horne, 19, who does not believe he has fathered any children, blames the girls in his neighborhood for having so many children so soon. "Tell all the broads to get their tubes tied," he advises, so young men like himself can have sex "every day without making no babies."

A pretty woman in a sheer white dress walks by. She is carrying a bag of groceries and has a toddler holding onto one of her hands.

"Hey baby!" Holmes beckons. "Hey sweet thing. You want me to carry that bag for you?" Holmes brings himself to his feet as the woman stops for a moment, smiles, then shakes her head as she continues to walk on.

"Hey," Holmes snaps, a frown coming over his face in answer to the rejection. "I ain't takin' no stepchildren. Just my own. But I take your aid check any time."

The rest of them start to laugh.

Holmes is 21. He is the only one on the corner who holds a job. He said he has a job working at a city parking garage a few blocks away, but he bides his time on the corner before and after work.

Lawrence Ivy's nickname is Spin because he dreams of being a radio disc jockey some day. He is the only one of the group still in school. Spin, 17, says he has had only one brush with the police: When he was getting some change out of his pocket at Collins High School, a marijuana cigarette fell out with the coins and a security guard saw it.

Spin explains that he once called a disc jockey, who urged him to stay in school and improve his vocabulary if he hoped to work at that job.

"He say I be capable," Spin recalls, "but I need to learn all those big vocabulary words like perspective and communism and point of view."

Spin is asked to define perspective. "Let me see. . . ." He thinks for a moment, then laughs.

Communism? "Say," he says, "you done got me there."

Point of view? "Let's see, now. Point of view . . . of a conversation. . . . Hey, I'm getting stuck here."

If he stays in school, Spin will graduate in June.

To travel to and from Collins, Spin and his friends have to pass through the territory of a rival gang. Spin, who displays the six-pointed stars and proudly announces his affiliation with the Gangsters, takes the Roosevelt bus west toward Collins. But unlike many of his classmates, he doesn't get off at the Sacramento Boulevard stop, which is directly in front of a building where members of the rival gang usually hang out.

Instead, Spin says he gets off at Kedzie Avenue, walks down to 13th Street, then walks two blocks east to the school, which is in Douglas Park.

It's not easy to get home, either.

One recent Friday afternoon, Spin and his friends got on the Roosevelt Road bus and rode west to Kedzie Avenue, where they usually transfer to make their way south. Standing at the bus stop, they found themselves approached by a group of about 30 boys whose clothing marked them as rival gang members.

Spin evaluated the situation as he looked down at the piece of paper he clutched his hand.

"I don't know about you guys," he told his friends, "but my transfer says we got some time."

He took off running, and his friends fell in behind him, the rivals chasing them a couple of blocks to a city parking garage, where Holmes' older brother and his pit bull came to the rescue.

When Holmes threatened to let the dog off its leash, the rival gang members ran the other way.

According to Linda Shumate, Shorty's mother, her son's basic problem is that he is too much like his father—headstrong in one sense but weak in another. His street friends, she says, are probably the biggest influence in his life.

Shorty insists he would do anything for his mother, whom he calls "Old Girl." But when she tells him to stay off the corner, he ignores her. The pop-pop-pop of gunfire brings her to her window late many nights, expecting to discover that the streets have claimed the life of her son just as they did that of his father.

"I can see the whole cycle revolving," Shumate explains. "He's his own man, just like his father."

Lots are empty as dying economy tightens grip

When big industry left, jobs and hope tagged along

N orth Lawndale never was meant to be a place where people ended up.

For its first 90 years, it was one of those tough, teeming Chicago neighborhoods where immigrants lived and worked until they could afford to move to some place better.

Now, for the first time, North Lawndale is the end of the road. Many of its residents, perhaps most, have lost hope for something better. Trapped by a disappearing economy and a malignant way of life, mired in welfare dependence, illegitimacy and violent crime, they are unable or unwilling to escape.

How did North Lawndale get this way? What economic causes led to this social catastrophe? Why do so many residents lack the ability to cope with the economic demands of modern life? Can the area ever find its way out?

In its good days, North Lawndale's economy was anchored by two giants—an International Harvester plant in the east, at 26th Street and California Boulevard, and Western Electric's famed Hawthorne plant in the west, at Cicero Avenue and Cermak Road. The Harvester plant employed 14,000 workers, Hawthorne, 43,000. In the middle, at Homan Avenue and Arthington

Left: Oliver Overton, 31, picks up a few dollars bringing scrap metal to a salvage operation in North Lawndale.

Street, was the world headquarters of Sears, Roebuck and Co., with more than 10,000 workers.

Harvester closed its operations in the late 1960s. A local development group called Pyramidwest bought it with federal money and tried to turn it into an industrial park, but no industry came. Today it is derelict—half prairie, half dump. The state's attorney's office plans court proceedings aimed at seizing the 53-acre site to satisfy more than $1 million in back taxes.

Most of the Hawthorne plant closed two years ago. The vast old buildings still are there, but the work force, down to 1,100, is being phased out. Soon, it will be empty. Western Electric has sold the site and the new owners plan to put in a shopping center, possibly with some industry.

In 1973, Sears built the world's tallest building in the Loop and moved most of its operations there, including the best-paying jobs. A catalogue distribution center in North Lawndale still employs 3,000 people, about three-fourths of them from outside the neighborhood. On a clear day, they can see the Sears Tower, 4 miles and a world away.

The rest of North Lawndale's economy echoes like a haunted house. Once there was a Zenith factory and an Alden's catalogue store, a Sunbeam factory, a Copenhagen snuff plant and a post office bulk station. All are closed now, all gone.

Lorean Evans remembers what it was like in the early 1960s when all those jobs kept money spinning through North Lawndale. "It was just a conglomerate of stores then," recalled Evans, who is head of Project-80, an economic development and job-training group.

"We had an auto center and banks, a York's department store, a Woolworth's. Roosevelt and Kedzie were both such good shopping streets. We had all kinds of specialty shops. There were grocery stores all up and down the street, an A & P and that Dell Farm food market."

And now? All these are gone, too. Fires, most of them set during the 1968 riots that followed the assassination of Rev. Martin Luther King Jr., burned out much of the Roosevelt Road shopping area.

That once vibrant strip never came back. About half of it is simply vacant. The rest is a travesty of an economy: a bank building now used as a disco, two hairdressers, stores with iron bars over broken windows, storefront churches, clinics and bars—a lot of bars.

North Lawndale has one bank, one supermarket, 48 state lottery agents, 50 currency exchanges and 99 licensed bars and liquor stores.

The reason is no mystery. More than half of North Lawndale's population is on public aid; in 1970 only one-third was. The official unemployment rate, about 20 percent, misses the vast numbers who have simply dropped out of the economy. A more accurate statistic comes from the 1980 census, which shows that 58 percent of everyone over 16 in North Lawndale is unemployed.

Not all of North Lawndale is destitute. A 58 percent unemployment rate means that 42 percent of the potential workers are working. Some small businesses have stayed.

But vacant lots, pervasive joblessness and a growing urban underclass population "tend to drag the whole community down," said Jerry Kelly, head of the Lawndale Business and Local Development Corp. "The people who are working see people on welfare who are driving a Cadillac, getting money from crime. They can't help but notice it."

Some community leaders claim the economy of North Lawndale has bottomed out and is improving. But the growing number of welfare cases, the continuing loss of jobs and recent closings of places such as Hawthorne and Sunbeam suggest otherwise.

"I'd venture to stay that, in the past 10 years, it's gotten worse," said Ruth Rothstein, president of Mt. Sinai Hospital, one of the community's few remaining big institutions. "It's very frustrating."

Without new jobs, the cycle of more people on welfare and a deteriorating housing situation will continue, Rothstein predicted. Youngsters, seeing little point in preparing for jobs that don't exist, will continue to drop out of school in alarming numbers.

"With no hope, how do you keep them in school?" Rothstein asked. "If there's no future, what's the point of the present?"

North Lawndale never was very wealthy, but it used to be a lot better than it is now.

"I always laugh when people say, 'Oh, the old West Side. It was wonderful," Rothstein said. "It was poor. It was poor.

"But it was a community."

North Lawndale is roughly the area south of the Eisenhower Expressway between Western Avenue and the city limits at Cicero Avenue. Its verdant name, suitable for a country club, was supplied by the real estate firm that laid it out in 1870.

One year later, the Chicago Fire took place. Industry, escaping the downtown ruins, began to move west into Lawndale. First to arrive was International Harvester, then called the McCormick Reaper Co.

Around the turn of the century, the elevated tracks came through, and Sears, Ryerson Steel Co. and Western Electric moved in. Workers at these and other industries moved into cottages or two-flats near the factories.

The first workers were Dutch, Irish and Germans. In the early part of the century, Jews moved west from Maxwell Street, and by 1930, North Lawndale was Chicago's biggest Jewish neighborhood.

It was tough and crowded. It had 51,000 people per square mile, twice the city average. But it hummed. It had 49 synagogues, a Yiddish theater, homes for the elderly and orphans and a well-stocked public library. Benny Goodman came from North Lawndale. So did Shelley Berman, Shecky Green and Adm. Hyman Rickover.

With the end of World War II and the subsequent movement into the suburbs, all this changed. In 1946, North Lawndale was 64 percent Jewish. By 1950, this was down to 42 percent and falling as Jews moved to better neighborhoods.

In their wake came the blacks. In 1950, 13 percent of North Lawndale was black. By 1960, blacks amounted to 91 percent of the population. Today, the figure is 97 percent.

North Lawndale's population hit an all-time high of 125,000 in 1960. It has been falling ever since, to 61,500 today. The loss has been due to not only the exodus of whites; middle-class blacks also moved out to better neighborhoods or suburbs.

The neighborhood's change from white to black coincided exactly with the decline in North Lawndale's economy and the loss of jobs there.

Some of the flight of business began early, as shopkeepers moved out and took their shops with them. But the real exodus took place after the riots, when storekeepers either found themselves burned out or unable to get insurance. The departure of Harvester was a milestone in the loss of industrial jobs.

A University of Illinois at Chicago study estimated that between 1960 and 1970, North Lawndale lost 75 percent of its businesses and 25 percent of its jobs. Between 1970 and 1980, it lost another 44 percent of the remaining commercial jobs and an astounding 80 percent of its manufacturing jobs. Factories, being harder to move, left last. Since 1960, the neighborhood also lost at least half of its housing units. Most of those that remain are overcrowded.

Even the sort of handyman or repairman jobs that most neighborhoods support are scarce in North Lawndale. Most absentee landlords are accused of spending as little as possible to keep up the buildings. With the notable exception of some streets where block clubs are active, most of the private homes show little sign of an owner's pride.

Unlike the old Jewish ghetto, North Lawndale today is no longer teeming. Rather, with its vanished factories and burned-out home lots, it is eerily empty.

"By the 1970s," wrote Lew Kreinberg, a longtime Chicago activist, "Lawndale's largest asset was its emptiness. . . . Mainly, land is vacant in Lawndale because people and industry would rather be elsewhere. Lawndale continues as an industrial slum, without the industry."

The loss goes on. An auto-repair garage, employing eight people, moved in last year. But a bakery, employing 60, went bankrupt and closed at about the same time. As businesses and jobs departed, so did almost everything else that held the community together—banks, theaters, newspapers, story-tellers and hangouts.

Communities need leaders and institutions. In the years since the sudden changeover from white to black, North Lawndale has had no shortage of leaders and institutions, but somehow they never have provided the kind of cement that holds a community together and makes it grow. Some of the most potent institutions—street gangs—have corroded North Lawndale, not built it.

The early years saw a flurry of plans and projects, all founded on high hopes.

Since the early 1970s, the federal government has poured $22 million into land projects in North Lawndale, and more millions into social programs. For the most part, it vanished like rain on the desert.

Early attempts at community-building produced the West Side Federation, which sponsored the Lawndale People's Planning and Action Council, which spun off the North Lawndale Economic Development Corp. This became Pyramidwest, which sponsored two big projects that never took off and a bank too poor to underwrite any real economic renaissance.

On the periphery were the Lawndale Industrial Council and the Lawndale Local Development Corp., now merged into the Lawndale Business and Local Development Corp., plus Project-80 and other self-help groups, all with too little money and expertise to roll back the tide.

And that, 17 years after the riots and fires, is about where things stand, with a roster of organizations, acres of empty land and, except for the bank, almost no progress at all.

Model Cities sponsored some social programs and improved some housing, but it appears to have done nothing to build an economy or create jobs. Pyramidwest built an attractive row of town houses and manages other housing, but again, it has had almost no noticeable economic impact.

Mt. Sinai and Ryerson still are big local employers. But both have cut back support of Pyramidwest and other economic development agencies. Instead, they are sponsoring another program, in their immediate area on the east edge of North Lawndale, that shows real promise of improving housing there.

Project-80 once issued a promising four-point program for job creation. But little came of it, and it is now focusing on job-training programs to give residents the skills to lift them from a life on welfare.

Rothstein laments this shift in focus, from job-creation to training for jobs that, at the moment, don't exist.

"Unless you train people with a reason at the end of the road, then you end up with the same frustration that you began with—maybe worse," she said.

VI
PRIDE AND COMMUNITY

Roots of the underclass: Racism and failed policies

Ghetto no longer just a place but a way of life

T he most compelling and angry fact about the underclass in America's cities is that the focus is almost entirely on the black family: unemployed black men and their unemployed sons, illegitimate children and their teenage mothers, young boys drifting into or recruited for crime.

Racial separation has transformed and hardened urban life. Only now, with the problems of the cities in an acute stage, is society beginning to face the truths and results of racism, government failure, welfare dependency and crime.

Black educators and some white social analysts are ripping away the myths that have prolonged, if not perpetrated, the decay of the cities. Alarmed that an underclass of urban blacks live separate from the white and black mainstream, they have begun to question economic failures more than racial discrimination.

Twenty years after the drama of the civil rights movement, they have become impatient with leaders who believe answers are contained in again expanding the benefits of the aging "Great Society."

Such notions are inadequate and impossible now, they say,

Left: Many specialists believe the problem of the black urban underclass has its roots in a uniquely American racism.

because the sore conditions of the underclass are too entrenched and middle-class values too weakened, or nonexistent, to lift people out of poverty.

Even more, the powers of the white majority in the United States are unwilling to support more social welfare programs targeted at minorities.

The talk is more about economics and international competition for jobs than about racial policy and discrimination. It accepts the historic symmetry that brought blacks to Northern cities for industrial jobs that were about to peak and falter.

It even accepts that discrimination against blacks—from slavery to Jim Crow laws to the civil rights era—has been more pervasive and destructive than against any other minority.

It also recognizes that the burgeoning Hispanic population, which may become the nation's largest minority, is more likely to overcome the enduring racism than blacks, who have suffered its effects for generations.

Tribune reporters have researched the problems connected with this underclass, finding that they span from the streets of the inner city to its schools to its tax base; to prisons and to crime statistics; to other areas of the city where people live in fear of crime and violence. At the same time, the research indicates a new and growing concern about the problem as policymakers try to identify the causes and find solutions. Many specialists believe the problem has its roots in a uniquely American racism.

Though a black middle class has evolved, the emphasis and concern is on an uncomfortably large number of blacks in the inner cities whose immediate past and forseeable future are far different from those of other minorities.

Eleanor Holmes Norton, former chairman of the Equal Employment Opportunity Commission, wrote recently: "The ghetto is not simply a place. It has become a way of life."

Reagan administration cuts over the last four years have forced the issue, because many black leaders do not expect federal help or innovative programs.

The attitude against granting money for social experimentation is stronger than ever, black leaders believe. The once-condemned "benign neglect" approach is perhaps the best to be expected.

Changes will depend almost entirely on local initiatives. As a social activist in Detroit said, the primary institutions—schools, churches and families—are to be left almost on their own to find solutions.

Politicians, black and white, generally have been too timid to face the problem of the underclass or even to recognize it publicly.

The election of black leadership in many of the nation's largest cities, including Chicago, further illustrates that though the urban underclass is black, the answers are no simpler for black leaders than for whites.

The federal government has ignored the specific social problem of the underclass, hoping a national economic recovery will dispel it. The White House was overjoyed in August when the number of Americans in poverty dropped to 5.1 percent and again in early September when the unemployment rate dipped to 7 percent.

Though blacks as a group are in those figures, the core of the jobless-welfare problem—the underclass—was not affected. It was another sign that this underclass, like a virus, has developed strong resistant strains to all efforts to eradicate it.

The current income figures outline the dimension of the problem among blacks in the cores of Northern cities. Median income for black families was lowest in the Midwest in 1984 at $14,370, lower than in the South [$14,860], the traditional bottom rung for income statistics.

The median income nationwide for black families is about 56 percent of that for white families.

Nationwide, some blacks enjoyed a decline in poverty in 1984 over the year before, but other key indicators of poverty revealed that the poverty rate remained at 46.5 percent for black children. The poverty rate for all black families was 30.9 percent, but it jumped to 51.7 percent for families maintained by women.

In this year's "Report on the State of Black America," by the National Urban League, Dr. James D. McGhee noted that nearly 42 percent of all black families were headed by women in 1983, up from 22 percent two decades earliers. Only one quarter of those are never-married females, McGhee reported, "so it is the disintegration of married-couple families . . . that accounts for the great majority of single, female-headed households."

The deteriorating life of many black families in Chicago was noted last May by Pierre de Vise, a Roosevelt University urbanologist. Two-thirds of Chicago's black children live in female-headed households, twice the rate of 1970, he said. Nearly 75 percent of black births in the city are illegitimate, up from 50 percent in 1970.

Of the births to black Chicago teenagers, 95 percent are illegitimate, compared with three-fourths in 1970. The rapid disintegration of black families is "more glaring" in Chicago's ghetto than anywhere else in the world where birth statistics are recorded.

In lectures at Harvard University this year, U.S. Sen. Daniel Patrick Moynihan [D., N.Y.] recalled an observation made in 1965, at the beginning of the failed "War on Poverty."

"From the wild Irish slums of the 19th Century Eastern Seaboard, to the riot-torn suburbs of Los Angeles, there is one unmistakable lesson in American history: A community that allows a large number of young men to grow up in broken families, dominated by women, never acquiring a set of rational expectations about the future; that community asks for and gets chaos. Crime, violence, unrest, disorder—most particularly the furious, unrestrained lashing out at the whole social structure—that is not only to be expected; it is very near to inevitable."

The problem is so acute that the Urban League's McGhee recommended sex education in the 8th and 9th grades. "We are aware that many communities object to the idea of sex education for children so young, but it is long past the time when the black community can afford to be squeamish or half-hearted about the problem of teenage childbearing or the methods that one employs to reduce it," he wrote.

Norton, now a professor at the Georgetown University Law Center, maintains that the transformation is a direct result of lack of jobs for young black men in a middle class society that links manhood with making money.

She said that in 1948, 87 percent of black males were in the work force, almost a full percentage point higher than for whites.

But between 1960 and 1982, the employment rate dropped from 74 percent to 55 percent, according to the Center for the Study of Social Policy in Washington. The problem, the figures show, is not going away. The overall unemployment rate for black teenagers this year is 39 percent, 2½ times that of white teens.

The proportion of black teenage males who never have held a job increased to 52.8 from 32.7 percent between 1966 and 1977; for black males younger than 24, the percentage grew to 23.3 from 9.9 percent.

Joblessness creates an aberration in the ghetto, Norton said in a recent article, that "transforms life in poor black communities and forces everything else to adapt to it.

The female-headed household is only one consequence," she said. "The underground economy, the drug culture, epidemic crime and even a highly unusual disparity between the actual number of men and women—all owe their existence to the cumulative effect of chronic joblessness among men. Over time, deep structural changes have taken hold and created a different ethos."

In his trilogy "The Americans," historian Daniel J. Boorstin outlined that the Irish, the Italians and the Jews generally began their American immigrant experience in the cities, and blacks who arrived as slaves primarily lived in rural areas for the "convenience of his white master or employer."

In the late 19th Century, depression and lack of opportunity in the South drew many to the North, but the outbreak of World War I and the cutoff of unskilled immigrants from Europe created more jobs there. Boorstin noted that Henry Ford and others sent their agents South and provided freight cars to bring blacks north to work in the factories.

"My own view is that historic discrimination is far more important than contemporary discrimination in understanding the plight of the urban underclass," William Julius Wilson wrote last year.

Wilson, chairman of the University of Chicago Sociology Department, has become an authority on the underclass. He has come under much "ideological criticism," he said, and the racial questions involved create a "very sensitive issue. But you have to have tough skin."

He has explained that black migration to the cities continued unabated unlike European migration, which was curtailed in the 1920s, or Japanese and Chinese immigration, which never reached proportions that threatened employment prospects.

Though their numbers are increasing, "It is just as possible that Hispanics will overtake blacks in the struggle for place and position in American society as that they will replace them at the bottom rung of the ladder," said Paul E. Peterson, editor of "The New Urban Reality," published this year by the Brookings Institution.

He said Hispanics don't carry the stigma of slavery and, like other immigrants, they bring with them ambitions, they are varied in skin color and national identity and they are less residentially segregated than blacks in the cities.

He also cites a number of other factors, including regional concentration, later childbirth ages and more intermarriage. He added that it is plausible that the language barrier will be less severe than color barrier.

In black demographics, Wilson reported, the black migration to Northern cities "skewed the age profile of the urban black community and kept it relatively young. The number of central-city black youths aged 16-19 increased by almost 75 percent from 1960-69. Young black adults [aged 20-24] increased in number by two-thirds during the same period, three times the increase for young white adults. In the nation's inner cities in 1977, the median age for whites was 30.3, for blacks 23.9."

Wilson added, "The importance of this jump in the number of young minorities in the ghetto, many of them lacking one or more parent, cannot be overemphasized."

In Snow Belt cities of the Northeast and Midwest, the white population dropped 13 percent in the 1960s and by another 24 percent in the '70s, Peterson said.

That came after the new migration of blacks whose population grew by 35.8 percent in the 1950s. "Clearly the processes of urban decline have been accompanied by an equally profound process of racial succession," Peterson wrote.

The 20th Century decline of cities is not new.

New York and Chicago each lost more than 300,000 manufacturing jobs from 1948 to 1977, more than half of them in the decade after 1967. Another 100,000 jobs in wholesale and retail trade in Chicago were lost in the same period.

In the same compilation, Gary Orfield, professor of political science and public policy at the University of Chicago, said residential segregation in Chicago and other cities is a "key contemporary institution for creating and maintaining inequality." The educational system also promotes segregation and inequality, he said.

The real median income of white families grew by 3 percent

last year to $27,690, it also grew for Spanish families, by 6.8 percent to $18,830. But there was no change for black families, which stood at $15,430. Even under other computations of the poverty level that use noncash benefits such as public housing and food stamps, which raise a number of white families out of poverty, there is no significant change for black or Hispanic families.

The government has not found a way to deal with the problem.

A program called Project Redirection, created by the Manpower Demonstration Research Corportion in New York City, was aimed at teenage mothers on welfare without a high school diploma. Though the program helped to keep the mothers in school, getting job training and avoiding pregnancy in its demonstration period, within a year the advances had been nearly wiped out.

In the State of Black America report, John E. Jacob, president of the National Urban League, noted that in 1975 black unemployment was almost double that of whites and 10 years later, it is more than double. That loss of opportunity, caused by influences from increased global competition to white flight to the suburbs, helped create the underclass.

There is a continuing debate about how many people fit under that "underclass" description, but they surely represent, to borrow a phrase, a large "dust of individuals" who simply fail at living in this society and at the same time cause enormous social problems.

Rev. William Cunningham, a Detroit priest who has directed the "Focus Hope" program since the late 1960s, prefers to call the underclass a "Third World cultural economy in the center of a first-rate world power."

He says that little has changed since the Kerner Commission report nearly two decades ago talked of two societies—one black, one white—moving in opposite directions.

Father Cunningham called the racial change in Detroit an "evacuation" that reduced the city from 1.4 million to less than a million and that is 70 percent black with a school system 95 percent black.

"And with the withdrawal of the whites go the white resources. . . . Racism is the radical disease, economics is only cosmetic," Father Cunningham said.

". . . The Great Society based on compassion is one of the

most screwed up attitudes toward human beings ... what society needed was some justice."

This brings up several divisive elements in the underclass debate. Though many see the issue as racial, others insist economics plays a far more important role.

Wilson said the problem cannot be corrected until the society is willing to admit "a racial division of labor" has been created because of historic discrimination and prejudice and that division is compounded by "impersonal economic shifts" in an advanced industrial society.

Added to all that is an internal rivalry among politicians, sociologists and civil rights activists for dominance in seeking remedies for the underclass or in reshaping goals.

"In a very real sense the civil rights struggle, envisioned by its founders and millions of American supporters, is over and won," black economist Walter E. Williams suggested to the U.S. Commission on Civil Rights in arguing against racial quotas.

"The new civil rights vision holds that the Constitution is color-conscious. ... Even if one were to accept the notion that disadvantaged people ought to receive extra privileges and benefits, numbers-based policy based on race is not only inequitable but inefficient as well," he said.

If that were not enough to anger those who fought to change unfair hiring patterns in city governments and in union hiring halls, Williams added: "... The evolution of the new civil rights movement is an effort by some to impose greater government control as a means to acquire more personal political power and wealth."

The neo-conservative black perspective has risen along with the Reagan administration and the signals Reagan's people have sent to political and academic powers.

Atlanta Mayor Andrew Young, former aide to Dr. Martin Luther King Jr. and United Nations ambassador under President Jimmy Carter, dismisses such arguments. "Every generation tries to discredit the last one," he said. "I call it intellectual cannibalism."

There has been legitimate questioning, however, of attempts to alter racial structure and bias in the city.

In Norfolk, Va., for instance, the school board, supported by a group of black parents, has petitioned the federal appeals court to severely curtail busing to achieve integration in that district, insisting it is harmful and disruptive for their children. The civil case is expected to reach the U.S. Supreme Court.

What many call the curse of isolated court-ordered solutions to the inner city is also evident in Boston, where the school district has shrunk from 93,000 students in 1974, when a federal judge ordered busing, to 57,000 students now. A decade ago, white children made up 65 percent of the school population; now they are 28 percent.

In five school districts surrounding the District of Columbia, blacks trailed white students by 20 to 48 percentile points in test scoring. This widespread failure has led to name-calling and complaints and countercomplaints that the problem rests with biased school districts or with black leaders and civil rights champions who failed to talk specifically about poor black achievement records.

Some black educators have said there is a residual fear that bringing up such problems publicly would have them used against blacks and would comfort opponents eager to reduce federal aid or programs.

Jeff Howard and Ray Hammond, coauthors of a current New Republic article on black attitudes of intellectual inferiority, reflect the change and the new openness about the particular problems of black society.

They prefer, however, to speak of it optimistically because, they believe, "the progress of any group is affected not only by public policy and by the racial attitudes of society as a whole, but by that group's capacity to exploit its own strengths."

It is a theme heard more and more, from church pulpits to school lecterns, because of the failure of state and federal efforts to deal with the urban underclass.

Government tried busing to solve the problem of the schools, welfare to solve the problem of income, public housing to solve the problem of ghettos and quotas to solve the problem of jobs. Those "solutions," in many cases, are now viewed as part of the problem.

Too proud to trade welfare for minimum wage

'People are afraid to get their hands dirty'

I t was late 1957, and Rev. Martin Luther King Jr. was at the airport in Atlanta.

Like other public buildings in the South, the airport had two restrooms for males. The sign on one read "Colored Men." The sign on the other simply read "Men."

As King later explained, "I thought I was a man, and I still think I am, so I decided to go into the Men's room, not the Colored Men's room."

No whites complained, but a black custodian became highly agitated.

"The colored room is over there!" he told King. "You belong over there. That's for the colored."

King refused to leave.

Later, in telling the story, he explained, "That fellow was so conditioned by the system that he didn't think of himself as a man."

Left: Out of work in North Lawndale. "It just seems that everyone here is down on their luck," says one man who lives there. "If everybody got together and wanted to have a picnic, it would rain."

Martin Luther King Jr. preached black pride. So did Stokely Carmichael, Malcolm X, H. Rap Brown, Ralph Abernathy, Elijah Muhammad.

The creation of that pride, a belief of blacks in themselves and in their dignity as human beings, was a fundamental accomplishment of the civil rights movement, which in an astonishingly small number of years achieved a social revolution in the United States.

Yet today, nearly three decades after King first told the airport story, pride again is a major problem for the black underclass of America's cities.

It is a complex problem exhibited in seemingly contradictory symptoms, a problem of too much pride and not enough.

It is a lack of self-respect that saps many inner-city people of the drive to improve their conditions. A loss of the work ethic that entices them to refuse low-paying work. An immensely inflated sense of expectations that tricks them into believing that they can achieve success without working for it.

The problem, ironically, is rooted in the increased opportunities that were made possible for blacks by the civil rights movement, opportunities that underclass blacks—unskilled, under-educated, ill-motivated—have been unable to take advantage of.

It is also rooted in the stubborn remnants of centuries-old racism in America.

It is a problem that is ugly and embarrassing for blacks who have made it to the middle-class, and for liberal whites who have championed social programs, many of which seem to have been a detriment, not a benefit, for underclass people.

Finally, it is a problem that, many longtime observers believe, will not be solved without another people's movement, similar to the one that won blacks civil rights—a new movement arising out of the underclass and demanding that underclass people take responsibility for their lives and their destinies.

● ● ●

"It just seems that everyone here is down on their luck," says Leon Collins, 35, who lives on general assistance in the West Side neighborhood of North Lawndale, home to many members of the black underclass.

"If everybody got together and wanted to have a picnic, it would rain."

For many members of the underclass, a lifetime on welfare, at the bottom of the American economic heap, has bred an aimless lassitude that, at its heart, is a form of self-hate.

"The self-hate," says former civil rights activist Al Raby, "comes from a psychological uselessness, a feeling of being discarded, that you're not needed in the society.

"How the hell would you spend 24 hours a day if you were on bare subsistence? How would it make you feel? The victims start blaming each other. That pushes it further and deeper."

One victim is a North Lawndale man who would identify himself only by his nickname, Bear.

"I was very interested in school when I was young," Bear says. "I thought I'd be somebody. I was an intelligent young stud."

But he began drinking and using drugs at an early age. Now, at 38, he lives on general assistance and hangs around a local vacant lot.

Bear is the father of four children—two by one woman, two by another. He is married to neither woman and does not live with either. But he does see his children.

"I hope things for them will be better than for their father," he says. "I don't want it to be nothing like it was for me, but what can I tell them?

"They're stuck here. I was stuck here, and it's going to continue that way. I would like it better, but there is nothing I could do because of the position I got caught up in."

Edward Williams is looking for the right job.

Williams, 33, has spent 14 of the last 16 years in prison—first, for shooting a man in a robbery, then for killing a man in another robbery.

In the last two years, he has gotten a number of jobs but has never held them for more than a couple of weeks. One he lost because he failed to show up on time. Another he quit because he didn't want to do manual labor.

"The right job," he explains, "would be anything that comes along that would start me off at $8 an hour. That would be the right job for me. I wouldn't have to worry then."

Despite his criminal history, despite his lack of skills, despite an unemployment rate for blacks in Chicago of 23 percent, more than twice that of whites, Williams is too proud to accept just any job. In this, among the underclass, he is not unusual.

"It's ridiculous," says Yvonne Gay, a caseworker with the Illinois Department of Public Aid. "A lot of people are offered a job at minimum wage. And they say, 'I ain't working for no minimum wage.' They haven't been to school, they have no experience and they say no to a job. I just can't figure it."

John Lewis, head of the Student Non-Violent Coordinating Committee in the early 1960s and now a councilman in Atlanta, notes that as a youth he worked as a janitor and "did it with pride and a sense of dignity."

Yet over the last two decades, he says, "something gave people the feeling that it is beneath them, that they're better than that. People are afraid to get their hands dirty. They think it would belittle their pride to work as a janitor or washing dishes in a kitchen.

"To tell a young black that he should push a broom or wash a floor or wash dishes, they talk like that's heresy!"

Most young whites also disdain such jobs. But few of them live, as do young underclass blacks, in circumstances where these jobs are the only ones available and in an environment where a welfare-based inertia is stronger than a job-oriented momentum.

Another example of this overdeveloped sense of pride among blacks is the sort of thinking exhibited by Iris Moore, a 17-year-old high school dropout and a recent mother.

Asked if she planned to return to school, she answered: "I don't have anything to wear. I'm not going up there looking like a bum. No way."

● ● ●

James Gordon is 17. He wants to be a movie star.

"I want to make lots of money and have a condo by the beach," he explains. "I want to move to Miami and be on 'Miami Vice' and have a big limo and lots of ladies asking for my autograph."

But Gordon has never acted or performed. He has never had a job. He says he is failing two courses at Manley High School, where he is a sophomore. For the last five years, he has been a street gang member.

"I know how to talk; that's all that matters," Gordon explains. "They have classes where they teach you how to walk and talk and stuff like that."

To become a movie star, he plans to borrow money from his uncle and fly to Miami. He does not plan to go to Hollywood.

"What do I want to go there for?"

James Gordon's dreams could be dismissed as the star-struck fantasies of a teenager if it weren't for the fact that such unrealistic imaginings are the only sort of planning for the future many young people in the underclass do.

"There is very little realistic future planning," says Denise Williams, a social worker at Tubman Alternative School. "I've had several tell me, 'I want to be a lawyer.' They're getting Ds in school. They have no conception of what it takes."

"Underclass people," notes Thomas Cook, professor of psychology and urban affairs at Northwestern University, "have the same values as the rest of society. They want to be so dreadfully, terribly middle class. They just don't know how to do it."

There are, of course, many poor blacks who do know what to do. When a McDonald's restaurant opened this summer in North Lawndale, more than 600 persons applied for the 100 low-paying service jobs that suddenly became available.

Gregory Webster, 24, was one of the lucky ones hired.

"I have a desire not to be on general assistance," he says. "Jobs are really scarce around here. Most people will settle for aid. I refuse to do that.

"A lot of people have too much pride to do jobs like this. They say these kind of jobs don't pay enough. But I say, 'Something is something.' Yeah, I'm working back there in the kitchen, but at least I've got a dollar in my pocket."

● ● ●

"The American Dream is a black nightmare," says Don Green, a longtime caseworker with the state Department of Public Aid.

"The dreams that it fosters are not really accessible to blacks in general. There's so much anger locked up in people, it's frightening."

Why shouldn't James Gordon dream of movie stardom? That's what American kids do. Why shouldn't Edward Williams refuse menial work? American kids are taught from birth to aspire to high-paying jobs. Why shouldn't Bear feel imprisoned in his poverty? Each day, he sees on television all of the fun, pleasure, fulfillment and success that other Americans are having.

Three decades ago, however, such questions would have been irrelevant, because for blacks, then called Negroes, the American Dream was irrelevant.

At that time, one of the best-known black movie stars was Lincoln T. Perry, a comedian whose stage name was Stepin Fetchit and who endlessly portrayed a lazy, wide-eyed, shuffling, drawling black, epitomizing the image that many whites—and many blacks—had of blacks.

There were black doctors and lawyers, and a black middle class, but they were few in number and generally required to live and work in black ghettos. Many more blacks worked lower-paying menial jobs as Pullman car porters, garbage men, janitors.

The custodian who criticized Martin Luther King Jr. at the Atlanta airport was holding a job that was considered fitting for blacks. He was also espousing a philosophy held by many blacks, in particular those who had carved out an adequate lifestyle: Don't rock the boat, keep out of trouble, stay in your place.

For many of these blacks, King's activism and the civil rights movement he headed were, at the same time, a stirring challenge and a threat. When random violence against blacks was a constant possibility, when the legal machinery was almost entirely in white hands, social activism seemed to invite retaliation.

Yet in the space of only 15 years, the civil rights movement shattered most of the legal barriers and social roadblocks that kept blacks from full participation in American society.

Suddenly, blacks were casting off the denigrating stereotypes and rejoicing in their blackness: Black was beautiful.

"You felt it. You saw it," recalls Lewis. "There was a great sense of pride which said, 'I'm somebody.' You could see it, that somebodyness. People were literally high on freedom."

Whites, many of them with a mix of guilt and fear, felt it, too, and gave blacks the greater respect they demanded.

The door to opportunity swung open, and blacks rushed to enter, aided by affirmative-action programs that were established to remedy past discrimination.

But as Lewis notes, "Some people didn't have the necessary tools, the necessary skills, to make it through the door." These people were left out in the cold, still filled with hope and expectations, soured by frustration.

"You had a new kind of black—all fired up and no place to go," says Dr. Alvin Poussaint, a psychiatrist at Harvard University Medical School.

As blacks were refusing to apologize for being black, poor blacks were refusing to apologize for being poor.

"During the 1960s, a large number of persons who once thought of being on welfare as a temporary and rather embarrassing expedient came to regard it as a right that they would not be deterred from exercising," writes James Q. Wilson in the latest issue of The Public Interest, a social science magazine.

"The result of the change can be measured: Whereas in 1967, 63 percent of the persons eligible for AFDC [Aid to Families with Dependent Children] were on the rolls; by 1970, 91 percent were."

That change in the status of welfare has had serious implications.

"To spend your whole life on welfare is very degrading, but I find this younger generation is proud about it," says Earlean Lindsey, president of the Westside Association of Community Action.

"I mean, the younger generation doesn't feel the embarrassment that an older person who has been in the workforce before feels when they have to go on welfare. A younger person who has never known any other way feels that's the way it is."

Since the civil rights movement, there has been a tendency by activist blacks and white liberals to blame all the new problems of the expanding underclass on racism and discrimination. Scholars and politicians, fearful of being branded racists, were unwilling to criticize the lifestyle of underclass blacks.

The fear was not unfounded: Daniel Moynihan was deluged with outraged criticisms when, in the mid-1960s, he wrote of the disintegration of the black family, a major element in the growth of the underclass.

Meanwhile, the civil rights movement ran out of steam.

"The mass of people that could be mobilized to demonstrate and march so that the walls of segregation would come tumbling down could not be mobilized over such issues as unemployment, welfare reform, better housing, improved health care," wrote Harry A. Ploski and James Williams in The Negro Almanac in 1983.

"The glamor had gone out of the Movement."

The young people today don't know anything about that movement," says Conrad Worrill, chairman of the inner-city studies department of Northeastern Illinois University and chairman of the National Black United Front.

"They don't even know who Stokely Carmichael was, who Malcolm X was. They hardly know who King was."

Nonetheless, he contends, the problems of the black underclass must be solved by blacks.

"Historically, white people have decided with each other what should be done with blacks," he says. "But black people have the ultimate responsibility for solving their problems. We have to take our destiny in our hands, to seize the time."

That was easier to do, John Lewis notes, in the 1950s and early 1960s, when all blacks were united by the common barriers they faced.

"We were all in the same boat," he recalls. "There was a greater sense of solidarity. Somehow, we have to find a way to re-create that sense of solidarity.

"Greater stress and emphasis and responsibility must be placed on the shoulders and backs of the blacks who have made it to become more caring and sharing and reach back to help the brothers and sisters who have been left behind."

More important, those in the underclass must take primary responsibility for helping themselves, says Al Raby, who in 1966 convinced King to come to Chicago to work for open housing.

"There's need for some kind of a movement," he says. "The only way the situation is going to change is if the victims, with the support and cooperation of other people, start doing battle."

Raby, director of Chicago's Commission on Human Relations, notes: "We have not currently got a leader yet who would pull together the frustration and concern and hope of these people and give it some direction.

"A major part of the movement today has to make some demands on the victims if they are to pull themselves out of the results of that victimization."

A system unable or unwilling to respond

'Promises, promises. That's all you get'

The streets of North Lawndale are littered with trash, broken bottles and junked cars.

Last year, Ald. William C. Henry's 24th Ward Democratic organization bought a second-hand street sweeper for $16,000 to augment the city's clean-up operations.

It makes a dent in the litter problem when it's working, but it often breaks down.

The street sweeper is much like the political organization that bought it. The organization sometimes tries, but it can't handle the extraordinary problems of the black urban underclass in North Lawndale—rampant crime, unemployment, ineffective schools, ramshackle housing and family decay.

The question for the 24th Ward—and for the other underclass areas in most of America's major cities—is whether government can deal with conditions that have created a permanent underclass. Can political leaders be concerned enough, creative enough and courageous enough to mobilize government toward a solution?

Bill Henry is one black leader who has worked his way up through the ranks of the regular Democratic organization. He

Left: Ald. William Henry was schooled in the white-controlled regular Democratic organization, but he believes his ties to Mayor Washington will help him address his ward's problems.

thinks that with the election of Chicago's first black mayor and with a potentially growing number of minority aldermen on the city council, he can use what he has learned to improve his ward, which contains more than three-quarters of North Lawndale.

But what he learned from his white mentors was the ward-level approach of government and politics—a few bucks to tide them over, a bag of groceries when the cupboard is bare, a used coat when the weather gets cold and a few jobs to ration out.

These were answers 50 years ago when generations of immigrants were working and struggling their way up through North Lawndale and the American way of life. But they are not answers to questions of the future. They only try, however pitifully, to address a small share of the immediate problems.

Another freshman alderman, representing a smaller part of North Lawndale, doesn't even have Henry's political experience. Ald. Wallace Davis [27th] was shot in the back several years ago by a Chicago policeman. He won a large financial settlement from the city in a civil rights suit, making him a kind of folk hero. Davis, without even the rudiments of political savvy, was elected in the black groundswell that put Harold Washington in the mayor's office.

At the higher levels of local government, the blacks who have reached new power find there is little left in a financially strapped city to give those who have been left behind.

And with the long history of neglect, some residents of the poorest wards accept politicians with flashy cars and fancy clothes who can do little to improve their world.

Carzella Donahue, 68, has lived in the community since 1947, and she said of Henry, "He's doing what he can, but I don't think there is a whole lot he can do."

As for city services, she says, "They're fair. They are no better or worse than they've been."

State Rep. Arthur Turner, an independent Democrat who represents the west section of North Lawndale, plus portions of Cicero and Oak Park, calls his fellow legislators' lack of interest in solving problems of the underclass a major obstacle to funding needed social programs.

"When you talk tax increases down in Springfield, it's the kiss of death," he said. "I've introduced legislation to raise taxes, and a couple of my colleagues call me the tax man.

"Telling people about their social responsibilities is hard to sell, especially when they have a misconception of who that money's going to help. They think the poor are lazy, shiftless, just make babies."

But State Rep. Juan Soliz [D., Chicago], whose district includes the eastern half of North Lawndale, said that even electing an official, such as a mayor, who is sympathetic to the plight of minorities, does not necessarily mean that all minorities will benefit.

"A lot of blacks who are employed in City Hall are from the South Side, which is being favored since the mayor comes from the South Side," Soliz complained. "All of us on the West Side are basically low priority.

"The West Side is less organized politically. It's taken longer for us to break the control that the old process had on the political apparatus."

On the national level, the sympathy of congressmen representing the wheat fields of Kansas or the deserts of Arizona does not extend into the burned-out sections of North Lawndale, especially as the country swings ideologically more to the right and becomes less patient with the social programs of liberal Democrats.

● ● ●

U.S. Sen. Paul Simon [D., Ill.] believes that the underclass and its problems are not high priorities in Washington.

A major roadblock in dealing with the problems is "our whole system of political contributions," Simon said.

"It makes government responsive to the wishes and whims of those who have the ability to be generous financially," he said. "People who don't have that kind of financial power too often get neglected."

If pressured to do so, the government could "guarantee a job for all Americans," Simon said, adding that the government could help finance adult education and literacy programs.

"It is costly, but it isn't costly when you compare the cost of what we're doing right now," Simon said.

"But government can't do it all alone. It has to be a concerted effort in a variety of areas, but government has to provide leadership."

Democrat Alan Dixon, Illinois' other U.S. senator, has found a lack of sympathy for solving problems of the underclass.

"When I came to Washington, I stayed near the Watergate in

the most affluent part of the city," he said. "I left the building and saw a man lying in the snow.

"I asked somebody, 'What is that man doing there?' and he said, 'That's a grate person. These people lie down for the night on grates because heat comes up from the metro.' That was a powerful influence on me, and I'll never forget it.

"They are not really part of the system, don't you see? One time I was in Mexico and gave some coins to a beggar. My friend said, 'I don't want to see that.' That may be a problem of our society—we don't want to see it.

"You can get a better-organized effort for cruelty to animals than for hungry people."

A problem with an area such as North Lawndale is that its representation in government often is divided. A state senator representing much of the area is Earlean Collins, a black Chicago Democrat who also represents portions of primarily white Oak Park and Cicero.

The other senator is John D'Arco Jr., a white. The interests of D'Arco, son of the powerful 1st Ward committeeman, are reflected more in the large Italian and downtown business community his district contains.

North Lawndale has no Cook County Board representative, as such, because city commissioners are elected at large, city-wide, and their political obligations to voters in a small area are small.

Former Mayor Jane Byrne said political leaders should work to dramatize problems of the underclass. She said her highly publicized move into the Cabrini-Green Chicago Housing Authority project was designed to do just that, to show a complacent majority the problems of a depressed minority.

"They're out there, they're in the communities. And it will spread," she said. "Politicians, government leaders, they have to show it and illustrate it."

Most of the political leaders in the 24th Ward through the 1950s were Jewish, in spite of the ward's ethnic mix, and they were effective. In the 1932 presidential election, the 24th Ward gave Franklin D. Roosevelt 21,270 votes to Herbert Hoover's 3,817. In November, 1940, Roosevelt got 26,215 votes to 1,914 for Republican Wendell Willkie. Roosevelt described the 24th as the most Democratic ward in the nation.

The ward has changed since then, with Jews, Italians, Irish

and Polish voters replaced by blacks, also voting heavily for Democrats.

According to the 1980 census, there were about 36,000 voting-age residents in the ward. About 13,000 of them voted in the presidential election that year. In 1984, after Washington had been elected mayor through a massive citywide voter-registration drive, nearly 20,000 votes were cast in the presidential election.

In the election that sent Washington to the fifth floor of City Hall, the 24th Ward gave him 99.5 percent of its vote.

In the presidential election last year, while Walter Mondale was being trounced by President Reagan nationally, in the 24th Ward, he received 19,430 votes to the President's 489.

Rev. Jesse Jackson said that his 1984 presidential campaign and the successful mayoral campaign of Harold Washington gave hopes to members of the underclass who had tired of giving traditional politicians their votes and receiving nothing in return.

The ward is still delivering after all these years, but is the political system returning the favor?

"The cities can't do too much, really," said the mayor, when talking of the plight of North Lawndale and similar communities throughout the nation.

"You need massive injections of programatically designed and oriented money, not just patchwork stuff dropping in periodically," he said.

"You need a beefed-up summer youth program, a beefed-up joint partnership and training program. Clearly, there has to be a training process, and then they have to be hired someplace.

"We make constant treks back and forth between here and Washington, D.C., pleading with Congress not to cut vocational-education money, not to cut nutrition money, not to cut housing subsidies."

The problem in Chicago, Washington says, occurred in other cities after the federal government became socially conscious in the 1960s and sent millions of dollars to urban centers: The money was misused, misdirected.

"In Chicago, what happened is they quietly did as they damned pleased until recently," he said. "A lot of those dollars that were supposed to go into the impacted areas didn't.

"What Reagan should have done was left the structure in

place and reformed it. The excesses were not in the programs. The excesses were in the way they were being dispensed and abused."

The mayor said he has encountered small thinking on the part of aldermen who represent poor areas, who want to operate as their white predecessors did.

"I told these guys, I said, 'Listen. That's a waste of time, looking for the penny-ante jobs. Patronage is dead,' " Washington said. "They have to get training, development, rehabilitation."

Byrne, too, said that during her four years as mayor, she told aldermen who came to her seeking patronage jobs that they should pay more attention to the have-nots, to the churches and community groups without political ties or government funds, who continue to work to better themselves and their community.

Henry said he is doing just that, organizing 160 block clubs in the 24th Ward, compared with the 30 that existed when he was elected in 1983. On Saturdays, volunteers in his ward organization, using forestry department equipment, trim trees around light posts.

"We give out garbage cans, but they cost $4 each, so we give them to senior citizens first," he said.

Kirsten Svare, a spokesman for the Department of Streets and Sanitation, said the city spends more money on areas such as North Lawndale than it does in more affluent areas, but the effect is not as apparent.

"In areas of heavy gang activity, we see gang members shooting out lights and shorting wires to make it dark so they can carry out their business," she said. "They also tear down signs."

Henry said his ward is getting a larger proportion of city and federal money, thanks to his allegiance to Washington. City services in the ward are good, he said, and will get better if Washington continues in office. The ward might be included in the experimental garbage-cart program in the future, and the 24th Ward will have 6 miles of streets repaved this year, instead of the 4 awarded to other wards, he said.

Some North Lawndale residents don't share Henry's description of increased political interest in the ward.

"He don't get out into the neighborhood much until it's time to vote," said Napoleon Burgess, 26, an unemployed carpenter who works with a group of other residents who spend their spare time cleaning up vacant lots the city has neglected.

"Sometimes you see the street-cleaning trucks coming down the street with no water in them," said Oliver Randle, 29, a cook in a neighborhood snack shop. "Just the brushes going round and round."

Frank Taylor, 24, a handyman who moved to North Lawndale 12 years ago, said he wasn't too interested in politics, but he did vote for Washington.

"When Harold ran, everybody voted for him because they thought there would be changes and jobs, but I don't see any," he said.

Mae Russell, 56, who moved to Lawndale from Mississippi in 1957, said she hadn't voted for years until Washington ran for mayor.

In the 1960s, she said, some people voted in Lawndale because they were given money to do so.

"I didn't understand why they would give money to vote," she said. "If I believed in the person, why would they have to pay me? But the city just let it fall down. They wanted our votes, but they didn't do anything."

Lawrence Grillier, 63, also moved to the area from Mississippi about 40 years ago, and he, too, is disenchanted with the political process.

He has been trying to get a sidewalk in front of his house fixed for 11 years, he said, but it is still broken and cracked.

"Chicago ain't nothing but a big Mississippi," Grillier said. "Promises, promises. That's all you get in this city."

Churches offer hope,
but only for the hopeful

'God's beautiful people are here in the midst of hell'

For more than a year, Betty Clay, 42, has been a member of Fizer Temple Church of God in Christ.

"It's the best thing that ever happened in my life," she explains. "Before I got saved, I was out there, and I would get high off beer, alcohol and drugs. I was looking for something. That's why so many people now get high on dope.

"I think this feeling of belonging and hope that the church gives is what the young people out there are really searching for."

Betty Clay, who works as a cleaning lady for a suburban family, may find peace and fellowship and a sense of community in her church. But many of her neighbors do not.

Betty Clay's life centers on her faith and the hope that it gives her. But for many of her neighbors, deeply embedded in the underclass, church and religion are irrelevant.

The heart of the black community has, for centuries, been its churches—where, with soul-stirring melodies, foot-stomping rhythms and convulsing energy, blacks sang out their longing for dignity and respect in the face of racism, discrimination and segregation.

Left: A moment of prayer at the New Rising Sun Baptist Church in a North Lawndale storefront. In the 5.5-square-mile community, there are about 50 churches and nearly 70 congregations that worship in storefronts.

It was in their churches that the black community celebrated its oneness, its joy in the midst of adversity, its endurance in the face of oppression.

Today, in North Lawndale and in other underclass neighborhoods of American cities, the church remains, for some, an anchor of stability in a roiling sea of social distress.

But others remain untouched. For them, there is no sense of community, nothing to unite them. For them, no church points the way to progress, lights the flame of hope.

They are caught up in the baseness of underclass living—casual sex, illegitimate children, crime and violence—antithetical to the teachings of religion and repugnant to those who believe in God.

And the churches, disdained and distrusted by the underclass, are left confused about what to do.

Ironically, the underclass, left behind and forgotten by much of the rest of society, may need the unifying effect of religion today as much as any group ever needed it.

The banks are gone from North Lawndale and the theaters. The parks are ruled by gangs. Vacant lots separating run-down buildings mirror the psychological and spiritual isolation in which many ghetto people pass their lives.

In a neighborhood such as this one, the churches could provide the sense of community that has been lost amid the other abandonments.

If the people of the underclass are ever to learn self-respect and self-reliance, ever to determine their own destinies, the impetus will have to come, at least in part, from black churches—much as these churches played a pivotal role in the civil rights movement two decades ago.

● ● ●

The turning point in Mary Taylor's life came two years ago.

"I got sick of myself and the things that were happening in my life," she explains. "There was nothing good there.

"I was wild. I drank, smoked reefer and followed the crowd and all the wrong that it did because I didn't have anything better to do."

So she returned to Fizer Church, in a storefront whose windows are painted over white, where her mother and stepfather worship.

"I like living right," Taylor says. "It's a lot of security being in church. It's an experience and understanding of life and its problems that you can't explain."

Taylor, who has a 4-year-old daughter and is expecting another child in December, is separated from her husband and living on public aid. She is studying to get her high school diploma.

"I'm longing for that day," she says. "I believe God is going to help me get into a better position so I get a job and get off welfare."

Taylor has been trying to persuade her estranged husband to return to church with her, but he has been resistant.

"A lot of people in church are big phonies," says Frank Taylor, a self-employed carpenter in North Lawndale.

"It seems that once you make a mistake, instead of helping you up, they treat you like the devil.

"There are some honest preachers, but there are some that are in it for the money. It seems like there is a lot of money in it for some of them.

"I think the church can help change the people here and make Lawndale better, but only if the people want to change. Just going, if you're not sincere, won't do it."

The collection plate seems to keep coming around," says a 37-year-old Baptist woman who has not been to church for three years.

"They always want you to donate a little more, a little more. That's what I hate. I think that's what put a lot of people out with the church—the constant asking for money.

"To me, you're paying your way to heaven."

The woman, who tries to support a large family on public aid, says "pride and the devil" are also responsible for her staying away from church.

"You don't want to go to church looking just any kind of way," she explains. "Sometimes you just don't go because you don't have decent clothes."

Like others in the underclass, the woman distrusts many ministers.

"When I see storefront churches, all I think about are crooked preachers," she says. "I know all of them aren't that way, but some of them are.

"A lot of preachers are phonies. You donate money, but where is it going?"

● ● ●

"God's beautiful people are here in the midst of hell," preaches Rev. James Wolff, the 32-year-old pastor of the Lawndale Christian Reformed Church on South Pulaski Road. "People carry a lot of crosses here. But in spite of everything, God has not abandoned us."

Nor, by one measure, at least, have the churches.

In North Lawndale's 5.5-square-mile area, where 48 state lottery outlets and 99 licensed bars and liquor stores testify to worldly fantasies and foibles, there also are about 50 congregations that gather in traditional church buildings and nearly 70 more that worship in storefronts.

Yet many of the congregations are small and not up to dealing with the problems of the underclass.

Many storefront congregations, for example, have neither the physical facilities nor the financial resources to provide much ritual beyond the Sunday worship meeting and a weekly Bible study.

And some of the established parishes, wary of vandalism and violence, have been leery of getting involved.

"When a person wants liquor, he goes to the liquor store," explains Rev. Amos Waller, senior pastor of Mercy Seat Missionary Baptist Church, 4015 W. Roosevelt Rd.

"When he wants to buy food he goes to the grocery. When he needs medical attention, he goes to the doctor or dentist. When he needs spiritual strength, he comes to church.

"They don't come to me to have a prescription on how to tell their son to get off dope. A woman doesn't come here for the church to help her get off welfare, because the church doesn't have the resources to do that."

Mercy Seat, in a large former theater on Roosevelt Road, is one of the more prosperous congregations in North Lawndale, operating on an annual budget of about $200,000.

"On a Sunday, we can have 500 to 600 cars parked around the church," Rev. Waller explains. To protect those cars from less-affluent local residents, the church employs security guards.

Rev. Waller, who established the church in a nearby storefront nearly 30 years ago, lives in a middle-class area in nearby Austin. He is one of many North Lawndale pastors who reside outside the blighted neighborhood.

"If you deal with poor-class folks all your life, you'll be poor class," Rev. Waller says. "If you deal with dope addicts, you'll end up being a dope addict."

For Rev. Waller, the challenge of trying to reach underclass people to show them a better way of life is insurmountable.

"We are living in an age where the whole society is throwing away its morals," he says. "The church can teach things on Sunday, but the people have six days to watch TV and see all the immoral things that are shown there."

● ● ●

Annie Marshall has been a member of Mercy Seat for 20 years. She lives a block away. Her late husband was a deacon at the church. Her three children, now adults, were baptized there and sang in the choir. Her daughter, Lisa, now directs the choir.

"As a Christian person, the church means a whole lot to me," she explains. "It is the basis of my life. It's very instrumental to me. Prayer, that's what keeps me living. If it wasn't for prayer, I couldn't make it. I can feel down, and when I go to church, it's uplifting."

Life was tough on the streets of North Lawndale when her children were growing up. Crime and violence were constant threats. Gangs were ever-present. Unmarried girls were getting pregnant and starting families on their own.

"When my children were growing up and in school," Marshall says, "I was afraid. I prayed that nothing would happen to them."

Such faith, the willingness to believe in God and follow moral tenets, is desperately needed in North Lawndale today, she says.

"There are a lot of problems facing people here, and we've got to reach the young people," she says. "If we could get all our children back to church and turn to Christ, this world would be a better place.

"And I believe that."

Many underclass people in North Lawndale "have gotten so far out of control that I don't know if the church can bring back the morals that have been lost," notes Rev. Cleveland Whittington, pastor of New Rising Sun Baptist Church, 3901 W. 16th St.

Over the last five years, his storefront congregation has lost $3,000 worth of equipment in four break-ins. "There just isn't the church influence or prayer influence in many homes today," he notes.

Nonetheless Rev. Whittington, a retired building engineer who has lived in North Lawndale since 1961, refuses to give up on the underclass.

He is trying to begin a youth program to attract more teenagers to his congregation, and once a month, he shares his pulpit with former drug addicts and ex-convicts.

Still, he concedes, "There are some people I can't reach if I take the Bible and read it from cover to cover."

Rev. Wayne Gordon, a graduate of Wheaton College and Northern Baptist Theological Seminary in the western suburbs, presides over the nondenominational Lawndale Community Church, which last year established a medical clinic that already has served more than 3,000 patients. He is one of several white churchman who live and work in North Lawndale.

"I identify with the people and their struggle and I try to struggle with them," says Rev. Gordon, 32, who founded the mission congregation 10 years ago. "We're looking for the people no one else is helping. God certainly has a heart for the poor, and that's why we do what we do. We're trying to take God seriously.

"The great commandment is to love God, and the second is to love my neighbor as myself. The church has missed loving our neighbor, the person who is really hurting, beaten up by the side of the road.

"It's a strong biblical mandate not just in the Lawndale community but for all the churches of the Chicago area. These are the neighbors of the suburbs and the Gold Coast."

Rev. Edward J. Maxa, who has been on the parish staff of Blessed Sacrament Catholic Church since 1969, asserts that it is the "call" of the church in the inner city "to be not only a set of buildings, but also a force in the community to give people a voice.

"We've seen a time of a crisis of faith, testing the ability of people to trust each other," he says. "We can preach that better things are coming, but we have to do things here and now."

Each of the seven Catholic parishes serving North Lawndale maintain parish schools, with a cumulative enrollment of more than 1,500 students, 80 percent of whom are non-Catholic. The schools' tuitions, often exceeding $900 a year, are among the highest in the archdiocesan system, effectively ruling out participation in them for "the poorest of the poor," Father Maxa concedes.

If you can change one person, it's all worth it," says Elder J.B. Fizer, founding pastor of Fizer Temple Church of God in Christ. "We mostly deal with the souls of people here."

Elder Fizer, still broad-shouldered at age 67, has operated the Pentecostal church for 10 years, driving up several times a week from his home in suburban Summit to dispense the essential message that "you don't have to stay down in the dumps. People can be somebody. Jesus can straighten their lives out."

The church is carpeted and filled with pews that could comfortably seat more than 100 adults. On a recent Sunday, however, there were fewer than two dozen people in attendance for Sunday School.

Elder Fizer is not discouraged. "Hundreds of souls have gotten saved since I got here," he says. "If they had stayed here, this church couldn't hold them all."

The preacher, who purchased the building from a younger pastor who transplated his congregation in Austin, says he is content in the storefront.

"The man sold me this building real reasonable," he says. "I'm not trying to move out. Churches cost a lot of money. I'm just planning on fixing this place up real nice. If I gave this up, the devil would try to put a tavern in here."

A memorial to dreams gone sour, social neglect

Public housing locks in woes it was supposed to cure

For more than three miles along the east side of the Dan Ryan Expressway they stand, one after the other, stark, silent and forbidding.

They are the Robert Taylor Homes, Stateway Gardens and Dearborn Homes: 54 public housing buildings, reaching as high as 17 stories.

They form a wall of bricks and glass that confronts the millions of Chicagoans, visitors and travelers who pass along this route each year.

This wall of housing projects, where 28,000 very poor black people live, also forms a civic monument of sorts.

With its crime, graffiti and garbage, with its grinding poverty, high unemployment and dead-end lives, it is a memorial to liberal dreams that went sour, to political expediency that looked the other way, to violent white racism that subverted its past and to social neglect that is determining its future.

This is not what public housing was supposed to be.

Public housing, as originally envisioned, was a place where people with low incomes could live while they saved enough to

Left: Public housing is a memorial to liberal dreams that went sour, fostering the conditions it was designed to eliminate.

Tribune photo by Chris Walker

move into better housing. It was supposed to be temporary. It was supposed to be integrated, and it was supposed to be a pleasant place to live.

Today, however, public housing, while inexpensive for residents, has most of the problems it was originally designed to eliminate: crime, poverty, poor living conditions and communal despair. Private housing for the very poor has many of those same problems but costs much more.

For half a century, government officials in Chicago and around the nation have struggled to eliminate urban slums. Instead, through naivete, misconceptions and calculated maneuvers, they have created new ghettos of segregated, substandard housing.

These new slums, whether a huge high-rise or a rundown neighborhood of dilapidated homes, are in many ways worse than the ghettos they replaced.

The earlier ghettos, although racially segregated, were economically heterogeneous. Doctors, lawyers and police officers lived in the same neighborhoods as those who worked at menial jobs or had no jobs at all.

But in the new urban slums, the very poor have no neighbors but themselves.

This has helped speed the growth of an urban underclass, mainly black, that has become so immersed in poverty, so reliant on welfare and so frustrated by unemployment and a lack of educational opportunities that it threatens to become permanent.

The members of this underclass often live in single-parent households headed by women. Their neighborhoods are places where crime and violence are routine.

The children have few aspirations because they have few, if any, job opportunities and few, if any, successful role models. Those with money are the gang members, drug dealers, pimps and prostitutes and those on welfare.

While the isolation of the new urban ghettos has insulated whites and middle-class blacks from most direct contact with the underclass, inner-city problems have important implications for society at large.

Billions of dollars are spent each year nationally in welfare payments and subsidies to the underclass, and billions more are lost from the American economy because so many underclass people are out of work.

The inability and unwillingness of underclass people and their landlords to maintain inner-city buildings drive down property values in and around the ghetto and drive up property taxes for all other property owners.

In addition, underclass crime, always threatening to burst out of the ghetto, breeds fear throughout American cities and suburbs.

And, despite $75 billion spent over the last 50 years to build public housing for the poor, the aging and deterioration of that housing and the swiftly increasing shortage of private housing for poor people means that, sooner or later, new homes will have to be found for the underclass at a potentially huge financial and social cost.

Officials estimate that $10 billion to $15 billion will be needed over the next five years simply to renovate public housing nationwide. In Chicago, renovation costs are expected to run as high as $750 million, according to Zirl Smith, executive director of the Chicago Housing Authority.

Yet since 1980, the Reagan administration has been trying to persuade Congress to cut public housing subsidies sharply. "It is only because of the Congress, primarily the Republican senators, that the program has been maintained," says Robert McKay, executive director of the Council of Large Public Housing Authorities.

Even now, the people of the underclass who live in private dwellings are facing a growing housing squeeze.

Just how tight that squeeze is can be seen in 1980 census statistics for households with very low incomes, those having only half the average income for the local area. Chicago has 265,094 such households, one of every four in the city.

Of such families nationwide, nearly one of every three is paying 70 percent or more of its annual income for housing.

Other census statistics show why underclass families must pay so much for housing. If those 265,094 very poor families in Chicago were to spend just 25 percent of their incomes for housing, the normal percentage, they would have only 114,711 units to choose from. In other words, there are more than twice as many very poor families in the city as there are affordable apartments.

A major reason for this has been the demolition of more than 60,000 housing units in Chicago over the last decade and the abandonment of tens of thousands more.

Although nearly as many housing units have been constructed in the city as have been demolished, Robert Slayton, a housing expert with the Chicago Urban League, points out: "The new construction is not going on in the places where the demolitions are going on. We're tearing down low-income units and replacing them with upper-income units."

The construction has occurred in such stylish areas as the Near North Side, Lincoln Park and the Loop, while the demolitions have taken place in the underclass neighborhoods of North Lawndale, Woodlawn, the Near West Side, West Town, Englewood, Grand Boulevard and East Garfield Park.

In those neighborhoods and others on the West Side and South Side, the vacant lots left by the demolitions and the broken-window facades of the abandoned buildings give the neighborhoods an air of decay and disorder.

Many of those vacant buildings have been abandoned by homeowners and fledgling entrepreneurs who, caught in the rising tide of black unemployment, could no longer afford to maintain the buildings or pay their mortgages.

In addition, real estate practices and city policies have long kept blacks, especially poor blacks, from looking for housing anywhere but in already black neighborhoods or areas undergoing sharp racial change. That has meant that despite the successful integration of a handful of areas, Chicago remains the most segregated city in the nation, according to numerous national studies.

And what that means for poor people looking for housing is that the housing they can find often is abysmal.

"Their rent is continually going up," says Ida McNeal, manager of a housing program of the Bethel Lutheran Church on the West Side, but "the buildings are continually going down."

Because the poor have no other options, landlords know that ghetto apartments will be filled despite the lack of maintenance. So when the paint chips, it is not repainted. When hallway lights break, they are not fixed. When rats and bugs invade, they are not driven out.

And, for many, the neighbors are a major problem.

"There are a lot of wineheads in this building," says one woman in the West Garfield Park neighborhood. "You hear yelling all night. I've been trying and trying to find another place to move to, but I pay $180 a month and I've got four rooms."

Fifty years ago, social reformers thought slum problems could be eliminated by the construction of public housing, and many such problems have been removed for those who live in public housing for the elderly or in some of the low-rise family developments.

Yet for poor families in the bulk of Chicago's high-rise projects and in high-rises throughout the nation, many of the same problems remain.

Bug infestations are common. Graffiti cover the walls in common areas, and garbage often covers the floors. Elevators, washing machines and other facilities are constantly breaking down, and the stairwells smell of urine.

Nonetheless, many residents take great care in making their apartments attractive and comfortable. "It's like they've created a safe island within a war zone," says a veteran teacher in a project elementary school.

As comfortable as the apartments may be, they can also become highly constricting for mothers with young children. The nature of high-rises makes it impossible for mothers to keep track of small children playing outside. The need to oversee such play is essential because of the presence of gangs and the prevalence of crime in the projects.

Many mothers won't let their children out to play. "It's like a prison," says one mother of five. As in other underclass neighborhoods, crime is an everyday fact of life in the projects. "Crime in public housing reflects the neighborhood it's in," says Winston Moore, head of security for the CHA.

Chicago police crime statistics indicate that residents of CHA high-rise buildings are slightly more likely to be murdered or raped than people living in other underclass neighborhoods, and much more likely to be threatened, beaten or injured in a nonfatal attack.

Nonetheless, they are less likely to be the victims of robbery, burglary or theft. In fact, people who live in all-white areas of Chicago are twice as likely to be theft victims as those who live in CHA high-rises. But those high-rise residents are 13 times more likely to be the victims of violent crime.

Even more than the underclass neighborhoods around them, CHA high-rises are highly concentrated and segregated communities of poverty, unemployment, instability and widespread hopelessness.

About 145,000 people are official residents of CHA housing, although there are as many as 100,000 or more unofficial residents. Given those numbers, as much as 8 percent of Chicago's population is living in CHA housing.

Nearly four of every five of the official CHA residents are on some sort of public aid, and more than three of every four CHA families are headed by a single parent, most often a woman.

A study of 1980 census information by Pierre de Vise, a Roosevelt University urbanologist, found that 10 of the 16 poorest neighborhoods in the United States were in CHA projects, 6 of them in that three-mile stretch of projects along the Dan Ryan Expressway.

In a section of the Cabrini-Green housing project on the Near North Side, more than 90 percent of the residents, 3,915 of 4,346, were living in poverty.

Across the nation, public housing residents tend to be very poor and very young and to live in female-headed families. [One major exception is New York City, where, because of a severe housing shortage and state policies that allow middle-class families in some projects, the heads of as many as 70 percent of the public housing families have jobs.]

And they tend to be members of minority groups. Nationally, 80 percent of families living in public housing are black or Hispanic. Unlike Chicago's CHA, many public housing agencies have projects with some significant white populations. In CHA family housing, 95 percent of the residents are black. Only 3 percent are white, and 2 percent are Hispanic.

As originally conceived, public housing was not supposed to be exclusively for the very poor or exclusively for blacks.

In fact, most of the residents of the first CHA buildings constructed in the 1930s and 1940s were white, and local liberals hoped and expected that, in addition to providing good, clean, inexpensive housing for the poor, the CHA would also promote integration.

Instead, over the years, the authority promoted and institutionalized segregation, as U.S. District Judge Richard Austin said in a ruling in Chicago in 1969.

This happened because whites throughout the city refused to accept poor black CHA residents as neighbors and because city and federal officials refused to carry out court rulings and legislative mandates to force them to do so.

Perhaps the most important turning point in the process came in August, 1953, when Donald Howard, a black postal worker, and his family moved into the previously all-white Trumbull Park development at 105th Street and Oglesby Avenue on the city's Southeast Side.

On the night of Aug. 5, whites gathered outside and pelted the Howard apartment with paving bricks and stones. The attacks continued daily, and on Aug. 9 the crowd swelled to 2,000 people.

The Howard family finally moved out of the project in May, 1954, but by that time other blacks had moved in, and the white riots continued. During one 24-hour period, nearly 1,000 police officers were on duty in the area.

The white riots frightened city officials, and a state law was enacted that gave to the Chicago City Council the power to determine sites of CHA housing. That, in effect, ended all hopes of an integrated CHA.

Elizabeth Wood, a former social worker who had headed the CHA and tried to use it to promote integration, was unceremoniously dumped from her job in August, 1954.

"The concept of the ghetto prevails in the city administration," she told a community group a short time after her removal. "It is the will of politicians to keep Negroes where they are."

Over the next decade, more and more housing units were needed for poor blacks as urban-renewal efforts leveled the slum buildings in which they lived.

But because of the threat of white violence, officials refused to allow those units to be built in white areas. Low-rise buildings were known to be better for residents, but they cost more per unit to construct and there was a tight federal limit on how much money could be spent in building public housing.

As a result, 168 high-rise buildings were constructed in the black ghettos to keep costs down and keep poor blacks out of white neighborhoods.

Later, middle-class and working-class blacks who had not been driven out by the problems and irritations of living in CHA high-rises were all but forced out by a federal law that removed a ceiling on public housing rents and required the payment of 25 percent, now 30 percent, of a household's income.

That meant cheap rents for the very poor on welfare, now an average of $85 a month, but increasingly high rents for anyone else. Thus, even the working poor fled the projects.

It did not help that for nearly two decades the CHA was the victim of politics and neglect, so much so that in 1982 federal officials called it the worst-managed public housing authority in the nation.

Today, more than a year after Zirl Smith took over as executive director, much appears to have been done to correct the CHA's problems. Efforts to evict criminals helped reduce the CHA crime rate during the first eight months of this year, and Smith is seeking $83 million in federal funds to beef up security.

He is also going ahead with plans to renovate some CHA buildings, although at a much slower pace because of residents' opposition.

Still, some wonder whether that's the right way to go.

"I'm pretty pessimistic about high-rises being used by families, even if you renovate them," says Devereux Bowly Jr., author of "The Poorhouse," a history of the first 81 years of subsidized housing in Chicago.

"The argument could be made that renovating high-rises for families is putting good money after bad. We should have learned by now that they simply don't work."

On the other hand, the only other suggestions for providing the poor with adequate housing have to do with finding them homes in middle-class neighborhoods and suburbs, a proposal long-fought throughout the Chicago area.

So the housing outlook for the underclass is bleak.

"The sad thing," Bowly says, "is that there really are no prospects that it's going to get better."

And if Bowly is right, the underclass and its problems will continue to grow and continue to drag on Chicago and the rest of the country and threaten to rip the fabric of the nation.

Community's housing in full state of collapse

25 years of neglect leave war-zone look

After 25 years of virtually unchecked housing deterioration, abandonment and demolition, North Lawndale looks like a bombed-out war zone. Almost half of the housing units there have disappeared since 1960.

Much of what remains is rundown or dilapidated. This is where the neighborhood's black underclass lives—with the Illinois Department of Public Aid paying the rent.

More than half of the residents of North Lawndale pay their housing costs with welfare money. Each month, landlords in the West Side slum collect an estimated $1.5 million from people on public assistance. The estimate is based on an average monthly rent per unit of about $240.

The growth of the underclass in North Lawndale has coincided with—and contributed to—the decline in the housing stock. In 1960 there were 30,243 housing units within the 5.5-square-mile community. Today only 16,287 units remain.

The total value of housing units lost in the last quarter-century is more than $350 million, based on the $25,200 average value of a housing unit in the area today, according to U.S. Census Bureau data.

Left: An 11-year-old dries his school clothes over a hot plate, the only source of heat in his North Lawndale apartment.

The cost in terms of disrupted lives and shattered families is incalculable.

In the last five years alone, North Lawndale has lost 2,303 dwelling units to the wrecker's ball, while only 61 new units have been built. That's a ratio of 38 units lost for every new one added.

Of the dwelling units left, at least one-third are seriously substandard. The city's Department of Inspectional Services has cited 5,521 units as falling short of minimum standards for human habitation.

Of the units cited, 1,417 are in the city's Housing Court because their owners have ignored repeated requests by tenants and the city to make necessary repairs.

The other 4,104 units are before the city's Housing Compliance Board, where the city attempts to mediate tenant complaints against landlords in the hopes of avoiding litigation. Many of these complaints are likely also to end up in Housing Court.

The number of substandard units may be substantially higher, because city inspectors long have been accused of being lax about citing violations.

An even grimmer picture resulted from a building-by-building survey five years ago that was conducted by an economic development group called Project 80. The survey found that:

● 9 percent [838 buildings] were on the verge of collapse.

● 38 percent [3,432 buildings] were in need of major rehabilitation.

● 42 percent [3,752 buildings] were in need of at least minor repairs.

● 3 percent [243 buildings] were abandoned.

● Only 8 percent of the 8,937 buildings remaining in the neighborhood were in good to very good condition.

"Fewer than one-third of the area's blocks contained predominantly sound buildings at the time of the survey," Project 80 researchers noted.

"Throughout most of the area, clusters of three or more adjacent vacant lots and substandard or abandoned buildings may be found," they said.

Many of the worst buildings have been demolished since the survey, but others, in need of only minor repairs five years ago, have deteriorated to the point where they too are now doomed to be demolished.

Newly constructed townhouses and high-rise complexes and entire blocks of well-maintained older houses and apartment buildings occasionally break the monotony of North Lawndale's depressing landscape. However, they are like a handful of roses scattered among acres of weeds.

Poverty is the primary reason North Lawndale has such serious housing problems. Because more than half of the neighborhood's residents are on welfare, there just isn't enough money available to support a healthy housing market.

"Residents of the community can't afford to pay the kinds of rents that landlords need today to adequately maintain their buildings," said George Stone, Chicago's first deputy housing commissioner. "Consequently, landlords continually defer maintenance on their properties until their buildings go down the drain."

Fewer than one-fourth of North Lawndale's housing units are owner-occupied, according to census data. When a majority of buildings in a neighborhood are owner-occupied, those communities tend to remain stable, most real estate experts agree.

On the other hand, in poorer communities where most of the buildings are occupied almost exclusively by renters, deterioration usually seems inevitable.

"In areas that are nice and well kept in North Lawndale, you'll find that those areas have owner-occupied buildings," said Mike Kingston, a supervising juvenile probation officer assigned to the area.

"If a person owns a house and is out there in his front yard picking up the litter, his neighbors are less likely to throw papers around. It's just a fact."

The age of the housing stock also plays an important role in the deterioration. Seventy percent of the existing dwelling units were built before 1939.

Furthermore, according to a University of Illinois at Chicago report issued in 1984, years of inadequate housing inspection and lax building code enforcement by the city and the courts also contributed to North Lawndale's housing decline.

"The disregard of property by tenants" was yet another factor, the report points out.

"Some of it is housekeeping and neglect on the tenants' part," city building inspector Fred Lopez agrees. "Many building owners in North Lawndale aren't doing what they should, but sometimes you have to blame the tenants, too. Just because you're poor doesn't mean you can't be clean."

Many also would argue that the city's financial institutions and insurance companies are also culpable because they dramatically reduced the availability of mortgage and repair loans, as well as insurance, after the West Side riots in the 1960s.

The practice of restricting or denying loans and insurance coverage in a specific area is commonly referred to as redlining. Banks, savings and loans and insurance firms literally drew a red line on a city map around deteriorating neighborhoods they arbitrarily decided they would no longer service.

A 1975 study by the Metropolitan Area Housing Alliance, a citywide coalition of community groups, found that North Lawndale was one of the "most severely redlined" neighborhoods in the city.

Because of the enactment in recent years of federal loan disclosure and community reinvestment laws, redlining is less of a problem today. Nevertheless, North Lawndale still suffers from a lack of housing loan availability, primarily because there's only one bank within the neighborhood, the Community Bank of Lawndale. With only $20 million in capital, it is one of the three smallest banks in the city.

The roots of North Lawndale's housing decline date to the 1940s, when the neighborhood's then predominantly ethnic East European Jewish population began moving to more upscale city neighborhoods like Albany Park and Rogers Park on Chicago's North Side.

In their place, black families began moving in, mostly blue-collar workers employed by railroads or the post office. By 1950 blacks made up about 13 percent of the population.

Because of restrictive property covenants in effect at the time prohibiting white homeowners from selling to blacks, most of the early black arrivals rented flats in the larger apartment buildings that were interspersed among the more common low-rise brick and stone buildings.

At first the blacks moving in were, if not openly welcomed, at least accepted by their white neighbors. In 1955, a community newspaper boasted that "new people are mingling with the old. The melting pot is bubbling again."

Carrie Moore, 50, a black woman who has lived in North Lawndale since 1953, remembers it as being "really nice" at that time. "It was clean, and there was grass and trees everywhere. There were no problems. You could walk the street without anybody bothering or harassing you. People said hello."

North Lawndale's experiment with integration, however, was short-lived. When the federal courts struck down the restrictive covenants, it touched off a mass exodus by whites.

"When that happened, a lot of the old-time Jewish homeowners in the neighborhood really got scared," said Max E. Stein, 76, a lawyer active in real estate in North Lawndale in the 1940s, '50s and '60s.

"They figured the area was going to go down, that it was going to be overrun by the blacks. They wanted to get out; so they were anxious to sell their buildings."

In this climate, real estate speculators flourished, using panic peddling and block-busting tactics to convince reluctant owners to sell quickly and cheaply. In turn, the speculators sold the homes to blacks at inflated prices.

White homeowners who couldn't or wouldn't sell right away ended up renting to blacks.

"It was either that or losing whatever money they had invested in their buildings," Stein recalled. "In the end, they couldn't charge rents high enough to keep them repaired; so they just dumped them on someone else or simply abandoned them."

By 1960, 91 percent of the neighborhood's population was black. Today, blacks account for 97 percent of the population.

When the panic selling by white homeowners first began, Stein said, the more reputable brokers attempted to seek out stable blacks, "people with jobs, good people," who could afford to keep the property repaired.

"But it wasn't long before the high-binder real estate dealer types moved in," he noted. "They didn't care who they sold to." They held mortgages for blacks who couldn't qualify for conventional mortgages or afford down payments.

"The result was the neighborhood declined," Stein recalled. "Then the worst elements came in—the gangs, the drug pushers—and it went from bad to worse."

The riots sparked by the assassination of Martin Luther King

Jr. in 1968 prompted many of the better-off black homeowners to leave the area.

"Since then, the area has just been a wasteland, just a wild area," Stein said.

As dwelling units vanished from North Lawndale's housing stock, the neighborhood's population also declined, to 61,500 in 1985 from a peak of 125,000 in 1960.

Most who remain there do so because they have nowhere else to go.

"People here are faced daily with the problem of living in buildings that have major problems with them," said Jesse Miller, a longtime neighborhood activist in North Lawndale and executive director of the Lawndale Peoples Planning and Action Council.

"Some don't even have heat, and if they complain or try to hold back rent until something is done, they are put out and have no place to go. Despite the tremendous loss of housing units here, some landlords still see Lawndale as profitable and are exploiting these buildings."

Tenants in a building at 1228 S. Keeler Ave. know all about living with major problems and getting little satisfaction from their landlord.

After four families living in the 15-unit building complained repeatedly to the city in 1985 about substandard conditions, Otis Flynn, their landlord, had them evicted.

On a cold and rainy September morning, they and their belongings were tossed out on the sidewalk. For almost an entire day, six adults and seven children, including two with chicken pox, stood or sat in front of the building with no idea of where they would go.

Representatives from Miller's community group and the city's Department of Human Services, meanwhile, frantically searched for a place to temporarily relocate them. At dusk, they decided to move the families back into their old apartments. It took several weeks before all were relocated.

Georgia Taylor, who was evicted with her three small children, said she had lived in the building for six years. She described living conditions there as "horrible" in the last few years.

"Back in March I had no heat and no water," she said. "The

pipes froze and busted, and I had to use my stove to keep warm. There was water leaking everywhere. It was so damp in my apartment that mushrooms were growing in the cracks of the bathroom floor."

● ● ●

According to longtime Chicago neighborhood activist Lew Kreinberg, most houses in North Lawndale today are "either prey to landlords of little means who can barely afford the building and have no funds for repairs, or owned by rich men who live in blind trusts and who refrain from spending profits on restorations."

Otis Flynn, who owns the building at 1228 S. Keeler Ave., falls somewhere between the two types Kreinberg describes.

Flynn, who is black, describes himself as a South Side real estate dealer and property manager who believed he could increase his investments by expanding his operation into North Lawndale.

He said he recently sold another building in the neighborhood, three blocks west on South Kolin Avenue, and is looking for a buyer for the Keeler Avenue structure.

"What I'm doing is pulling out," Flynn said. "It's just a bad situation. Everywhere else I own or manage buildings, I look for tenants with good rent payment histories and families that don't have any gang-age children.

"But in North Lawndale, it's hard to find those kinds of people. The gangs there are bad. Eighty to 90 percent of the people live on welfare, so frequently they don't pay their rent. Consequently, there just isn't enough money coming in to fix up a property as it should be fixed.

"You can't attract quality residents in an area like that. That's just the way it is.

"There are landlords who are making it in Lawndale and are increasing their investments there. Apparently, they know something I don't."

City housing officials doubt that any of the remaining landlords are making huge profits off their property in North Lawndale.

"The big slumlords got out years ago just like everyone else," Stone said. "It's just the little guys who are left."

Over the years, there have been some limited attempts to

address North Lawndale's housing problem. But while they resulted in upgrading small areas within the community, none, thus far, has spurred a neighborhood housing resurgence.

As far back as 1954, the Chicago Housing Authority opened Ogden Courts, a 136-unit public housing complex on the east end of the community.

More recently, the minority-owned, North Lawndale-based Pyramidwest Development Corp. completed a federally subsidized, $7 million townhouse complex—Lawndale Terrace—at Roosevelt Road and Kedzie Avenue.

However, it is very unlikely that any new subsidized housing will be built, because the administration of President Reagan has eliminated funding for such efforts. It also has trimmed funding for the rehabilitation of existing subsidized units.

"We still have community development funds, which we can use to leverage investment in low-income housing by private investors in areas like North Lawndale," Stone said. "But the funds we have are pitifully limited compared to the need out there."

But no matter how much money is poured into North Lawndale, the neighborhood's housing is not likely to be significantly improved unless the community first experiences an industrial and commercial renaissance.

North Lawndale once was a thriving industrial and commercial neighborhood, but like a lot of the housing, most of the businesses and factories have vanished.

"If everyone in North Lawndale suddenly had a good paying job," Stone acknowledged, "there would be no housing problems."

VII
THE CHOICES

Despair, dependency tow underclass into the vortex

Society reawakening to severity of deep-rooted problem

The existence of a permanent black underclass in America's cities defies the most basic promise of the civil rights movement and the national conviction that this land offers opportunity, unbridled and absolute, for those who seize it.

This new, firmly rooted underclass has changed that conviction along with the character of the cities. It has sharpened racial divisions, and it is breaking down black family life while it erects new barriers between poor and middle-class blacks.

It has absorbed billions of dollars and persisted through all Great Society programs. Now it has helped create a backlash at the failure of some of those programs. An angry resentment exists throughout the nation today, and there is accepted scorn for notions of liberalism and social legislation aimed at the disadvantaged.

That said, however, there is a movement of concern current among academics and politicans, both liberal and conservative. The pendulum may be slowly swinging back.

New legislation again is taking aim, sometimes indirectly, at the expanding underclass. Often it is two-edged—the federal school voucher proposal is the most recent example, in that

Left: Children watch a softball soar above gang graffiti in a vacant lot. If current trends continue, few underclass children will ever leave poverty behind.

public funds are offered to aid low-income individuals and families, but the national effect may debilitate the entire public school system and hurt the neediest.

Other proposals for a subminimum wage, welfare tied to work and even complex tax legislation for families on the doorstep of poverty are creating a new national debate. Some proposals are sharp and focused; others are mere ideological toys. In either case, motives are being formed now more by society's self-interest than by compassion for the underclass. Many of the voices raised say that is just and right. The issue clearly is not black versus white; if anything, the underclass harms the black middle class far beyond public perceptions.

The permanent black underclass is a group of undetermined number in the central cities joined by ignorance, crime [either as criminal or victim] and poverty. The common characteristics are joblessness, teenage pregnancy, illegitimate births, female-headed families, serious crime and welfare dependency.

For America, members of the group represent the reverse of the immigrant image of vigor and rising expectations, for they are the continued failures and reflect expectations of nothing.

The future of the underclass has already crystallized.

If current trends continue, less than 30 percent of black men will be employed by the turn of the century and by then 70 percent of all black families will be headed by single women. What alarms the Joint Center for Political Action in Washington is no less than the disintegration of the black family in America.

Welfare dependency, a kind of social narcotic that alters behavior and is a hallmark of the underclass, becomes more ingrained each year. Social scientists suspect generational dependence on welfare, but Kathleen McKelvy, a teacher in a Harlem storefront school, is convinced of it. When she asked her young students where they would go if they needed money, 9 out of 10 of the children replied: "To the mailbox."

Crime has created enclaves of lawlessness and random killing. In the Watts ghetto of south central Los Angeles, for instance, the major cause of death for males up to age 34 is gunshot wounds. Last year at Dr. Martin Luther King Jr. Hospital there daily admissions averaged four gunshot wounds, three stabbings and three cases of "blunt assault" to the head.

One barometer of social pathology may be in the way

children are harmed. Two doctors published a study on juvenile gunshot victims admitted to the Dr. King Hospital during the decade between 1974 and 1984. There were 300 children, all under the age of 15, most of them between 10 and 15. There were 18 victims under age 10; one-third of those were unborn fetuses. More than half the victims were shot by one of their parents or by their mothers' companions. Sixteen percent were victims of random gunfire or indiscriminate drive-by shootings. Many of the rest were believed to have been caught in crossfire or other gang-related shootings.

Society is bound to react to such mayhem. The states' prison systems, where 47 percent of all inmates are black, will consume greater portions of the public dollar. Each $100 million spent on prison construction ultimately costs $1.6 billion in salaries, operating costs and debt retirement over the next 30 years.

Society already appears to have made some choices and apparently is relying on prisons to handle social problems. There has been a 40 percent growth in the number of inmates at federal and state prisons since 1980, the Justice Department reported, though the FBI crime index showed an overall drop in crime, with violent crime down 7 percent from 1981 and property crime down 12 percent during the same period.

The National Conference of State Legislatures reports spending on corrections is increasing more than on any other state agency. There were 34 new prisons built in 22 states in 1984 at an average cost of $10.9 million for each facility. Another 111 prisons planned or under construction are estimated to cost more than $2 billion. Illinois alone added nine new prisons in the last eight years.

Education in the cities is constantly threatened from within and without. Private schools will flourish, taking the brightest of the black public school students and leaving inner city schools with the poorest, the most ignorant and the most vicious. It is a selection that has long since begun. Currently, for instance, 70 percent of Chicago's public school population is from poor families. Though the city is 49.7 percent white, only 14.7 percent of the public school enrollment is white.

The dropout statistics are chilling: Among low-income black high school students, the national dropout rate is 57 percent. That figure from the Census Bureau is close to another, private study that claims 58 percent of black youths are "functionally illiterate," which means they cannot read at a 6th-grade level or fill out an application form for a job or anything else. An ancillary statistic—two-thirds of all inmates of Illinois prisons also are functionally illiterate. Many of these obviously are among the two-thirds who reported they were unemployed before sentencing last year.

Michael P. Lane, director of the Illinois prison system for the last five years, said: "The ignorant tend to come to prison again and again and again and again. The educated tend to stay away."

A study by the Chicago Panel on Public School Finances estimated the annual costs to society for the 12,616 students of the class of 1982 who dropped out before graduation. This one class of dropouts—there is a new one each year—will mean about $7.3 million in lost taxes each year, $50.5 million in welfare payments and $1.6 million in crime costs.

The costs to society are not only hurtful, but expensive. Public housing projects, which now act like cages for both criminals and their victims, will absorb still more money. Officials claim $10 billion to $15 billion will be needed to renovate public housing projects nationwide over the next five years, with $750 million of that needed in Chicago alone. In some projects there is a five-year waiting list to get into scattered public housing and out of the high-rise nightmare apartments.

Even when people want to help themselves, bureaucracy can get in the way and the costs go beyond dollars. In Chicago's Washington Park housing project some years ago a rapist roamed almost at will. Finally a group of local men who normally spent time "shooting craps, drinking liquor and smoking their pot" organized to stop the rapes. Mrs. Hattie Williams, a 63-year-old community activist, recalled how they found a suspect and dragged him to the apartments of several victims, who identified him. He was then beaten and given to police.

"The women were very proud their men would do this," Mrs. Williams remembers. "They voted to each give $1 from their monthly checks to the men" to continue the patrol. But the local effort was suppressed as the Chicago Housing Authority sent in two hired guards, who ordered the volunteers to disband.

The cost of the underclass also is reflected in the financial consequences of teenage pregnancy. Illinois alone pays about $188 million annually in AFDC and Medicaid for teenage mothers and their 37,000 children, according to Janet Reis of Northwestern University's Center for Health Services and Policy Research. The statistics point to a serious imbalance in black-white ratios. The black teenage pregnancy rate is exactly double that of whites, and 62 percent of the state's AFDC recipients are black.

Beyond the financial consequences, there is fear that ultimately an unchecked underclass will prompt truly draconian measures. The voices of anger and frustration are still relatively faint, content to cut programs, insist on tighter eligibility and work rules and build more prisons. Others are willing simply to ignore the deterioration as long as it doesn't touch them. But that may be only prelude to less humane alternatives. An elderly crime victim, such as the 82-year-old black women who called the newspaper, is upset and fearful when she recommends sterilization of young black criminals. But it is more forceful when Atlanta's Mayor Andrew Young leans back in the Brumby rocking chair in his office and says he believes people really are considering options like that.

There is a lingering fear among many liberals, and fewer conservatives, about talking about the underclass, noted William Julius Wilson, chairman of the University of Chicago's sociology department, who has been in the forefront of underclass research. People are reluctant to describe behavior "that might be construed as unflattering or stigmatizing to ghetto residents either because of a fear of providing fuel for racist arguments or because of a concern of being charged with 'racism' or with 'blaming the victim.' "

But the problem is so acute and the social consequences so disturbing that a reexamination of the War on Poverty and the Reagan administration's reaction is beginning to emerge.

Actually, the intense anti-welfare policy in the last five years may have injected a new enthusiasm into the national debate. For those who care, the obstacles are as numerous as the opportunities. It is a phrase that may be reversed for those who prefer optimism.

As a Detroit priest, Rev. William Cunningham, insisted earlier: People do not need compassion from society, they need justice. It is entirely possible that some programs failed because true compassion may not be shared with groups but only with individuals and our society was too naive to understand that.

"I believe what happened was after the Great Society we went through a period of saying nothing works and then there was another evaluation and now we are in a period where we can see that some things worked better than others," said Martin Rein of the Massachusetts Institute of Technology. Studies by the National Academy of Sciences, universities and private research companies back that up.

In retrospect, it was foolish to believe one exhaustive mid-'60s effort would solve the problems of the underclass, would somehow magically instill middle-class values and norms of behavior in a group that lives on the hungry, mean edge of society.

Even well-intentioned programs have unforeseen backlashes. The Reagan administration and some local governments have proposed vouchers for housing and schools and even jobs. In a recent experiment in Dayton, Ohio, however, welfare recipients were given vouchers that offered their potential employers either tax credits or cash payment for hiring them. The plan failed because, it is believed, the employers didn't consider voucher holders as good prospects and it stigmatized them.

Good intentions don't always mesh with reality. And the underclass has become especially resistant to programs either created by government largesse or designed to force the poverty-stricken to get off the dole. The questions are obvious but the answers, if indeed there are any, remain obscure.

There are loud choruses already in this debate. Since the decade began liberals have seen their promises and projects falter and public sentiment turn against them. They reached, to use a phrase from the Brookings Institution's Henry J. Aaron, "an intellectual and political cul de sac."

On the other hand, the initial agenda and social program cutbacks of the first-term Reagan adminstration have been halted, and conservatives are realizing their vision needs not only Democratic but liberal votes.

The debate is especially strident among black professionals who take radically different approaches to dealing with the underclass.

Wilson, for instance, has a pragmatic liberalism that believes "unless we deal with joblessness, we will have very little impact. . . . [To] achieve reforms there can't be race-specific legislation. It has to capture the attention of the white middle class and that will not be accomplished by affirmative action programs for minorities. We have to look at programs to get all Americans back to work, to tie manpower programs to a universal package of programs."

Arthur Brimmer, a private financial consultant and former member of the Board of Governors of the Federal Reserve System, has a similar assessment: "We do need to spend money on these people—not giving them dole. We need to spend money to train them.

"There's one thing that stands out. The lack of employment today is due far more to a lack of skills than to discrimination. Race discrimination still exists, but it's far outweighed by a lack of skills. If you're looking for a pressure point, somewhere to break into this vicious cycle, it has to be education.

"The improvement that we see in jobs and income is nearly entirely in the [black] middle class and above. They are the ones with the marketable skills, and they are the ones with the two-earner families."

Those improvements don't necessarily help the black underclass, Brimmer cautioned, especially "the large number of blacks in female-headed households. The gap between blacks and whites has been narrowing moderately and has become less severe. But the gap within the black community has been growing deeper. The black schism has been growing deeper."

Brimmer wrote in a paper to be published by the Joint Center that the top fifth of blacks took in 46.9 percent of all black income last year, while the bottom fifth took in only 3.7 percent. That disparity is wider than the difference between rich whites and poor whites.

Black neoconservatives on the many-sided national debate prefer to see the solutions through a "bootstraps" approach, demanding changes first within the black underclass community.

After Glenn Loury began publishing his ideas on the black underclass, several of his Harvard colleagues stopped speaking to him. Loury, a political economist, said the idea that racial discrimination is to blame for the existence of the black underclass is a "fiction." Instead, he argued that the growing number of alienated, impoverished blacks is caused by social problems within the black community.

Specifically, Loury believes there is a lack of values, and that the absence of those values has been excused for too long.

"I contrast that with the conventional civil rights strategy that puts the onus on society, the government, white people. That's not to let people off the hook, but it is a fiction that discrimination is to blame for the underclass," he said, adding that traditionally "black political and intellectual leadership feared that acknowledging any complicity in the problems would be to undermine their political base of support."

Dr. Alvin Poussaint, associate professor of pyschiatry on the Harvard University Medical School faculty, is an expert on black-on-black violence, another hallmark of the underclass.

"They are frustrated by being poor and not making it and they take it out on each other. That adds to the [powder] keg," he said. "And my feeling is that a lot of anger and rage comes from the fact that people in the community are abusing each other. They don't see whites directly there as the people messing over them. You don't hear black kids standing around saying, 'Let's get whitey.' It is other blacks who burglarize them, other blacks who rape them, other blacks who kill their sons."

Charles Willie, a Harvard professor of education, rejects the entire notion of an underclass and calls Loury "an apologist for the system as it is."

"Poor blacks have been harmed enough by people unlike them, and they don't deserve to be dumped on by one like them," said Willie, who describes Loury as "the glamor boy of the conservatives."

The intellectual debate appears almost sanitized, however, compared to life in the projects.

In the Cabrini-Green public housing project on Chicago's Near North Side, Carolyn Shelton sits behind a desk in a project office painted welfare green with steel security screens over the lower windows. Across the room sits Clarence Walker, who has lived in Cabrini all 37 years of his life. He has just dropped in for some advice from Shelton before he heads for an afternoon job interview.

Shelton tells him: "The reality is there are college graduates working as store clerks because there aren't any jobs out there. You are a black man. You have to try harder. You have to kick those doors in, and you can't kick them in Shaft-style. You have to look good. Feel good about yourself. Smile. Convince them to hire you."

Shelton, who has worked in Cabrini for two years under a state contract as a "motivational counselor and job developer," thinks it's harder for the youth of today to make it out of the ghetto.

"Years ago," she said, referring to her childhood, "you didn't have as many handouts. You had to become a survivor. Basically our people have forgotten how to earn a living.

"It takes more than a check. They expect the check today. They don't expect to see you. We have to have black people that care about black people."

Shelton attempts to recruit black professionals to come to Cabrini to spend time with kids "so they can see some positive role models." But "they're afraid to come to Cabrini," she said, noting the notorious and well-deserved reputation of the housing complex as a vicious jungle where life is cheap. "And I can't blame them."

Shelton said that one of the first youths she placed in a job last year quit after he received his first paycheck.

"I asked him why," she recalls, "and he said: 'Because they were cheating me. They were only giving me about half of what they said they'd pay me.' He didn't understand that he had to pay taxes. So I told him: 'Well, you know your friends who are getting $144 a month [in general assistance], where do you think that money is coming from? And the girl who lives next door and spends all day watching soap operas with her boyfriend? Where do you think her check comes from? That's what you're paying for now.' But he had no idea."

She turns to Walker, the man bound for a job interview, and asks him what sort of job he is applying for.

"It's just a clerical job," he said.

"Don't say 'just a clerical job,'" she responds. "Let me tell you something. We are out of style. We walk around with a 'you-owe-me attitude,' and all sorts of other minorities are out there taking jobs we won't take. And they're smiling."

Shelton has found jobs for 29 youths in the two years the program has been in operation. Only about "11 to 15" are still working.

"We have to let them know ... that Cabrini is not a homestead. That it's temporary. That there are ways out," Shelton said. "And that's why it's important for [middle-class] blacks to come back here."

The imperative to do something about the underclass raises its own pointed questions: Many middle-class blacks who had and seized the opportunity for education and work may feel guilty and resentful, both for failing to return to the ghetto to help the disadvantaged and for being expected to return. They fear, often justifiably, that their place in a predominantly white society is hindered by an unfair association with the worst stereotypes of the underclass; people still see the color of skin before they recognize a face.

"The relative income position of blacks as a group has moderately improved, [but] the gains have not extended throughout the black community," said Brimmer in a paper on the economy. "Instead, the gap between the better-off and worse-off is getting wider."

Last year, Wilson wrote: "Race-specific policies emanating from the civil rights revolution, although beneficial to the more advantaged blacks [i.e. those with high income, greater education and training, and more prestigious occupations], do little for those who are truly disadvantaged, such as the ghetto underclass."

In Chicago and elsewhere it is increasingly rare for the black middle class and poor to share the same neighborhoods. "No upwardly mobile group comes back to their origins. The Italians don't come back to the ghettos. The Jews don't go back to their ghettos," said Mayor Harold Washington, whose own roots are middle class. "If you're out, you're out. If you're in, you're in. We can empathize with you, but no one goes back to the scene of the crime. They just go. The black middle class is not going to go back to the heart of the ghetto unless it is regentrified."

Nonetheless, there are small pockets where the two economic groups mix.

Around the corner from a cement wall covered with the violent proclamations of street gangs, Hattie Williams presides over her home and South Side neighborhood, as she has for more than 30 years. Before she and her late husband bought their house, they and 10 other families shared the dwelling in illegal one-room apartments hurriedly constructed within the grand, old home by a landlord seeking to profit from the post-World War II housing crunch.

For a number of years, the neighborhood was a bastion of the black working class. During the 1950s, in an effort to do away with the eroded, illegal conversions of the once proud homes, the Oakland area on the mid-South Side was declared a slum area to be cleared. Giant brownstone and graystones were bulldozed and replaced with public housing.

Many black families fled. And when the black street gang wars of the 1960s were producing regular and copious blood-baths on her streets and those around her, Mrs. Williams, too, considered moving.

Her 18-year-old son was shot as he walked behind the Oakenwald Elementary School just across the street from her home. He recovered. The youth who shot him "was out walking the street in 12 weeks," Mrs. Williams recalled clearly.

"I thought, how can we escape? I had five sons and a daughter. And then I realized that to move wouldn't really make any difference. The problems follow blacks wherever they move en masse," she said. Only those "who truly have some means" move to neighborhoods that remain integrated, she believes. "The others, they just become block busters. The attitudes among the [white] working class are, 'The niggers are coming.' That's still the thing."

Mrs. Williams has been trying to change the world around her with projects that bring white church members in from the suburbs and food distribution for those who need extra help.

Mrs. Williams thinks she is doing her part and wonders why other middle-class blacks are not, especially the churchgoers.

At Grant Memorial African Methodist Episcopal Church on Drexel Avenue, the church she referred to, the cars are indeed parked three deep on a Sunday morning but it is because many of the members are elderly and fragile and need to be helped out to the service. There are fewer than 1,000 church members now, and most live far from the old neighborhood. They are in the dilemma of declining membership as well as being in an area that is increasingly foreign to them. "I thought we ought to go for about the last five years," said Pastor Roy L. Miller.

"We are not the kind of church that attracts the masses," he added, explaining the church's commitment to self-help and higher education. "This is a thinking man's church. We don't shout. We think."

"A large minority of blacks, when they move up, harbor a contempt for the underclass," Mrs. Williams said.

To come back and deal with the problems of a community they left, she is convinced, "reminds them too much. It's a hurt that they'd rather forget."

The Catholic bishops have recognized the chasm between the poor and the middle class. In their second draft of a pastoral letter on the economy, the American Bishops Conference describes as "morally unacceptable" the current 7 percent level of unemployment [representing 8.4 million people] and poverty that encompasses more than 33 million Americans.

That combined voice of 300 Catholic bishops may influence the power structures but, the University of Chicago's Wilson said recently: "It is the storefront churches that are gaining increasing importance because of the breakdown of other institutions such as the schools and large churches, the exodus of established families, and the middle and upper classes. The storefront church is all that's left to provide a minimal structure and institution."

Not surprisingly, other voices—Louis Farrakhan's Nation of Islam among them—are heard more and more on streetcorners. The racism and bigotry of his message are reported in the newspapers, but for listeners the self-help is important, a matter of pride for those left with little of it.

A middle-aged black woman in Harlem explained the difference among the self-help preachers: "Farrakhan sees into my soul as it is. Jesse [Jackson] sees it as he wishes it to be."

On Madison Avenue near East 127th Street in Harlem, Russell "Fat Man" Fields has no trouble defining his role. He hustles vegetables to the underclass. With a devotion most common in new American immigrants, Fields tends his business in an 18-foot rusted, red truck parked on the street. Fields, who is 46, is a classical entrepreneur, only slightly illegal, in the ghetto. Instead of drugs, he peddles rutabaga and raw peanuts from Vidalia, Ga. Fields came up from Delaware when he was young. Once Harlem started downhill, he retreated with his wife and five children to the Bronx for the next 21 years. Now he is back to live among the gutted, city-owned apartments and broken sidewalks because, he said, most merchants left years ago and, if he works hard enough and his children help out, it's possible to make a decent living. Fields has hustled all his life, sometimes stolen goods, but mostly trinkets at ballgames, knife sets, anything that helped keep his kids in school, including the daughter now in college. The younger girls still help on the truck on weekends and holidays.

He has a middle-class view that sees something wrong with government welfare policy and the people who accept it. "These people, they don't want to do nothing," he said as he weighed a parcel of greens for several elderly customers. "They'll stand for a meal or stand for [government-subsidized] cheese, I don't need no meal that bad. . . . What you're doing is making these people irresponsible. They get hungry, they just get up and get a meal. It don't make sense. You ought to see the stampede when they got free cheese or chickens."

His work is hard, he said, describing getting up at 5 a.m., and often not sleeping till midnight. "If you leave this area and move into a middle-class area, you gotta work. There's no cheese lines there. You gotta pay a mortgage and lights and everything. Every once in awhile, the police come and give me a ticket for parking here. It's $25, but I think of it like paying rent."

He has a hard but not unsympathetic view of the world around him and his family: "Some of these people are lost, you can't reach them. You have to start with the young ones. You get people who are 25 or 35, and they're set already, they're wasted."

Before he finished speaking, three young men, obviously under the influence of some drug, walked by holding onto each other. The middle man wore high heels and all his front teeth were missing. One of Fields' eyebrows went up and he commented, "The No. 1 thing here is to get rid of the drugs. You do that and you lick 75 percent of the problem."

That is a problem that demands confident leadership and commitment.

In the spring issue of the Review of Black Political Economy, author Monte Piliawsky reported that the number of black mayors climbed 150 percent in the last decade, from 101 in 1974 to 252 last year. Black mayors now govern 20 cities with populations over 100,000, including four of the six largest cities in the U.S.: Chicago, Los Angeles, Philadelphia and Detroit.

While he examined the administration of Mayor Ernest "Dutch" Morial in New Orleans, Piliawsky described numerous studies of black urban leadership. "Even under a black mayor, public jobs and contracts go mostly to the middle class; and . . . the black underclass is left on public welfare with little hope of escape," he said.

Instead of concentrating energy directly on the underclass, he wrote that Morial and Mayor Washington, along with Andrew Young of Atlanta, Coleman Young of Detroit and Newark's Kenneth Gibson, "have made corporate investment the keystone to their urban development strategies" in order to create jobs and raise the cities' eroded tax bases.

Piliawsky also claimed that black mayors often use two forms of rhetoric. The first "is the exhorting of blacks to achieve upward mobility through individual striving, enhanced self-esteem and the work ethic." Secondly, he said, "They make a show of standing up to the white establishment by accusing white institutions of racism. While charges of racism are often well founded, the purpose of these attacks is as much the generation of personal political support for the black leaders as it is an effort to ameliorate racist practices."

Politics of racism has many angles. The mediagenic Jesse Jackson advocates a new Marshall Plan for inner-city neighborhoods. He also insists that as long as poverty is associated with blacks little will be done.

"We must whiten the face of poverty to get a substantial reaction," said Jackson, but " . . . if the Reagan forces can identify poverty with blacks, they can isolate it as something peculiar or congenital to the black people."

Washington touts long-term solutions such as job training and job development. He said the city is attempting to address the problems of the underclass but admits its efforts are "not much more than patchwork. We don't have the money."

In Chicago's North Lawndale neighborhood, where the plight of the underclass has been spotlighted for several months, some residents have criticized Washington for not making even a symbolic gesture to aid them.

Washington identified what he believes is the greatest political obstacle to helping the underclass. "You have a large core of middle-class people represented by politicians who are afraid of what reaction they will get and are either too lazy or lack the ingenuity to come up with the kinds of ideas that can be attractive and sold.

"I don't think it will take too much arguing in a few years to convince people that the Lawndales of the world are going to spread and multiply and infect the whole body politic. We're going to have chaos in these cities . . . unless something is done."

While he opposes Reagan-era cutbacks, he faults earlier administrations. "The excesses were not in the programs, the excesses were in the way they were being dispensed and abused. And the problem with the progressives and the liberals was that they didn't recognize it. And they didn't change it. So they were easy ducks for Reagan to come along and knock them over," he said.

The black mayors of the nation are not escaping criticism from their white or black constituents. Robert L. Woodson, president of the National Center for Neighborhood Enterprise, for example, is critical of "jobs, peace and freedom [black] mayors" who have not lived up to the "special expectations" of the blacks who elected them.

"We should particularly hold their feet to the fires because of their promises," said Woodson.

If the cities cannot deliver, it is unrealistic to look to the federal government as a savior. In the New York Review of Books, sociologist Christopher Jencks wrote an incisive response to what has become known as the "conservative bible," a book called "Losing Ground," by Charles Murray.

Americans may think the government "pampers the poor," but ". . . total government spending on 'social welfare' programs grew from 11.2 to 18.7 percent of GNP between 1965 and 1980. If all this money had been spent on the poor, poverty would have fallen to virtually zero," Jencks wrote. "But 'social welfare' spending is not mostly on the poor. It includes programs aimed primarily at the poor, like Medicaid and food stamps, but it also includes programs aimed primarily at the middle classes, like college loans and military pensions, and programs aimed at almost everybody, like medical research, public schools and Social Security. In 1980, only a fifth of all 'social welfare' spending was explicitly aimed at low-income families, and only a tenth was for programs providing cash, food, or housing to such families."

If that is not enough evidence to resist putting all faith in the national government, mark these words: "We in America today are nearer to the final triumph over poverty than ever before in the history of the land. . . ." They were spoken by Herbert Hoover when he accepted the Republican nomination for president, in 1928.

Education for the underclass is most perplexing because of its importance and its fragility.

Recently U.S. Secretary of Education William Bennett announced a new administration proposal to give parents an average $600 a year in federal funds that they could use for tuition at the public or private school of their choice. The money would come from a $3.2 billion fund already used for "educationally deprived" children from low-income areas. At present the money goes directly to the public schools.

The proposal immediately was condemned as a sugar-coated attack on public schooling that would leave city schools as the dumping ground for children unable to get a private school education. Bennett defended it as a chance for the poor to have a choice in schooling and to create a more competitive atmosphere among complacent public schools.

That is only one of many ideas percolating in the school issue that will be debated in the coming months and years. Michael Bakalis, former Illinois school superintendent and now dean of education at Loyola University, said some proposals may lead to the disappearance of public education in the cities, but "let the free market work."

"I wouldn't have said that 10 years ago if you had asked me," Bakalis said. "But the sentiment is growing. The frustration is growing."

The black-white divisions in education are profound and, as the cities become more populated by young blacks and elderly whites, the split starts at the ballot box for school funding. In early November, voters defeated a $155 million bond issue needed for physical improvements to the crumbling schools of the St. Louis school district, especially those in the largely black north side of the city.

The bond proposal, which needed a two-thirds majority, lost with 56 percent of the vote. It got overwhelming support in the north, but only weak support in the predominantly white southern areas of the city. The defeat, the third for the bonds, led School Supt. Jerome B. Jones to say: "If I were a parent and had children in public schools, I would begin to explore other options and alternatives. It is clear that the kind of voter support you need for quality education does not exist at this point in time."

Other options already are being explored: This year 7,100 black students from St. Louis schools are attending schools in 16 county school districts; 550 white children from county schools are being bused to inner-city magnet schools.

Two of the black children voluntarily bused are 9-year-old Latonya Tolen and her sister, Natarra, who is 7 and a 1st grader. "The area we lived in was kind of rough," said their mother, Juanita Tolen, describing the old neighborhood before they moved up to a resident-managed housing project, "Latonya was really too smart for the school she was going to. The new school is just great. When she is out at the school [a half-hour bus ride away] she comes home excited about what they do. She didn't do that at Mitchell. She said they just did baby work."

Then Mrs. Tolen voiced the worry most parents, black and white, share. "The only real problem I have was catching that bus and hoping they made it safe both ways."

There are no easy solutions—for either the underclass or the schools they attend.

The school questions prompt a loud, often discordant, chorus:

"We don't hold the institution accountable, we don't hold the students accountable," complained Earl D. Craig Jr., former president of the Minneapolis Urban League.

"Tougher school standards help the underclass. We really need to rethink this question of what is a compassionate position. A mushy, non-toughminded position is not necessarily a compassionate one."

Back in Chicago, Joe Kellman, who founded the Better Boys Foundation and who also owns a string of auto glass shops, presented his argument about schooling for the underclass. "It's the only case I know where we blame the product rather than the management. You couldn't survive in the business world with inferior management people and inferior production people."

The interest of businessmen in the school and underclass debate ultimately may take it on a radically new course, injecting business values into what has been a closed system.

Eugene Lang, a technology exporter with a Walter Mittyish white mustache and thinning white hair, burst onto the education field with a simple promise of money.

Five years ago, Lang made a promise to 61 sixth-graders at his old Harlem school, P.S. 121, that if they graduated from high school, he personally would pay for their college educations.

The promise was not made public until two months ago when the school announced that 52 students, most of them black or Hispanic, who are still in the school are indeed preparing for college and taking up Lang's offer.

Normally only one or two students would have gone on to college in such a class, but now the entire class is taking exams and applying to colleges where, ironically, many of them will qualify for tuition scholarships.

"I stepped into the lives of these kids at a very important juncture," Lang explained in his Manhattan office. "They were 12-year-olds facing two paths. One, they could become functional members of society or, like 80 percent of their peers, they could let the pressure of the streets fill in the vacuum. . . . What I did really was to get them to recognize that each student must have a dream and work for that dream."

The essential part of Lang's effort, however, was not just money but a commitment to take part in the students' lives. They were invited to call him and come regularly to his office. He worked with the school and even hired an older student to help the class stay together and help each other over rough spots.

Schooling, or the lack of it, as a child affects a lifetime of work. For that reason, three years ago the Boston Compact was created.

Businesses in Boston wanted the schools to provide them with a better trained and educated workforce. The schools wanted the businesses to provide jobs for the kids who did graduate.

Both sides agreed that each would have to tolerate some problems for the short-term. Employers would have to employ youngsters not fully prepared, while school administrators would scramble to improve the quality of education.

Since the Boston Compact was signed, daily school attendance in the city's 17 public high schools reached 83.3 percent in 1983-84 compared with 78 percent in 1981-82; achievement scores were up with nearly 52 percent of high school students reading on grade level in 1985 compared with 38 percent in 1981.

The foundation for all work and school is the experience at home with the family.

For the underclass that can be so destructive.

It was Oscar Lewis who explained the culture of poverty best 20 years ago when he wrote that poverty "tends to perpetuate itself from generation to generation because of its effect on children. By the time slum children are age 6 or 7 they have ususally absorbed the basic values and attitudes of their subculture and are not psychologically geared to take full advantage of changing conditions or increased opportunities which may occur in their life-time."

The crisis of the black underclass family is evident just driving through neighborhoods.

"You don't see many men hanging out in the streets unless they're addicts," observed McKelvy, who directs a preschool in Harlem. "And another one of the things that's scary is that money means a lot. As if it's the only way to judge self-worth."

The trauma inflicted within some underclass families prompted Los Angeles Mayor Tom Bradley to suggest last summer that children be placed in mandatory urban kibbutz-like settings where they could study and learn values. Because of criticism, he quickly backpedaled on the idea, saying such programs must be voluntary.

That is part of the conundrum of government involvement: Can it influence without dictating?

Sen. Daniel Patrick Moynihan [D., N.Y.] has proposed a "family bill" aimed at easing the tax burden on families in or near poverty. President Reagan's moribund tax reform proposal also raises the personal exemption level on taxes that affect the family. Individual states have strengthened laws or enforced existing ones on child-support payments.

Another current proposal is the subminimum wage. Brimmer and others suggest a "two-tier minimum wage . . . a lower wage for youth—75 to 80 percent of the present minimum of

$3.35 per hour—would provide an incentive for employers to put more of them on the payroll."

There are disputes between the White House and the individual states over the entire welfare sytem; the latest involves the federal government fining states millions of dollars for too much fraud or abuse in managing their programs. Such wrangling is not confined to a technocrat's combat zone; its real-life effect creates new de facto welfare policy by tightening eligibility and reducing staff. There are other perceived assaults on past Great Society or civil rights legislation, including three cases in the Supreme Court in which the Justice Department, speaking for the Reagan administration, is a protagonist and has aggressively sought to limit affirmative action benefits to the actual victims and not to entire classes suffering discrimination.

Such policy decisions are joined by administration supporters on Capitol Hill who want to set, for example, stricter limits on Small Business Administration loans to minorities.

"It's very clear there are going to be no new initiatives," said Tom Cook, a social scientist at Northwestern University who questions the growing disparity between the large number of children in poverty while the aged population, through private pensions and cost-of-living increases in Social Security are better off as a group than ever before. "This is not a one-year-agenda," said Cook. "A 10-year agenda is needed to deal with these problems."

"To make genuine progress in the future . . . reduce poverty among black families headed by women," Brimmer wrote in a recent report. "Reflecting their desperate situation, these female-headed black families [representing 4.6 percent of all families in the nation] got 29.9 percent of all the public assistance and supplemental income in 1983."

That was the same year the Joint Center in Washington issued A Policy Framework for Social Justice that read: "Family reinforcement constitutes the single most important action the nation can take toward the elimination of black poverty and related social problems."

In late October, California and New York acted on workfare proposals.

California Gov. George Deukmejian signed a workfare bill that was a hard-fought compromise between conservatives and liberals that legislated workfare, but added an annual $142 million in the state budget to subsidize day-care centers for both welfare and working families.

New York state officials announced new job requirements for welfare recipients. Most new welfare applicants must enter job search or training programs. If they cannot find jobs they might have to work at public or nonprofit sector jobs for up to six months or they could lose their benefits.

The program does not apply to mothers with children under 6 years old, who comprise about 80 percent of the 1.1 million recipients of federal and state money.

While the protection of young motherhood remains as established as apple pie in society at large, there is less sympathy for poor welfare mothers getting state money to stay at home with their children in an era when 61 percent of all women with children under 18 are now working.

Some federally financed programs are highly effective, but Judith Gueron of the Manpower Demonstration Research Corp. in Manhattan said, "It is very hard [for state and federal programs] to do it right the first time."

Chicago has much first-hand experience. In early October, an independent University of Chicago study declared a city-run retraining program for dislocated workers, financed by a $1.5 million grant, spent almost twice as much as the state average to retrain workers and more than twice the state average to find the worker a job. Still, the program had the lowest placement rate of all areas in the state with only 23 percent of the 1,433 people finding work.

On the other hand, Massachusetts Gov. Michael Dukakis credits his state's cut in welfare caseload and a saving of $60 million in welfare and Medicaid costs to the Employment and Training [ET] program that began two and a half years ago.

While the federal government is promoting the Job Training Partnership Act, which replaced the politically discredited Comprehensive Employment Training Act [CETA], the subtle fact is that most money is targeted on people who have had job experience and normally would have found a job in any event, federal program or not.

So it is the underclass who do not benefit substantially from these programs. In addition, they are more likely to fail in programs compared to others who have had job experience.

The catch is the future of those programs is dependent on its successes, not its failures.

Last month the National Academy of Sciences declared, as others have, that the "Jobs Corps" is actually an effective program despite administration efforts to kill it. It cost $824.5 million in fiscal year 1985 and served 40,000 young people. For up to three years after graduation, Job Corps youths earned higher wages, took fewer unemployment and welfare benefits and were less involved in criminal activity, the academy reported.

It pointed out, however, that during the late 1970s, 23 separate youth job programs cost about $2 billion and reached 6 million youths and still "not much was learned about how to reduce the long-term employment problems of American youth." It examined these programs and said, "It appears that at the beginning of 1985 the employment problems of youth were of about the same magnitude and configuration as they were in 1978."

While some initiatives are being directed at the plight of the underclass, James Compton, president of the Chicago Urban League, explained some essential obstacles. "A lot of people—both black and white—don't want to come to grips with it," he said.

"I just don't think there are enough whites who really know the depths of the underclass problem and how people live on a day-in, day-out basis," he said. "I'm thinking about good people and honest people as well as those who practice discrimination.

"People whose lives are confined to the Loop and the North Shore, even if they know intellectually, they have to be sensitized to the depth and embeddedness of it. The lives of a lot of Chicagoans are very circumscribed. The people locked in the ghetto don't get out of the ghetto. The people who make decisions downtown very often don't get out of downtown."

McKelvy, who has worked in the ghetto for five years, understands the problem: "We've allowed the professionals to replace the passion." It is the same sentiment expressed in the Book of Revelations, preferring either hot or cold, hating the lukewarm.

Woodson objects to policymakers who think they have all the answers and that "poverty not only makes you dispirited and destitute, it makes you stupid." He said that most poor people can propose solutions and create change if given the opportunity. "Malice is easy to deal with," he said, echoing past wisdom in the statement. "But how do you tell them their good intentions are injuring people?"

Dr. Martin Luther King Jr., in his famous letter from a Birmingham jail, saw that clearly. "Shallow understanding from people of good will," he wrote, "is more frustrating than absolute misunderstanding from people of ill will. Lukewarm acceptance is much more bewildering than outright rejection."

VIII
AN EDITORIAL

Courage and brains can grind a millstone into dust

Giving the young the tools to break a chain

Millstone is a hard, cold word. Its most famous literary reference is in the New Testament, where Matthew says that rather than offend God through his children it is better to hang a millstone around the necks of offenders and toss them into the sea.

Whether it grinds down or pulls under, the millstone is a heavy burden. And no single word more precisely describes a unique group of Americans whose misfortune has been the subject of an extraordinary series of stories by Tribune reporters during the last year.

The essence of this story is unpleasant and unwelcome.

For the first time in the history of this country a segment of an immigrant minority has carved out a permanent place for itself in the basement of the American dream. Unlike all the ethnic groups that followed the same path in search of the same opportunity, a relatively small number of black and Hispanic Americans have become hopelessly entrapped in the centers of our nation's largest cities, unable to break the chain of poverty and despair.

Even worse is that also for the first time in our history, America appears to have accepted the plight of these people as the inevitable result of their own making. Not only is this unconscionable for a nation this moral, it is unbelievably stupid for a nation this smart.

The American Millstone, the Tribune series has shown, is precisely that. In hundreds of interviews with dozens of experts, including social workers, law enforcement authorities and business, labor and political leaders, the same message comes through: Wherever there is a costly, seemingly insoluble problem plaguing America, you find the same small group of desperate, deprived citizens at the heart of it.

It doesn't take long to realize that the cost of tolerating the status quo is far greater, financially and morally, than doing something about it. And there are things that can be done.

It will take a combination of personal missionary work, a dramatically altered welfare system, a new program of pilot projects targeting the most troubled urban centers and a commitment from all segments of the community, public and private. Above all, it will take a kind of political courage that has been sadly lacking for a long, long time.

Personal pride

Of all the characteristics that those who have escaped poverty hold in common, nothing stands out like their personal pride. Almost all tell little stories of some parent or friend who gave them pride or, at least, presented a model of success, no matter how humble, that they could look up to and emulate.

Without pride, nobody can believe in himself or his own ability to improve his condition. Even with it, people still need direction because pride itself can turn into a burden.

Examples abound. The unemployed, unskilled, poorly educated youth who turns down a job because "it pays only the minimum wage" turns down the type of opportunity that has helped countless other urban poor people to take their first step up the long climb to success. A young welfare mother who refuses to go to school because she cannot afford attractive clothing also shows misdirected pride.

Welfare was intended to be a temporary stopgap for the poor. But social researchers now find more welfare recipients than ever expressing less shame than ever about their condition. It is not because they want to be freeloaders. It is because welfare is the only source of income they have known. They do not worry about upward mobility. They worry about survival.

Government and the business community have an obligation to help provide an escape hatch for the underclass. But black or Hispanic pride cannot be built by white business leaders and politicians. The burden of this campaign must be borne by people who have felt the pain of poverty but did not let it keep them down.

Education and jobs

Of all the profiles in tragedy sketched by The Tribune's Millstone series, one vividly conveys both the depth of the problem and the most promising solution. A 2-year-old boy wanders half-clothed through an apartment filled with his pregnant teenage mother, her boyfriend, his young aunts and uncles, his grandmother, three TV sets turned up loud and the scoldings and spankings of his relatives as they push him out of their way.

What chance does this small boy have to break out of his family cycle of chronic dependency and lead a productive, rewarding life? Without intervention, very little. But with the right motivation and stimulation, he can make it. His neighborhood, bleak as it is, is dotted with stories of men and women born into poverty who excelled in school and built successful careers. All got something that, so far, no one has given to this little boy: motivation to move up. Somebody kept saying, "Try." And somebody gave hope that if you do try, you will be rewarded with a much better life.

If that motivation can't be found in the family, it can be provided through early childhood education. A wealth of experimental projects proves that children from the most disadvantaged homes will thrive academically and socially if they are stimulated early enough in special preschool programs.

Mental malnourishment is a hidden epidemic among the underclass and the leading cause of its social pathologies. Early intervention can cure it. But wait too long and the disease will spread from parent to child down through succeeding generations.

Without adequate learning stimulation, the brain does not develop optimally and intelligence may be dulled for life. Corrective measures to foster the development of intelligence are most effective when the brain is growing most rapidly, and the brain grows at a decreasing rate from birth on. Kindergarten, first grade, even Head Start come too late and offer too little.

The best way to reduce the numbers of the underclass is through mental stimulation in a loving, secure environment beginning as soon after birth as possible, and especially between the ages of 12 and 36 months.

Such programs should include a visiting teacher who goes once or twice a week into the home soon after birth, or even before, to show mothers how to play learning games and encourage language development; a child-parent center where teachers work with babies and toddlers and mothers can learn parenting skills; a Head Start nursery school or day care center based on Montessori methods starting at age 2 or 2½; and full-day kindergarten with serious learning and reading goals.

If children can reach first grade with a well-developed brain and a mind able to succeed, they can take full advantage of school opportunities, job training and all the other bootstraps this society provides.

Early learning programs are expensive, but the money can be found to provide them for neighborhoods with large concentrations of dependent families. Businesses can contribute a small fraction of the money they pay for security services and the dollars lost through absenteeism, poor work habits and special training programs. Every major employer in a city like Chicago knows the toll. City, state and federal governments can contribute a small portion of the huge amounts they spend on coping with the pathologies of the underclass—crime, drug addiction, teenage pregnancies, remedial education.

In a few years, early learning programs will pay for themselves many times over in the reduced costs of school failures, delinquency, dependency and violent behavior.

The children of the underclass also need role models to prove that work is more satisfying than a welfare check. They need to know that work is available to them. Helping the adult members of the underclass get and hold a job is more difficult than stimulating the children through early learning classes, but there are steps that can make it easier. Vocational education in public schools has withered to the point where it is worse than useless; it's a cruel joke, evidence that you're better off having a baby and getting on welfare than staying in school. Local businesses should work with the public school system in developing realistic, updated, job-related courses.

The federal government can provide the next step by renewing and expanding the tax credits available for employers who hire and train economically disadvantaged young people. As experience proves, this is one tax loophole that adds to government revenues.

Other ways to provide more jobs for the underclass involve no government spending, but it will take political courage to push them through. These include repealing minimum wage laws and revising rigid building codes that discourage housing restoration and hold down the number of construction jobs.

Adequate public transportation to suburban industrial jobs is vitally important and virtually nonexistent. And cities like Chicago must offer attractive incentives and tax structures to encourage industrial growth within their boundaries.

But new industry won't hire the unemployed of the underclass if they don't know how to read and write adequately and aren't motivated to learn. That leads back to the single most important step in breaking the chain of poverty and despair: early childhood education.

Financial incentives

If this nation had set out to lure people into dependency and keep them there, it couldn't have devised a more effective means than the American welfare system. The giant program known as Aid to Families with Dependent Children could be renamed Aid to Create Dependent Families.

Over the years, state and federal rules and a series of court orders have given it a perverse twist. It rewards failure and punishes success. Irresponsibility gets a bonus. But the family that stays together starves together.

The system will continue to foster generation after generation of dependent families unless it is turned inside out. The incentives to get on welfare and stay there must become disincentives. Welfare checks should come with strings attached, and those strings should lead to self-sufficiency—if not for the parents, at least for the child; but, preferably, for both.

Now, virtually the only requirements for getting Aid to Families with Dependent Children are poverty and a baby on the way. Welfare rights groups and their legal advisers have seen to that. They argue that attaching conditions to welfare checks violates a civil right. What about the right of every boy and girl to have a crack at fulfilling their potential? Isn't that what this country is all about? The welfare system should be restructured to restore that basic human right to the children it supports. If, as a result, the parents it also supports have to suffer some inconveniences, so be it.

First and most important, welfare mothers who seem headed for chronic dependency—in particular, the young and unmarried—should be compelled to enroll their children in early education classes and see to it that they attend regularly.

If the mothers are poorly educated and unskilled, they should be required to participate in job-training programs, finish high school or study nutrition and child-rearing while their children are in school. These programs are available through the public school system, city colleges and city government. Getting a welfare check should be contingent on participating in one or more of them. The mother, the child and the taxpayers who provide the welfare check will all be better off in the long run.

Next, the punishments imposed by the public aid system on people who try to improve their lives should be turned into rewards. Two-parent welfare families should get a bonus for staying together. Now, 24 states won't give a welfare check unless the father disappears; Illinois will, but applying is more complicated and the father must be unemployed if he lives at home. There should be a bonus, too, for attempting to be self-supporting. For example, jobless welfare parents who manage to find part-time work should be permitted to keep everything they earn; now, all but a small portion of their wages is deducted from their welfare checks.

If the welfare recipients find full-time jobs, they could be rewarded with supplemental payments enabling them to get better housing.

And why not give supplemental payments to welfare parents whose children have consistently good school attendance records and good grades?

A variety of rewards and bonuses should be built into the welfare system to encourage parents to stay together, raise their children together, motivate their children and strive to be self-supporting. The dollar amount would not be prohibitive. The long-run savings in social costs and the gains in individual pride and dignity would be enormous.

Community commitment

To speak of a "permanent underclass" implies that the group is hopeless. Hope may be in short supply, but the situation is far from hopeless, especially if business, labor and other elements of the community pick up with private resources where government antipoverty campaigns left off.

For business leaders and labor organizers, the underclass poses a problem so deeply rooted—and without obvious reward—that they have left it largely to the social workers. Almost every free-standing institution has fled neighborhoods like Lawndale except for the black church. And many of those, from the big neighborhood edifices to the storefront chapels that line Madison Street or Roosevelt Road, have pastors who say their prayers and then leave.

Yet if anyone is to provide the leadership that can help the left-out develop their communities, it is business and labor, the people who know productivity best. And if anyone is to provide the moral leadership to coordinate the drive, it is the church.

It will take more than appeals to the conscience to mobilize community resources into a stepladder out of the underclass. Some of the most important programs will cost money, and the cities and states with the largest populations of dependent families don't have the tax resources to provide all of it. Additional federal help is necessary. But, to make sure the money is spent in productive ways, it should be contingent on a broadly based, cooperative community effort.

New federal block grants for early childhood education, job training and development and bonuses for welfare families that stay together should be narrowly targeted. Only cities with large concentrations of poor people should be eligible. And to get the money, the cities would have to raise a matching grant from state and local tax sources, private foundations and charitable organizations and the business community.

Part of the matching grant could be services instead of dollars. Civic groups such as Chicago United could provide administrators, perhaps recruited from the area's talented pool of retired executives. Neighborhood organizations, labor unions and churches could provide additional volunteers.

In the past, federally funded antipoverty programs have been diluted because Congress made too many municipalities eligible, needy or not. Other scarce federal funds were siphoned off to pay the salaries of layer upon layer of new bureaucrats hired to run the programs. Those abuses can be prevented through precise targeting and stringent rules for community involvement.

Political courage

America's political leaders have reacted to the phenomenon of chronic dependency in one of three ways. Some refuse to see the brutal realities; they still cling to the old cures of more money fed into failed social programs. Others see the depth and complexity of the problem and are overwhelmed; all we can do, they say, is provide subsistence support and isolate ourselves as best we can from these hopeless misfits.

And then there are the demagogues who exploit the wasted lives and the doomed children to boost their own careers, poisoning the nation's political and social climate in the process.

There is another way to respond—the right way. It takes courage and creativity rarely found among today's political leaders—whether federal, state or local, black or white or brown, male or female.

What's needed are politicians who will be forthright in acknowledging the problem in all of its painful, dangerous dimensions; who will admit that not every member of the underclass can be reached, but for many the chain can be broken; who will argue, with hard facts and figures, that providing the resources to break the chain is one of the smartest investments this nation's governments and businesses can make; and who will repeat, as often as necessary, that America can no longer afford this burden on its budgets and its conscience.

This may seem like a tall order for a politician, one with scant appeal to the general public. Yet the opposite is true. The violence, dependency and family breakdown that permeate the underclass extract a terrible price from the rest of society. Americans from one end of the political spectrum to the other have a vital stake in reducing those costs. The budgets in cities like Chicago and states like Illinois are clear proof that the millstone must be lifted: Police departments, prison systems, support payments, health care for poorly nourished children born prematurely to other poorly nourished children—all are siphoning off ever-greater portions of the tax dollar.

And no one, no matter where he or she stands in the political spectrum, should ignore the tragedy of young children who will never realize their potential because they never had a chance.

Yet almost every political leader from President Reagan down hides from the truth or exploits the misery. The first ones with the courage to illuminate the problem and galvanize support for the solutions will earn a lasting, respected place in American history. They will give the underclass what it needs the most: not more welfare dollars or more pity or more preaching, but the chance to be productive citizens participating in the American dream.

Authors

In order to lift a millstone,
you first must see it
By James D. Squires

The American Millstone
By Timothy J. McNulty

A family tradition
with no hope for tomorrow
By Bonita Brodt and Mark Zambrano
Contributors: Don Terry, Jerry Thornton
and William Recktenwald

North Lawndale blues:
Day with the down and out
By Mark Zambrano and William Recktenwald
Contributors: Bonita Brodt, Jerry Thornton,
Don Terry, Gabe Fuentes, Cheryl Devall,
Terry Armour and Stanley Ziemba

Crime in the ghetto:
Everybody pays the price
By Patrick Reardon

One short, wayward life; one horrid crime
By Patrick Reardon

**Violence rules the day
in troubled North Lawndale**
By William Recktenwald and Bonita Brodt
*Contributors: Jerry Thornton, Mark Zambrano,
Don Terry, Mark Eissman and Philip Wattley*

**Parole system putting
crime back on the streets**
By Mark Zambrano and Bonita Brodt
*Contributors: Don Terry, William Recktenwald,
Jerry Thornton and Mark Eissman*

**Addicts slip out
the back door of reality**
By Jerry Thornton and Bonita Brodt
*Contributors: Don Terry, Mark Zambrano,
William Recktenwald, Philip Wattley and
Edward Baumann*

**Even money can't
seem to cure poverty**
By Timothy J. McNulty

**Checks bring basics
and a dead-end emptiness**
By Bonita Brodt and Don Terry
*Contributors: Mark Zambrano, Patrick Reardon,
William Recktenwald, Jerry Thornton and
Hanke Gratteau*

**Welfare warfare:
The victim is the family**
By Timothy J. McNulty and Hanke Gratteau

**A social worker's
losing battle to help hopeless**
By Bonita Brodt and Mark Zambrano
*Contributors: Don Terry, Jerry Thornton
and William Recktenwald*

**Another child is born
without a fighting chance**
By Bonita Brodt and Mark Zambrano
*Contributors: Don Terry, Jerry Thornton
and William Recktenwald*

In the delivery room,
poverty cycle starts again
By Bonita Brodt and Jerry Thornton
Contributors: Mark Zambrano, William Recktenwald
and Don Terry

Schools outclassed
in a battle with failure
By Patrick Reardon and Jean Davidson
Contributor: Casey Banas

Poverty and crime
hold education hostage
By Mark Zambrano and Don Terry
Contributors: Bonita Brodt, William Recktenwald,
Jerry Thornton and Jean Latz Griffin

Du Sable's students learn the laws of survival
By Jean Davidson

Escape is a struggle,
but some will pay the price
By Mark Zambrano and Patrick Reardon
Contributors: Jerry Thornton, Don Terry,
Bonita Brodt and William Recktenwald

As jobs disappear,
what remains is despair
By R.C. Longworth
Contributor: Rogers Worthington

A land of broken glass
—and broken promises of '68
By R.C. Longworth

Futures of three men
get junked in a vacant lot
By Don Terry and Jerry Thornton
Contributors: Bonita Brodt, Mark Zambrano,
William Recktenwald and Philip Wattley

Youths spin their wheels
in the streets of despair
By Jerry Thornton and Don Terry
Contributors: Bonita Brodt, Mark Zambrano
and William Recktenwald

The lots are empty
as dying economy tightens grip
By R.C. Longworth

Roots of the underclass:
Racism and failed policies
By Timothy J. McNulty

Too proud to trade
welfare for minimum wage
By Patrick Reardon
Contributors: Mark Zambrano, Jerry Thornton,
Don Terry, Hanke Gratteau and Jean Davidson

A system unable
or unwilling to respond
By Robert Davis and John Camper
Contributors: Bonita Brodt, William Recktenwald,
Mark Zambrano, Don Terry and Jerry Thornton

Churches offer hope,
but only for the hopeful
By Jerry Thornton and Bruce Buursma
Contributor: Patrick Reardon

A memorial to dreams
gone sour, social neglect
By Patrick Reardon and Stanley Ziemba

Community's housing
in full state of collapse
By Stanley Ziemba
Contributors: Jerry Thornton, William Recktenwald,
Don Terry, Mark Zambrano and Bonita Brodt

Despair, dependency tow
underclass into the vortex
By Timothy J. McNulty and Hanke Gratteau

Acknowledgments

Chicago Tribune reporters and writers involved in The American Millstone series included Terrence Armour, Edward Baumann, Leigh Behrens, Bonita Brodt, Bruce Buursma, John Camper, Jean Davidson, Robert Davis, Cheryl Devall, Mark Eissman, Gabe Fuentes, Hanke Gratteau, Jean Latz Griffin, Richard Longworth, Timothy McNulty, Patrick Reardon, William Recktenwald, Don Terry, Jerry Thornton, Phil Wattley, Rogers Worthington, Mark Zambrano and Stanley Ziemba.

Photographers, artists and graphics personnel included Linn Allen, Dodie Anderson, Ron Bailey, Chuck Berman, Ovie Carter, Ernie Cox, Michael Fryer, Phil Greer, N. Jane Hunt, Anton Majeri, Jose More, Karen Olson, Bill Parker, Mario Petitti, Nancy Reese and Chris Walker.

Editors who put it all together were Thomas Cekay, F. Richard Ciccone, Jack Corn, Jack Davis, Jim Gallagher, Doug Kneeland, Charles Madigan, James D. Squires and John Twohey.

Book cover design by Mare Earley.

The material in this book first appeared in The Chicago Tribune between September 19 and December 1, 1985.

About the photographer

When Tribune photographer Ovie Carter was in his teens, his family moved from a small town in rural Mississippi to the North Lawndale neighborhood on Chicago's West Side. "We were poor and hungry for a better life," he recalled. "Most people in North Lawndale struck me as hungry for a better life. I hoped to someday have the opportunity to use my talent to make other people aware of just how bad things had become there."

The chance came in the fall of 1985 when Carter was asked to be the principal photographer for The Tribune's "American Millstone" series, which detailed the plight of the urban underclass by concentrating on North Lawndale.

To obtain his remarkable photos of poor people in this troubled and crime-ridden neighborhood, Carter frequently ran the risk of verbal abuse and physical harm. But he viewed the assignment as one of the high points of a successful career that already includes a Pulitzer Prize for foreign reporting for coverage of the 1974 famine in Africa.